The Orillia Spirit

For Janice and Rebecca

The Orillia Spirit

An Illustrated History of Orillia

Randy Richmond

Dundurn Press
Toronto • Oxford

Editor: Wendy Thomas
Designer: Sebastian Vasile
Printer: Webcom

Canadian Cataloguing in Publication Data

Main entry under title:

Richmond, Randy, 1958-
   The Orillia spirit

Includes index.
ISBN 1-55002-240-7

1. Orillia (Ont.) – History. 2. Orillia (Ont.) – History – Pictorial works.   I. Title.

FC3099.O74R5 1996   971.3'17   C95-932915-3
F1059.5.O74R5 1996

Publication was assisted by the **Canada Council,** the **Book Publishing Industry Development Program** of the **Department of Canadian Heritage**, and the **Ontario Arts Council**.

Care has been taken to trace the ownership of copyright material used in this book. The author and the publisher welcome any information enabling them to rectify any references or credit in subsequent editions.

Printed and bound in Canada

Printed on recycled paper

Dundurn Press
2181 Queen Street East
Suite 301
Toronto, Ontario, Canada
M4E 1E5

Dundurn Press
73 Lime Walk
Headington, Oxford
England
OX3 7AD

Dundurn Press
250 Sonwill Drive
Buffalo, NY
U.S.A. 14225

CONTENTS

ACKNOWLEDGEMENTS

This book would have been impossible to write without the help of hundreds of people.

James A. 'Pete' McGarvey set me on the road into the past and for that I am ever grateful. He and other notable Orillia historians, Sue Mulcahy, Don Hunter, Don Jenkins, and Joan and Jay Cody gave me advice and research and answered my seemingly endless questions.

All those I interviewed for this book showed remarkable patience and grace and getting to know them was reward in itself.

This history owes a great debt to the many historians, researchers, storytellers and story collectors of the past, many of them members of the Orillia Historical Society. The Society's tireless work is the foundation upon which much of this book rests, and I thank all its members, past and present and especially past-president David Boehme, for their help.

The unsung storytellers of this city are the reporters who have called Orillia home at one time or another. Without their sharp eyes, my look into the past would have been veiled. The current crew at The Packet & Times deserves my thanks for continuing to research the past and jot down the notes that will make up our history. At The Packet, publisher Bruce MacIntyre and managing editor Jeff Day, and my reporting staff allowed me the opportunity to write this book and put up with an editor often pre-occupied by the past and not the present.

My heart felt thanks goes to Sean Rogers for his valuable research on the Depression and the Second World War, without which I would have pushed my deadlines even more than I did.

My second home for the past year has been the Orillia Public Library, where the staff, especially Fran Richardson, Paul Blower and Gail Ward, gave me the freedom to rummage through anything I wanted, borrow whatever I needed and ring up a huge photocopying bill without a word of complaint.

The staff at the Simcoe County Archives, especially Bruce Beacock and Ellen Millar, also gave essential help.

Kirk Howard and the staff at Dundurn Press have shown considerable patience with me and considerable creativity in their handling of the material I dumped in several stages on their desks.

All my friends and family gave me encouragement and help in the past year and a half. I thank most of all my wife Janice and daughter Rebecca who offered love, patience and understanding beyond measure.

R.R., Orillia, 1996

FOREWORD

A week after I arrived in Orillia in April 1947, I picked up a booklet at the Board of Trade Office. It bore the title, "Orillia, the Town on Two Lakes!"

As Randy Richmond makes so brilliantly clear in the pages of "The Orillia Spirit," it could have been titled "The Town with Two Personalities," with equal accuracy.

With candour, a keen journalistic eye, and even keener editorial perception, the author has chronicled three centuries of Orillia's ambivalent existence, carefully separating fact from myth and assigning each the value it deserves. It's a prodigious performance; what results is a work that will endure far longer than any "official" municipal history. This is authentic communal lore, social analysis, economic profile, all in one, and much more. The rich anecdotal overlay alone assures its permanence.

Orillia's true identity has been a matter of debate since at least the turn of the century. Are we the place much of the world thinks we are, the mythical "Mariposa," basking in Leacock's perpetual sunshine? A place of innocence, historic lore, civic boosterism, bucolic charm? Or are we the "town ahead" (to use the boast adopted in the town's pioneering push for Daylight Saving Time)—a bustling industrial/commercial centre elevated by home-grown hydro from lumber-village obscurity to Golden Age prosperity in a single generation?

Who better exemplifies the Orillia "Spirit"—industrial and civic mogul James Brockett Tudhope, or the bemused professor from Montreal, Stephen Butler Leacock, creator of Mariposa? Oddly, "Sunshine Sketches of a Little Town," published in 1912, contains no hint of the existence of a major automobile manufacturing plant within the borders of the mythical municipality. A strange omission in a book that borrows freely from all of Orillia's leading institutions (churches, lodges, banks, stores) and engaging characters. Police Magistrate/Mayor John McCosh is the fictional Judge Pepperleigh; Canon Richard Greene is Dean Drone. Barber Jeff Shortt is barber Jeff Thorpe, and Josh Smith, proprietor of the Mariposa House, is the real life proprietor of Orillia's most popular watering-place of 1912, whose surname was also Smith. But where was James Brockett Tudhope, at the time of writing the most eminent and powerful Orillian of all?

Like Leacock's cast of characters there's always more than meets the eye to Orillia's prime movers and shakers. Champlain, the noble figure atop a block of granite in Couchiching Park, had a vision of a common nationhood for Europeans and aboriginal Canadians. But he blew it in a shabby expedition against the Iroquois, plotted in Orillia in 1615. When the Iroquois took their vengeance a generation later, the dream went a glimmering and a long dark night descended on the land. The lumber barons of Orillia's mid 19th century brought employment to the masses, but little social conscience to the community. Drunkenness and debauchery flourished. The architects of Orillia's Golden Age—Charles Harold Hale, Erastus Long, the aforementioned James Brockett Tudhope among them, combined extraordinary vision, communal pride and personal generosity to fashion visible declarations of Orillia's uniqueness (The YMCA, Opera House, Soldiers' Memorial Hospital, Champlain Monument), but also subscribed to a feudal code of low wages, no unions, and a social/ruling order reserved to the corporate, professional and political elite of the little town on the two lakes. Those celebrated demagogues, Ben Johnston in the thirties, Wilbur Cramp in the fifties defied the establishment and successfully rallied the left-outs and have-nots, but in the end betrayed their constituencies through greed and personal weaknesses.

The nose-thumbing of authority and the flouting of convention have been features of Orillia's public life from the very start. A few weeks after the village council convened for the first time in 1867, a meeting of the local literary society was disrupted by "Doc" Slaven, the village pharmacist, pouring scorn on both the speaker's research (he was discussing some aspect of a Shakespearean play) and the air of intellectual superiority assumed by the membership. The story in the Northern Expositor doesn't relate if strong drink figured in Slaven's outburst. We're only told he brought proceedings to a crashing conclusion and no one knew how to deal with him.

It's been that way ever since. We've never been sure how to deal with rebel spirits and populists. I was among the Orillia aldermen in the 1950s who spent much of their time frustrating the outrageous schemes of Wilbur M. Cramp. In most showdowns, it was seven members of council against the mayor. But they were hollow victories. At election time, the wily Cramp would turn it all around—simply including council as a co-conspirator in the plot of the "ginger group" to destroy the community. The folks lapped it up. He spoke their language.

In more recent times Mayor John Palmer enjoyed much the same communion with voters, but unlike Cramp, was an honest broker, if often judgmental and bombastic. He sought no material reward from his office.

Contrary characters abound in Richmond's history. Scoundrels as well as swashbucklers, schemers as much as dreamers, have played roles in Orillia's checkered saga. As a good reporter Richmond relishes their stories. Each proves that Orillia, like most communities, is a mix of good and band, of humbug and humility, bunkum and heroism, inspiration and depression.

Charles Harold Hale gets a lot of space in this book and deserves it. More than any other person of his time he moulded the Orillia we know today. The long-time editor of the Packet, a friend of Stephen Leacock's for fifty years, my friend and mentor for fourteen years, understood Orillia's split personality perfectly. He sold the merits of the Orillia Hydro scheme to his townspeople in the pages of The Packet before the turn of the century and led most of the crusades for Orillia's betterment over the next fifty years. He was responsible for the Public Library, the Champlain Monument, Soldiers' Memorial Hospital, the Board of Trade, the Canadian Club, the Historical Society, the Leacock Associates and in the last years of his life the movement to persuade the town to acquire and restore the Leacock home. If there were controversies, scandals or blunders in any of the great schemes of the past, they were well-kept secrets with C.H. Hale. In my many conversations with him, he spoke only of super achievements of selfless citizens—the universe unfolding as it ought. He moralized in print on the evils of alcohol, but never once criticized (in my company at least) the celebrated imbibing of Stephen Leacock. As a seasoned reporter and editor, no one knew the grim social and economic realities of his community better. Or managed to conceal them more. In the enticing literature that drew summer visitors to Orillia in the 1930s, all of it composed by the Packet's editor, there's no suggestion that this centre of recreational delights—blue skies, crystal clear waters, fishing, swimming, sailing, cottaging, was also home to a score of foundry industries, sub-standard wages and widespread unemployment. Far more than Stephen Leacock, Hale created the myth of Mariposa. But in truth he was the champion of both Orillias—the community of bustling enterprise as well as the centre of vacation fun. And he was far more a hustler than he knew—accenting the positive and eliminating the negative in the pitches he contrived for both factions. Nay-saying was unproductive. It was a slogan he lived by.

The Orillia Spirit manifests itself not only in the lives and deeds of past movers and shakers, but as a kind of Element "X" in the very air and water of the community. How else to explain the astonishing list of achievers who have departed this place and gone on to national and international acclaim? Franklin Carmichael, an original of the Group of Seven; Gordon Lightfoot, Canadian troubadour to the whole world; Leslie Frost, "Old Man Ontario;" Floyd Chalmers, the greatest single benefactor Canadian music and drama have known; Sculptor Elizabeth Wyn Wood; the Jake Gaudaurs, Senior and Junior, and in our present generation, Donald Tapscott, author and guru/futurist to corporate giants, Peter Baillie, president of the Toronto Dominion Bank, Tayler "Hap" Parnaby, News and Public Affairs Director of CFRB, the nation's most listened-to radio station. It infects those who stay behind just as much. I think of Gordon A. "Skid" Watson, father figure to generations of young Orillians at the YMCA, Archibald "Mac" Carter, who led the movement to build our own community centre, Jim Dykes and Jim Storey, heroes of the Leacock Boathouse project, Doug Little, the creator of pageants to keep Orillia on the map. There are hundreds of latter day heroes on my list—volunteers of every stripe, the promoters and pursuers of good causes from literacy instruction to the Sharing Place. And good and decent people—to be found in every church and service club, in the corridors of Soldiers Memorial, at the Legion, and in every lodge hall in town, doing their bit to build a healthier, happier, more caring community.

Element "X" has yet to be isolated, yet it's there, still infecting ordinary people and moving them towards the extraordinary. While the Leacock Boathouse project of 1995 is cited as the latest example, the author errs. The latest example is this very volume. Randy Richmond has given his adopted community a gift for the ages—a mature and humourous (as any book about Orillia should be) account of its storied past, and with it a reminder that what once was can be again.

The Spirit moved him.

Pete McGarvey, Orillia, May 1996.

PROGRESS ORILLIA

A GRAND VISION

rillia's story begins with a grand vision, a questionable decision, and a holocaust.

When the great French explorer Samuel de Champlain travelled through the lands around present-day Orillia in 1615, he marvelled at the richness of the 30,000-strong Huron nation. "This country is so fine and fertile that it is a pleasure to travel about in it," he wrote in his journals. "And this small extent of territory I have observed to be well peopled with a countless number of souls, without reckoning the other districts which I did not visit, which by common report are as thickly settled as those above mentioned, or more so..."

Thirty-five years later, the powerful Huron nation was reduced to 300 people so hungry they dug bodies out of graves to get something to eat. Jesuit Paul Ragueneau, who lived with the survivors wrote: "Mothers fed upon their children; brothers on their brothers; while children recognized no longer, him whom, while he lived, they had called their Father."

Famine had crept in behind the armies of the Hurons' fierce enemy, the Iroquois. The two great native nations had come from the same stock. Centuries earlier, the tribes that eventually made up the Hurons had spread north from Iroquois country, south of the Great Lakes, to a territory bordered by present-day Orillia in the east and Georgian Bay in the west. Some of the fish weirs at The Narrows are 5,000 years old. Even before European explorers reached the New World, the Hurons and Iroquois had battled. It is unclear why, and historians can see whatever they want in the nature of the conflict. Writing in the late 1800s after the destructive Civil War, American historian Francis Parkman saw the Iroquois as the 'good Indians'. These American-born Indians were democratic, yet nationalistic, just like the victorious Northern States. The Hurons were a loose confederation of tribes, much like the South, and obviously weaker for it.

During the Cold War in the 1950s, the Hurons made a bit of a public relations comeback. The Canadian Hurons were the good Indians, according to former Ontario premier and historian E.C. Drury. The Hurons were peaceful and democratic, like the West in the 1950s. The Iroquois were totalitarian and war-like, like the Soviet Union and the Eastern Bloc. The

Samuel de Champlain included these sketches of Huron men in his journals. Figures A and C show Huron men ready for battle.
Courtesy of The Champlain Society, Toronto, Ontario.

clash between the Iroquois and the Hurons was started, as usual, by the totalitarian tribe trying to overrun the peaceful, freedom lovers, said Drury.

Whatever the reasons for the initial rivalry between the Huron and Iroquois, the coming of whites to North America and the growth of the fur trade intensified the conflict. Whatever tribe controlled the fur trade earned the most of the Europeans' guns and other goods. The Hurons occupied a key position, at peace and trading with the agricultural tribes of Petuns and Neutrals to the south, and the hunting Algonquin tribes to the north. As middlemen, they controlled the fur trade that moved pelts from Georgian Bay up the French River to Lake Nipissing, then down to the Ottawa River to the St. Lawrence and Quebec. The Hurons' rudimentary tools and belief in a spirit world were enough to convince the French the natives were inferior savages. But Champlain saw more than savages in the Hurons. After all, they were generally peaceful, and organized into clans and villages with clear forms of government. They cleared land and farmed corn, beans and squash. And they understood commerce. Champlain intended not to destroy or enslave the Hurons, but to forge a new nation of French settlers and converted, educated natives.

Before Champlain fixed that vision on the Huron nation near present-day Orillia, he helped the Hurons in a battle against the Iroquois in 1608. He tried to persuade the Hurons to let him visit their home territory, but the Hurons were reluctant. By 1615, they were not so reluctant. Iroquois raiding parties were making it difficult for the Huron fur traders to reach the French. Hurons meeting him at Lachine Rapids that year asked for Champlain's help against the Iroquois and invited him to visit their villages.

Champlain agreed to help, explaining in his journal that he did so:

Both to engage them the more to love us, and also to provide the means of furthering my enterprises and explorations which apparently could only be carried out with their help, and also because this would be to them a kind of pathway and preparation for embracing Christianity. For which reason I resolved to go and examine their territory, and to help them in their wars, in order to induce them to let me see what they had so often promised me.

That summer, Champlain, two other Frenchmen, and ten natives in two canoes travelled the French River route to Lake Huron and Matchedash

Bay, arriving at Carhagouha, a palisaded town near Nottawasaga Bay in August 1615. For the next three weeks, Champlain travelled from village to village, working his way from Georgian Bay to Lake Simcoe.

Not knowing what to expect, Champlain was pleased with the fertility and size of the Huron nation, which must have further strengthened his vision of a great alliance. The greatest village of all was Cahiague, with 200 large longhouses and 5,000 people protected behind a triple palisade. Champlain arrived at the village, a few miles from present-day Orillia, August 17. The Hurons prepared feasts and dances to celebrate Champlain's safe arrival and the march against the Iroquois. Champlain stayed in Cahiague until the main body of warriors was assembled, then on the first day of September, made the short trip to The Narrows between Lakes Couchiching and Simcoe.

When the most part of our people were assembled, we set out from the village on the first day of September and passed along the shore of a small lake [Couchiching], distant from the said village three leagues, where they make great catches of

Champlain in Huronia: The parting with Etienne Brule at The Narrows, 1615. A painting by Rex Woods. No authentic likeness of Samuel de Champlain exists, but his explorations have fed the inspiration of artists for centuries.

Confederation Life Collection

fish which they preserve for the winter. There is another lake immediately adjoining [Simcoe], which is 26 leagues in circumference, draining into the small one by a strait, where the great catch of fish takes place by means of a number of weirs which almost close the strait, leaving only small openings where they set their nets in which the fish are caught.

The small army stayed at The Narrows for a few days, waiting for the rest of the Hurons. When they had arrived, two canoes of twelve Hurons and French

In spite of superior weapons and a shooting tower, the French and their Huron allies could not seize a strong Iroquois fort in what is now New York State. French involvement in the battle in 1615, shown here in a sketch from Champlain's journals, angered the Iroquois. Eventually, the Iroquois destroyed the Huron nation and drove the French out of present-day Ontario.

Courtesy of The Champlain Society, Toronto, Ontario

interpreter Etienne Brule set out to sneak through Iroquois country to reach about 500 allies of the Huron that had promised help. Champlain and the army made their way along the lakes and rivers of the Trent Valley to Lake Ontario. Once they crossed Lake Ontario, they were in Iroquois country, so they hid their canoes on shore and worked through the forest to an Iroquois stronghold near or on Lake Onondaga.

Champlain quickly realized it would be no simple task to overwhelm the Iroquois. Thirty-foot-high palisades enclosed the village. A nearby pond gave the Iroquois fresh water for drinking and to put out any fires. The battle was a disaster for the Hurons and French. Arrows fell down on them like hail. Champlain wrote that the Hurons promised to obey him in the battle. But from the start, the Hurons' less organized style of fighting frustrated the French. The Hurons and French managed to build a cavalier, a ten- to twelve-foot tower on which the French shooters could stand to fire their guns over the Iroquois palisades. The allies also built a mantelet, a large, movable shelter that could shield a group of warriors from Iroquois arrows as they moved in and laid siege to the fort. But the Hurons broke ranks, setting small and useless fires, wrote Champlain. The first attack ended in a stalemate, with several wounded and killed on both sides. Champlain received two arrow wounds, one in the knee and one in the leg, yet tried to convince the Hurons to attack again, in an organized fashion. The Hurons would agree only to wait a few days for reinforcements. In the skirmishes that followed over the next few days, the Iroquois shouted at the French that they should not interfere in Iroquois and Huron battles - a prophetic warning.

The reinforcements did not arrive, so the Hurons and French left. Champlain begged the Hurons to take him back to the settlement at Quebec, but the Hurons said they could not spare the canoe. Champlain wrote, "I perceived that their plan was to detain me with my comrades in their country, both for their own safety and out of fear of their enemies, and that I might hear what took place in their councils and meetings..." This Champlain did, spending the winter visiting Huron and Algonquin villages, such as Cahiague, cementing the alliance.

That alliance turned out to be deadly to the Hurons. Thanks in part to Champlain's efforts, French Jesuits eventually set up missions throughout Huron country. The Iroquois grew increasingly frustrated at French interference in their affairs, the pressure of white settlement on their territory and the Hurons' stranglehold of the fur trade. The French feared a Huron -

Iroquois alliance would free the Hurons to send furs to the rival Dutch, so they broke up any moves by the two native nations to establish a peace treaty between themselves.

Disease gave the Iroquois an advantage over the Huron. Smallpox, brought by the French, raged through Huron country in 1637, killing thousands and reducing the population from 30,000 to about 12,000. Shaken, the Hurons gathered north into their strongholds that stretched from Lake Couchiching to Georgian Bay. The missionary work continued, and fur brigades of canoes laden with pelts still travelled down the Ottawa and up the St. Lawrence Rivers to the French. Iroquois attacks on the brigades intensified in the 1640s. In

1642, the Iroquois slipped into Huron country itself, burning the village of Contarrea, a few miles south west of present-day Orillia, and killing all the inhabitants. (Cahiague, the capitol village Champlain had visited earlier, was abandoned sometime before 1624, either because nearby resources had been depleted or the two clans that made up the village had gone their separate ways). Over the next few years, the Iroquois began isolating the Hurons by destroying their allies, the Petuns, Neutrals, and Algonquins.

The final destruction of the once-proud Huron nation began July 4, 1648, with an attack on Teanaostaiae, called St. Joseph by the French, a mission town of about 2,000 in what is now Medonte Township. About 700 Hurons were killed. The Iroquois slipped back home, apparently satisfied with their success. That fall and winter, hundreds of Iroquois began moving into the forests of eastern Ontario. The French and Huron had no idea their enemy was marching quietly toward them. A thousand warriors suddenly attacked St. Ignace, near present day Waubaushene, March 16, 1649, killing most inside. Only three men escaped, fleeing half-naked over snowy fields to nearby villages. Next the Iroquois took St. Louis, one more village on the road to the main mission village, Ste. Marie. For some reason, the Iroquois fell into a strange panic and left a few days later, torturing prisoners on the way home. The Jesuits had no other explanation for the sudden fear among the Iroquois other than the fact it was St. Joseph's Day.

Over the summer of 1649, with 15 of their villages destroyed, the surviving Hurons fled to Ste. Marie on the Wye River near present-day Midland. But no one felt safe there anymore, and on June 14, the surviving Jesuits and Hurons burned the mission and headed across Georgian Bay to St. Joseph Island, now called Christian Island. The island had little food to support the 8,000 survivors and the Iroquois hunted down any Hurons who tried to come to the mainland. It was a horrifying winter, as Father Ragueneau reported to his superiors:

> Another mother, perceiving that she would be the first to die, left - with the same peace as if she were falling into a sweet slumber - upon her bosom two poor orphans, who continued to suck from her after her death, and who died upon their mothers as quietly as formerly that had slept there, when they drew from her both milk and life."

Champlain's travels gave Europeans new knowledge about the lands west of French settlement. His map of 1616 shows present-day Lake Ontario and the Ottawa River. The Great Lakes lie to the west.

Courtesy of the Champlain Society, Toronto, Ontario

About 4,000 Hurons died of famine that winter, Ragueneau reported. Hundreds more died of exposure and starvation. The Iroquois killed many Hurons the next spring as the starving survivors braved the thin ice of Georgian Bay to reach the mainland. Those who survived fled to find shelter with other tribes. In the spring of 1650, a straggling band of French and Hurons fled this area for Quebec. Out of the 30,000-strong nation that would have been the foundation of Champlain's new world, only 300 remained.

The Iroquois victory destroyed one nation, the Hurons, and weakened another, the French. If Champlain had left the Iroquois alone, or succeeded in beating them, the face of North America would be different today. Canada today might be a French-speaking nation. The Hurons might have thrived. But one cannot blame Champlain for trying, and his dream of a peaceful alliance stands in marked contrast to the violent methods Europeans often used in in dealing with natives. At least Champlain tried. About 300 years before anyone coined the phrase, his vision can stand as the first recorded version of the Orillia Spirit - the desire to take a risk and do something different.

Orillians dreamed of turning the site of Cahiague into a research centre and tourist attraction. Richard Shultz, a University of Toronto student, gave other students a tour of the grounds in 1967, but by then funding for the dig had begun to fade away. In this photograph, Shultz is standing on an area where a longhouse for six families stood.

A FORGOTTEN VILLAGE

The misfortune that followed Samuel de Champlain's stay in Cahiague in the 1600s cast a shadow on the village itself in the twentieth century. Debate about the location of the chief Huron village appeared settled in 1947, when the remains of a huge native settlement were found near Warminster, a few miles outside Orillia. For the next twenty years, students and archeologists, mainly from the University of Toronto, dug at the site. Professor Norman Emerson, chief of the archeology department of the University of Toronto, suggested the village was indeed Cahiague, one of the largest native villages in North America.

Orillians dreamed of a unique tourist attraction, a reconstruction of that village. In 1964, Premier John Robarts, announced the province would spend $1 million on the first part of a multi-million dollar project to rebuild Fort Ste. Marie, not Cahiague. Professor Emerson received the usual $4,000 summer grant to pay for student research. Orillians pointed the finger at the petty politics of academia. Midland-based archeologist Wilfrid Jury and researchers with the University of Western University had developed the Ste. Marie site. They were rivals to the University of Toronto, which had developed the Cahiague site, and had more influence with the provincial government. Premier Robarts himself was a Western graduate. Midland received money to re-build a historic site, while Orillia had to struggle on a pittance.

Interest in Cahiague sputtered on for another decade, and the province promised in 1974 to help make the site a tourist attraction. But researchers gave up on the site, and Professor Emerson died before completing a report establishing the site as Cahiague. A Metis and non-status native association tried to develop the site in the early 1980s, but that effort too failed. Today the site is a field, silent and almost forgotten, perhaps the most fitting memorial to the fate of the Huron nation.

WHAT'S IN A NAME? IN ORILLIA, CONFUSION

No one is really sure how Orillia gained its name, although the most likely theory has as the source the Spanish word Orilla, meaning the lesser shore. Oro means the greater shore. Many of the soldiers who settled in the area on half-pay retirements had served with Wellington in the Peninsular Wars and knew some Spanish. They or soldiers still in service might have given the area around Lake Simcoe the name Oro, and the area around smaller Lake Couchiching, Orillia.

The name Orillia was used officially as early as 1820. That seems to rule out another theory, that early settler Gerald Alley named the place after his sister Aurelia. She had given him the money he needed to buy land west of the Indian Village, which he sold to other settlers. Alley was an ambitious man and it would not be out of character for him to take it upon himself to name the community.

Natives called a red berry growing in the area Orelia, and some claim that as the ancestor of the name. Another theory credits the name to Jean Orillat, a Montreal fur trader who worked in the area in the 1700s. Others argue the name is a corruption of aureula, the Latin term for beautiful rose. The city could be named after Orillion, a technical military term for a waterfront fortification. An even stranger claim has Orillia named after a mythical robber, magician, and son of an imp, Orillo. Apparently Orillo could replace his limbs or head if they were cut off, which at least offers hope that no matter what, Orillia will always survive.

AN INEVITABLE CLASH

The diaries of Captain John Thomson, who settled at The Narrows in 1832, provide in places a succinct description of pioneer life. For example, "12th June, 1835, Friday. Mrs. Thomson presented me with a second daughter at a quarter past five this afternoon. Men at the potatoes."

Today, most people likely wouldn't include a grocery list in the same entry as the birth of a child. But for the first white settlers at The Narrows and the bush around present-day Orillia, raising a family depended on raising the crops. Life wasn't easy for the retired military officers, like Thomson, the tradesmen, or even the government employees drawn to

Settlement in the Orillia area began in the 1830s. The Chippewas were settled on what is present-day downtown Orillia, and whites gathered at The Narrows between lakes Simcoe and Couchiching. Henry Byam Martin, working in pen and brown ink, captured these "Gentlemen warming their toes, the Narrows, at the head of Lake Simcoe on the 26th day of September A.D. 1832."

H.B. Martin, National Archives of Canada/C1150113

fledgling communities at The Narrows, the channel between Lakes Simcoe and Couchiching, in the 1830s. They came and stayed in the area to teach, to preach, to farm — some even came for love. In their spirit, politics, eccentricities, strengths, and weaknesses, they set the foundation for life in Orillia.

Few whites even saw the area for the 200 years after the Hurons left. Some white historians say a Dark Ages fell over the area after the destruction of the Hurons, with no natives daring to cross the land. Others argue more convincingly that the Iroquois, using the former Huron territory for hunting, clashed with the Chippewas there, just as they did in other areas of Ontario. A story passed down for generations tells how the Chippewas, while driving out the Iroquois, stopped briefly at The Narrows in order to get food, wait for reinforcements and get ready for the rest of their march. One warrior, perhaps a medicine man, made a painting on a rock near Lake Couchiching that predicted the defeat of the Iroquois. A version of that painting, in wampum, is held by the Royal Ontario Museum.

Chippewa storytellers say the connection with The Narrows stretches back even farther than the painting. Long before the coming of white men, on a great migration down the St. Lawrence and into Ontario, the Chippewas came across the Hurons living and fishing at The Narrows. The Chippewas and Hurons became friends. When the Hurons clashed with the Iroquois years later, the Chippewas came to their aid. Some of the Hurons who did not flee to Quebec in 1650 were adopted into the Martin clan of the Chippewas. The Chippewas pushed the Iroquois out of the area. At The Narrows, the Chippewas flourished and became renowned as the people of the fish fence, Mnjikaning. The Narrows became a healing centre, where different, even rival, tribes could rest on their journeys. Many tribes helped mend the fish weirs, the fish fences, that guided fish through The

Resting at The Narrows on a march against the Iroquois, a Chippewa warrior made a rock painting that predicted a victory for his people. A wampum version of this painting is held by the Royal Ontario Museum.

Courtesy of the Royal Ontario Museum.

Iroquois. The other took travellers along the ancient Taronto Portage, from Lake Ontario up the Humber River and overland to the Holland River, which flows into Lake Simcoe. Through The Narrows, traders and soldiers alike could head up Lake Couchiching, then into the Severn River and Matchedash Bay on Lake Huron, or overland to Lake Huron along the Coldwater Trail. Governor Simcoe and his force took the Taronto route on their 1793 expedition to Penetanguishene Bay to select a site for a fort.

The area was rich in furs, and in 1800, attracted the attention of a French nobleman. Laurent Quetton de St. George, a lieutenant in the service of Louis the Fourteenth, had fled the French Revolution to England in 1789, then emigrated to Upper Canada with other French aristocrats and soldiers two years later. These French gentlemen tried farming on land north of York, now Toronto. Most of them failed and returned to England. Quetton St. George stayed and became a trader, with his headquarters and one house in York, and north of that community, a chateau, with a private lake, called Glen Lonely. Quetton St. George grew rich, with branches from Kingston to Niagara trading tea, whiskey, tar, buffalo robes and salt cold for furs, flour, butter and cheese.

In 1800, Quetton St. George set up a little post at The Narrows. He learned the Chippewa language. They affectionately called him "White Hat", as he usually wore a white hat in summer. The trading post seemed to earn its keep. A clerk's record from March 8, 1800, kept in the Simcoe County Archives, shows the following purchases of pelts: sixty-nine martens, twelve bears, two foxes, and one beaver. Other trading firms, such as Borland and Roe, may have used the post. After the battle of Waterloo in 1815, which saw the defeat of Napoleon and the return of the monarchy to France, Quetton St. George returned to his native land, a rich man.

By then, the territory near The Narrows had attracted the attention of the British government. Worried about continued trouble with the United States, Britain bought about 1.6 million acres in Simcoe, Grey, Wellington, and Dufferin counties from the Chippewas in order to ensure a safe route to the west that avoided the Great Lakes. The 1818 purchase cost the government a yearly payment of $1,200 in goods. For years the Chippewas continued to roam the lands at will. Early settlers in Simcoe County huddled along the sound end of the Penetanguishene Road, which was opened in 1813, and ran from from Kempenfelt Bay on Lake Simcoe to Penetanguishene on Georgian Bay. Few settlers wanted to go much farther north.

Narrows into Huron nets. According to Chippewa tradition, the language of the Mnjikaning people took on the singsong rhythm of the water flowing between the two lakes. The Chippewas at The Narrows gained the admiration of all tribes for their healing powers.

It appears most of the battles between the Iroquois and Chippewas took place northwest and southeast of present-day Orillia. The Chippewas had driven the Iroquois out of the area by 1701, and were settled in the area when the first fur traders, soldiers, and explorers came through The Narrows — the junction of two north/south routes from Lake Ontario and the Hurons' main/east overland route, the Coldwater Trail. One north/south route took travellers from Lake Ontario through the Trent Valley, the way Champlain and his Huron allies had travelled on their expedition against the

"They have six or seven months dead winter, and then four months of cold winter," the Reverend Thomas Williams recalled one settler telling his family when his father was considering moving north of Lake Simcoe in the 1820s. A few of the hardiest souls did brave the north, and a few of the sharpest saw in junction of The Narrows a natural place for future settlement. Honore Bailey patented 500 acres of land beside the lakes in 1826, although he never settled on a lot himself. A year later, voyageur, fur trader, and ex-soldier Antoine Gaudaur paid Bailey $25 for a lot close to where today's Highway 12 bypass reaches the Atherley Road, in 1827. It's not clear why the adventurous Gaudaur settled at The Narrows, but it might have been for love. On his travels, Gaudaur had met Mary Shilling, the daughter of a Chippewa chief, Big Shilling. (Gaudaur and Shilling, representing two of the founding nations of the country, started a family that became prominent in Canada. Grandson Jake was a world champion oarsman and a great-grandson, also Jake Gaudaur, became commissioner of the Canadian Football League.) Antoine Gaudaur and Captain John Thomson, whose diary begins this chapter, became neighbours, with a typical neighbourly relationship. They argued over fence lines, but when two of Thomson's cows fell into Smith's Bay on Lake Simcoe, Gaudaur and his two sons helped rescue them.

The two families gained more neighbours in the 1830s, as a wave of immigration from Britain reached Canada's shores. Britain was experiencing a period of unrest, and travellers returning from Canada sparked new interest in the colony. In 1830, as settlers began moving north, Sir John Colborne, the lieutenant-governor, gathered about 500 Chippewas in three bands on to a reserve of 9,800 acres stretching from The Narrows to Coldwater. The Coldwater Trail was cleared into a road. One Chippewa band was moved to Coldwater, where a mill was built for them, and one to Snake's Island. A third band, the Reindeer clan, lived around The Narrows and was led by Chief Muskquakie from his home on what is now called Chiefs Island in Lake Couchiching. Chief Muskquakie, or William Yellowhead as he was known to the British, had to move his band to the site of present-day, downtown Orillia on Lake Couchiching. (From his name come the word Muskoka, an area of cottages lakes north of Orillia.) The government hired teachers and builders to teach the natives white ways, such as growing crops and milling grain. Just getting to the area proved difficult for these early white immigrants. Jacob Gill, hired by the British

government to build a frame house for Chief Yellowhead and a mill on the reserve, moved his family to the new Indian Village on Lake Couchiching in 1832. His daughter described the journey many years later for a newspaper. The family had a head start on most pioneers, beginning their journey from Newmarket, rather than York. The first day they took a stage to Holland Landing, staying overnight in an old log house. The next day they took a schooner down the Holland River and up Lake Simcoe as far as Bell Ewart. The family built a fire on shore, ate a supper and "made [their] beds with the sky for a roof, and slept until morning." It took another day to sail up to Eight Mile Point just south of the Indian Village. There was no wind, so the men had to row the boat from Eight Mile Point to the village. The family arrived at 10 p.m., taking three full days to travel from Newmarket to Orillia, about a 45-minute car ride today.

The teachers and government workers heading to the Indian Village had to land at The Narrows or at Shingle Bay at the foot of present-day West Street and walk through bush and swamp. The first white child to arrive in the village came in the arms of the Chippewas. The child's father, Robert Bailey, moved his family to the village so he could work with Gerald Alley, the government employee who was teaching the Chippewas how to farm. The boat the family was on got stuck in The Narrows, and the passengers and freight were put on a bateau and brought closer to shore. The Chippewas carried the young Bailey girl the rest of the way to shore through water and waist-deep mud.

The Indian Village was a relief to these first settlers. At least here there was some form of civilization. The Indian Village stood about 200 yards from the Lake Couchiching shore. The layout of the sixteen log houses formed a triangle, with the base parallel to the lake and the peak a frame meeting/schoolhouse. Each log house, built to accommodate two Chippewa families, was twenty-eight feet long and fifteen feet wide, with a fireplace in the middle. Gerald Alley and a succession of Methodist ministers each had a slightly larger log house. Shanties and wigwams lay scattered here and there, with most of the residences south of Coldwater Road. Gill built Chief Yellowhead's frame house near the corner of Coldwater Road and present-day Neywash Street. By 1833 about 250 Chippewas, 130 of them Christian converts, lived in the village. Alley helped them cultivate about fifty acres of potatoes, corn, beans, and oats in a field adjacent to present-day Neywash Street near Yellowhead's house. The village stood north of present-day Mississaga Street and east of present-day West Street to Lake Couchiching. About 100 whites lived along the edge of the village and nearby.

It did not take long for conflict to arise between the whites and Chippewas, or for the Chippewas to get caught up in white politics. No sooner had Yellowhead's band been moved from Chiefs Island to the village, than British government officials and the Methodist ministers, sent up by their church to convert the natives, began fighting over who was to do what. The ministers and British bureaucrats argued over who should teach the native children, where the schoolhouse should be built, and when it could be occupied. Caught in the middle of an argument over who should teach the children, "...poor Yellowhead was so confounded... that the perspiration rolled from his face and finally could not say anything on one side or the other," reported Captain Thomas Anderson, the federal government's Indian Agent in 1830.

The whites' opinion of the Chippewas was typical of the time. Methodist missionaries, a kindly lot from most accounts, viewed the Chippewas as children. Settlers saw them as savages. The Chippewa women were "very plain when young and hideous when old," wrote Millicent and Ellen Steele, the daughters of a prominent settler, in their 1833 diary. The British government saw the Chippewas as a reclamation project, and not an easy one at that.

"...it is hoped they will become industrious and useful subjects. But as long as they are permitted to ask and have whatever their fickle minds may desire, they will be just as long before they will be either useful to themselves or to society," concluded one government surveyor in an 1833 report.

Many white settlers rejected the idea that the Chippewa should be taught anything, or even go to Christian church on Sunday, recalled the Reverend Thomas Williams. His family had moved to Simcoe County in 1822, when he was 12. Before he answered the call to religion, Williams worked as a settlers' guide for the Canada Company, a British agency charged with settling Huronia. Many years after he retired, he wrote his recollections for The Packet, an Orillia newspaper. Williams recalled walking from the land agency office at Bass Lake each Sunday to the Methodists' Church Service for the Chippewas. Mission teachers gave Sunday school lessons to the children from 9:30 to 11 in the morning. Then the mission teacher "or some strong lunged Indian would take a long tin horn and produce from it trumpet-like sounds, which would seem to echo in all directions. Then look! There would be a stir at the door of every Indian house as the people began to move towards the central schoolhouse to take part in holy worship."

Many of the white settlers, traders, and teamsters refused to attend church. It's true much of the service was conducted in Chippewa, but scriptures and preaching was done in English, recalled Williams. And many of the whites could have used the instruction, he observed. "The prevailing disposition was not religious, and many wanted the Chippewas out of that," Williams recalled.

The Chippewas did not accept the animosity with indifference. They allowed some white settlers to live in the two-family log houses for awhile, but made it clear who owned the house and who was visiting. As more whites moved into the area, the Chippewas stood their ground. Indian agent Wellesley Ritchie decided in 1834 to build on a lot north of present-day Mississaga Street, west of West Street. The Chippewas felt that was too close to their houses and refused to let him build. Ritchie waited until the Chippewa men were away hunting, brought in his workers and built a large house of hewed cedar logs. The Chippewas were so angry when they returned, they burned the house down.

Yet the same British system that ensured a certain amount of snobbery also guaranteed the Chippewas protection under the law. Captain Thomson brought together some Chippewa and white men together in the spring of 1834 to raise him a barn. The work was plagued by rain and delays. During one supper break, a playful wrestling match broke out between a Ronald McDonald and a Chippewa, Joseph St. German (sic). McDonald threw St. German on the floor in the kitchen. St. German was mortally injured and died within eight minutes.

"He was a young, strong, active Indian, but from habit and education more like a Canadian," Thomson wrote in his diaries. The next day a jury, assembled mainly of the barn-raisers, found McDonald guilty of manslaughter. Constable John O'Connor refused to take McDonald to jail, because he would not get paid for doing so. So Thomson sent McDonald to Toronto, where it appears he served some time before a proper trial. The only good thing about the accident, concluded Thomson, was that it kept a group of wet, cold, and unhappy barn-raisers on his property another day to stand for jury duty, and they more or less finished raising the barn.

In spite of a few disputes, life in the Indian Village and surrounding communities moved along as normally as it could. The farmers cleared their land by burning the trees, visited each other when they could, and tried to thrive in a land riddled with pests ranging from mosquitoes to bears.

"Could not sleep from the mosquitoes," reads a July 14, 1833, entry in the diary of Millicent and Ellen Steele. "Life is not worth having in their company. They are the only drawback we have found in this country." The two were daughters of Elmes Steele, who built Purbrook, a house about nine miles from the Indian Village. Their neighbour, John Drinkwater, had equally bad luck with bears. He lived in a house and grounds called Northbrook, a few miles outside of the village just north of present-day Highway 12. Determined to catch a bear that had killed some livestock, John and his wife Sarah hid in their barn, with a shotgun aimed through a crack in the wall at the carcass of one of their cows. They sat until midnight, when they heard a commotion outside. John shot off the gun, but he and Sarah would not go out until daylight in case the bear was merely wounded. The next morning they walked out of the barn to discover they had killed their one and only bull. John had to walk to Bond Head to get a new bull, taking three days to get it and bring it back through the bush.

Life was becoming slightly more civilized in the Indian Village. Methodist teacher Andrew Moffatt took on the job of postmaster, keeping letters addressed to The Narrows, Lake Simcoe, in a little birchbark basket. Moffatt took whatever mail there was to a log in front of his house and chatted with people while he thumbed through the contents of the basket, looking for their letters. The Connecticut Missionary Society posted Moffatt to the Indian Village in 1833 to teach the Chippewa men and boys. He was well-suited to pioneer life. On his way to his new posting, Moffatt grew so delighted with the beauty of the countryside, he had his baggage sent on by stage, and walked all the way from Toronto to the Lake Couchiching. His partner at the school, Mercy Manwaring, taught the Chippewa women and girls, and was equally suited to life in the village. Manwaring was posted to the Indian Village in 1832 and became proficient in the Chippewa language. She and Moffatt married in 1834 and gave birth a year later to Thomas, the first white child born in the village.

Several villages vied to become the centre of white settlement around the Indian Village. In the 1830s, Newtown arose at the foot of West Street on Shingle Bay, where some settlers landed. The Narrows also laid claim to becoming the true centre of activity. Leading settlers and natives met in a council meeting January 6, 1834, in a tavern at Newtown to consider certain bylaws. Two chiefs, Yellowhead and Big Shilling, attended the meeting, presided over by Constable O'Connor. At that first meeting, council passed two bylaws, one allowing swine, cattle, and horses to roam freely and the other describing in detail to the inch how local fences must be built. The community's clerk was told not to worry about tax receipts, because no taxes were to be collected that year. There wasn't really much for a council to do in a community of a few hundred whites and Chippewas, so it met only once a year for the next few years. Yellowhead became a warden of the community, showing how much the white settlers respected the diplomatic chief. As the Indian Village's importance grew, Newtown's faded, and by 1835, the council was calling the community around the village and The Narrows, Orillia. By then, councillors had also had enough of bulls, rams, and goats running freely, and passed a new bylaw restricting their movements. Aside from the livestock, council had few other concerns. In 1836, fines for breaking the livestock rules and others gave council $9 in revenue, with $5 still in the bank at the end of the year.

Even the Rebellion of 1837 caused only a small stir in village life. In December, word reached Orillia that radicals were marching on York to overtake the government. Most Orillia area settlers were appalled to hear the news. Captain Thomson, Captain Drinkwater, and Alley swore several men in as constables and ordered the local blacksmith to make pikes. Some men went to Barrie to join the loyalist forces, but they were too late to help. The rebellion had fizzled. There was some sympathy for the rebellion. The Reverend Williams wrote years later that the system of land grants was unfair to those without connections to the government or military. And it's recorded that someone less peaceful than Williams burned down the house of a local loyalist leader, Captain William Kersop, while he was off leading the local militia against the rebels.

Armed rebellion isn't the British or Canadian way. The increasing friction between whites and Chippewas resulted in the removal of the band by paperwork, not force. The settlers were tired of travelling through swamp and bush from The Narrows to the settlement beside the Indian Village. Their community of log cabins edged the west side of West Street and both sides of Colborne Street from West to Andrew, unable to spread closer to the lake. The Chippewas refused to let them build a landing on the lake and had built their own store and wharf. In 1836, white settlers petitioned the government to move the Chippewas off the village site. The government agreed to the petition and Chippewas surrendered their land in November, 1836. Some whites wanted to have the Chippewas settled on Manitoulin Island, but Yellowhead's band refused, deciding to settle as close as possible to The Narrows. By the end of 1839, Yellowhead and his band of 184 Chippewas had completed their move to 1,621 acres of land on the other side of Lake Couchiching, land white settlers had earlier abandoned. The Chippewas bought the land for twelve shillings and six pence per acre (about $4,000 in total).

The settlers who forced the Chippewas out soon petitioned the government to survey and sell the land in the former Indian Village. Andrew and Mercy Moffatt were among the first to move into the village, opening up a store at the corner of present-day Front and Mississaga Streets, where the Champlain Hotel stands, and building a house on Mississaga Street between Matchedash and Front Streets. (The house was torn down in 1959) The population of the village grew slowly over the next thirty years. Drawing people to Orillia were good land and a market of farmers and shantymen working the bush to the north. In 1844, Orillia was made up of

What is now Bay Street in Orillia was once a cabin and fields, as seen in this 1844 drawing by T.H. Ware. That is Chiefs Island on the right. The cabin was the residence of Captain St. John, an earlier settler. Lake St. John, or Cingin, was named after him. The property was eventually purchased by Henry Pellatt, who built Casa Loma in Toronto. Pellatt's Southwood was used a summer home for the family for many years. It is now Southwood Circle off Bay Street.

Metropolitan Toronto Reference Library, Repro T 14374

about 100 people, mainly mechanics and labourers, living in about thirty frame houses. For about $35, you could buy a half-acre lot in a town that boasted two doctors, two mills, one clergyman, and as yet, suffered no lawyers, reported Titus Herbert Ware, a lawyer himself, who toured and sketched the area in 1844. Besides his invaluable sketches, Ware gave an interesting written account of the village. There were plenty of jobs and wages were good. Farm servants could make $10 a month, besides free room and board, and female servants could make $5 a month. Immigrants to Canada preferred jobs in more southerly communities, creating a shortage of labourers in places like Orillia, said Ware. The high wages allowed labourers to soon own farms or businesses of their own. Ware seemed pleased with Orillia. The frame and log houses were pleasant, the farms self-sufficient, though not large enough for market farming, and many families respectable. Hard work in spring, summer, and fall was replaced by visiting and other amusement in winter. The only problem in paradise, said Ware, was the attitude of common labourers that they were the equal of the upper class, "the equality notions which the lower orders in a manner imbibe with the American air they breathe, the notions which the servants and the laboring classes generally entertain is that 'Jack is as good as his master'."

In some ways, the labourers had it just as good, or rather, as bad, as their masters. Differences in wealth did not necessarily translate into differences in lifestyle. Just about everybody in 1844 owned a horse or a pair of oxen, and a cow, according to the assessment roll of that year. And everyone, rich and poor, struggled through streets that were mud in spring and dust in summer, not to mention a pasture for the cows. Much of present-day Orillia lay in bush or swamps. Hard times demanded innovation. For example, there were no rivers nearby with the power to run mills, but that proved to be no problem for Frederick Dallas. He simply dammed a small creek, flooding much of the land around present-day Memorial Avenue. The dammed waters gave him enough power to run a saw and grist mill.

And life was good enough to draw more people. The population grew to about 300 in 1854. Already the rugged beauty of the village was attracting attention. An article in the Barrie Magnet of 1851 described Lake Couchiching as romantic and the situation of Orillia as beyond equal. The community had by now built two churches, two schools, four general stores, two taverns and one lockup house, and provided work for two blacksmiths, a tailer, a tinsmith, a wagon maker, a tanner, a cabinet maker, a butcher, a shoemaker, several carpenters, a physician, and a surgeon. Mail arrived three times a week in summer by steamer, and three times a week in winter by stage.

But the Magnet posed a question that has echoed in Orillia since, why was the place growing so slowly? "It may appear so strange that a village and township so well situated and so desirable for settlers should be at a standstill these few years back." The Magnet's writer blamed the province for directing immigration to Owen Sound. For many years Orillia remained a small pioneer community, serving nearby farms and northern lumber camps, surrounded by homesteads and the woods. One visitor recalled that the most exciting moment in daily village life arose with the arrival of one of the steamers that plied the lakes.

Albeit slowly, the village did grow, and so did the aspirations of its residents. By 1866, they believed Orillia should stand on its own, separate from South Orillia Township. A petition signed by 122 ratepayers persuaded Simcoe County council to pass a bylaw on November 22, 1866, separating Orillia from the township and incorporating it into a village. The election in the Temperance Hall early the next year named James Quinn as the first reeve, head of a council of four. The township and village began an immediate rivalry, which still flares up occasionally. Both sides claimed ownership of some tools and the library, housed at the Temperance Hall. A county judge settled the matter, giving the tools to the township and the library to the village. The township also refused to contribute to the building of a drill hall, so the village was forced to ask its residents for more money. Confident of their village's growing importance, Orillians handed over the money. Council was careful with it. Expenditures for the first year totalled $400. About $161 of that was for road work, and $180 for salaries. When the census taker refused to provide each member of council with a copy of the census, council refused to pay his $8 fee. About $1,500 in taxes was collected that first year.

By the time Confederation came on July 1, 1867, Orillia had laid down the foundation for the calm and steady growth that typified Ontario's villages in the 1800s. The lumber boom rocked that foundation. The fuel for the explosion was the great Canadian pine belt that stretched for thousands of miles north. The fuse was the coming of the railway. And the spark was the enterprise of the village's first kings, the lumber barons.

Mississaga Street in 1864, likely from the West Street intersection looking east.
Simcoe County Archives

By 1867, Orillia was large enough to break away from the township and become a village. A brewery and several hotels supplied thirsty travellers, citizens and shantymen from nearby lumber camps. The market stood near the waterfront. The railway did not reach Orillia until 1871, so the line marked on the map may have been the proposed route.

Courtesy of Orillia Historical Society

FROM HOTEL TO ASYLUM

One man's mistake gave Orillia its largest industry and a certain amount of character. Henry Fraser, an innkeeper at Prices Corners near Orillia, figured tourism would be the village's mainstay some day. So in the 1850s he threw his money into building a luxury hotel on the shores of Lake Couchiching, about where the Champlain monument stands today. Fraser could picture his three-storey brick hotel, with its two wings and lake frontage of 118 feet, full of tourists seeking the clean air. If he pictured them getting there, he did so with blinders on. The railway was 20 years away. The only way to get there was by stage and steamer. Frazer ran out of money and gave up the project before the hotel was completed. About the same time, the province began looking for a building to handle the overflow

at the Toronto Lunatic Asylum, and in 1859, bought the hotel and property for $16,800. The Orillia Lunatic Asylum opened in 1861 and soon had 140 patients. From the description of a visitor in 1869, it sounded like a well-managed institution with compassionate caretakers and a surprisingly relaxed attitude toward security. Mrs. Ephriam Post came to the asylum to visit a friend she had not seen in 11 years. The elderly groundskeeper who let her in explained she was too late to visit patients, but agreed to take her on a tour of the grounds. They came across the gardener, who took delight in giving Mrs. Post lengthy descriptions of the flower beds. As they returned to the asylum building, Mrs. Post was shocked to learn from the groundskeeper that the gardener was actually a patient who believed he was the gardener. When the groundskeeper introduced her to the matron of the asylum, Mrs. Post was further shocked to learn he too was a patient, who happened to believe he was the groundskeeper. Nine years after opening the asylum, the provincial government paid some favors in London by opening a new branch there. Orillia's asylum was closed and remained an irritant to village council. As a newspaper article in the 1870s pointed out in the brute language of the day, there were still a lot of idiots in the province with nowhere to go. So in 1876, the province turned the building

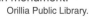

Henry Fraser's dream of a luxury hotel on Lake Couchiching in the 1850s soured, so the government bought the building for the Orillia branch of the Toronto Asylum for Lunatics. The Champlain monument stands where the asylum once did. The grounds were beautifully landscaped and turned into Couchiching Beach Park after the asylum was closed. The waterfront was already filling in with boathouses. The outline of the foundations of Fraser's hotel are still visible on summer days in the dry grass near the Champlain monument.
Orillia Public Library.

The province moved its Lunatic Asylum to London, Ontario, but eventually built the Asylum for Idiots on Lake Simcoe. That asylum became the Ontario Hospital School, then the Huronia Regional Centre, still in operation in 1996.

into the Orillia Idiot Asylum. Within two years, the province had to put the overflow from the Orillia institution in the Queen's Hotel downtown. The province began building a new Idiot Asylum in 1885 on the shores of Lake Simcoe, opening it in 1891. The new Idiot Asylum held about 550 patients. The village bought Asylum Point on Lake Couchiching and turned it into Couchiching Park.

Over the years the number of those patients and their treatment changed. Teaching and training the patients became the key to treatment, and the name of the institution was changed to the Ontario Hospital School in the 1930s. The Ontario Hospital School was transformed into the Huronia Regional Centre, one of the city's largest employers, in 1974.

A COUNTRY WITH NOTHING BUT TREES

Few of the settlers who moved near the Indian Village had any experience homesteading. Many of them were military officers retired on half-pay and a grant of land. Said one Irish ex-sergeant when he came across his choice lot of 200 acres: "The trees, the trees; I never saw the likes of them. Oh, the trees, the trees, if they had been stones I would know what to do with them."

The Reverend Thomas Williams recalled that story and many more for The Packet in the late 1800s. As a young man in the 1830s, he had worked as a settlers' agent for the Canada Company, which was charged with settling the area. The work of building a simple house in present-day Orillia was often dangerous, as the missionary's tale of the shanty-building for an experienced Captain Wood reveals. Wood was living with a Chippewa in one of the Indian Village houses, but feared he was going to be evicted before winter. He demanded the Canada Company help him move, so Williams was ordered to find a shanty boss and gather up a building party.

Lawyer T.H. Ware sketched these log cabins in Orillia during a September, 1844 visit. These cabins were likely near Chief Yellowhead's house, roughly where St. James Anglican Church stands today. Built properly, the cabins provided warm and dry shelter, although many settlers spent a few cold months before learning from neighbors how to build a fireplace and chink the walls.

Metropolitan Toronto Reference Library

I had learned from an Indian that Couchiching had frozen over, so that it would be safe to walk down the shore to the place I wished to reach. We, the eleven men of us, took the ice and walked down, the men carrying their provisions and camping necessaries. I directed the men not to gather into groups, but to keep some distance apart, which they did orderly enough until we nearly reached our destination. When I judged we were near the place, I took out my map and spread it on the ice to compare the shores with the map. While I was intent on this work the men forgot my caution, and gathered round me. All at once I felt the ice bending; I picked up the map and ran out between the men, crying "Scatter for your lives the ice is bending." They were not slow to do this, and it certainly saved us a cold bath at least, for after we left the place the water came up over more than an acre of space.

The shanties were built of logs from eight to twelve inches in diameter with roofs of overlaid scooped-out basswood logs, similar to today's tile roofs. Typically, a foreman and his crew of nine axemen would cut out the space for a door for the new homeowner and leave it up to him to put in a door, windows, and floor.

"...and though they could never be made into a handsome dwelling, with skill, care and some taste, they were often made very cosey (sic), very comfortable in the inside," recalled Williams. "I have put in a good many evenings and nights with great comfort and pleasure in such dwellings."

Captain Wood and his wife found little pleasure their first winter, according to accounts from another pioneer, Hester Gill. Wood and his wife spent the first months without a fireplace, building a fire at the end of one room. He had not chinked in the spaces between the logs to keep the wind out. The family wasn't poor, but the shanty builders and other labourers had dispersed for the winter, and there was no way to get away from the area when the lake was frozen. Fortunately for the Woods, a hunter from the north came down to the area for the winter, and stayed with the family. Knowing more about life on the frontier, the hunter built the family a fireplace and filled in the gaps between the logs.

THE LUMBER BOOM

In the summer of 1874, the Oddfellows Society took its annual excursion on Lake Simcoe, and a party of shanty roughs took theirs on the streets of Orillia. The Oddfellows excursion aboard the Lady of the Lake epitomized, according to the weekly Orillia Times, fellowship, grace, and good humour:

Lumber turned Orillia from a sleepy village to a bustling town. This illustration from 1875 shows the location of the Orillia's churches, public school, hotels, flour mills, sawmills and two rail lines. The illustration at the bottom of the map shows the Orillia Asylum for Idiots from the Midland Railway wharf at the foot of Mississaga Street.
Simcoe County Archives

The Orillia Brass Band accompanied the excursionists and discoursed music sweet and soothing. Dancing was kept up nearly all the way out with commendable vigor, and arriving at their destination the party at once scampered in all directions in search of some shady nook wherein to partake of the contents of hampers supplied with everything to tempt the most sluggish appetite. Games of numerous kinds, idling, flirting and other recreations equally interesting and pleasant beguiled the hours until the whistle warned the merry crowd that it was time to start for home.

According to the newspaper, the shantymen's excursion also epitomized fellowship and good times:

A crowd of shanty roughs took possession of the village last Monday. It is perfectly amusing, were it not for their innate and unbearable brutality, to witness the abandon which they will buckle down to the task of reversing the conventionalities of society and making the time hideous to the orderly portion of the community generally.

The two social events of the season drew their people and their money from the same source - lumber. Trees built Orillia, its industry, its future, and a split personality that continues to be a source of amusement, frustration, and tension among city residents even today. The 100-foot tall white pines of the Shield country were chopped, cut, planed, and sliced into millions of dollars for everyone: a few thousand millworkers, farmers, shantymen, cooks, tanners, and butchers; a few hundred clerks, artisans, tavern owners, merchants and newspaper men; a dozen or so wealthy businessmen and their society wives, and a few rich lumber kings. Lumber gave Orillia a timber-rough core and a veneer of gentility, with every kind of texture of society in between. The railways, the newspapers, industry, and a sense that Orillia was destined for economic greatness — lumber brought it all.

Simcoe County had been lumbered as early as the 1780s, when masts for British ships were taken out of the Coldwater area. But little organized lumbering took place until the 1840s and 1850s, as settlement pushed north. Settlers saw trees as both a nuisance and a potential small income, burning the trees and selling the ash for soaps. A few sawmills in and around Orillia produced the lumber that was necessary for the community's buildings and houses. In the mid-1800s, the lumber trade in Ontario began to grow. Settlement in the United States was pushing farther west. Booming cities like Chicago needed more and more wood, as settlement consumed the forests of Ohio and Michigan. Ontario lumbermen were working their way through the forests of eastern Ontario, approaching Orillia. And in 1853 the Northern Railway reached Allandale near Barrie, linking lakes Simcoe and Couchiching, and the rivers and smaller lakes reaching into the great Canadian pine belt with Toronto.

Dozens of mills sprang up. In 1846, there were twenty-nine sawmills in Simcoe County. By 1871 that had jumped to 114. A small self-sufficient community on the border between farm country and the towering pine forests of the north, Orillia naturally became a centre for supplying camps with food and equipment. Huge lumber companies, such as Dodge and Co. of New York, opened offices and yards here. Ambitious men began building mills in Orillia to make money milling the logs before they were shipped south. One such man was Andrew Tait, who started by making cedar shingles with his wife in a small building on Albert Street south of Colborne Street. He made the shingles with a hand-powered machine and his wife bundled them up. From that simple start, Tait built a tidy lumber empire. The Tait and Carss Lumber Company mill, driven by steam engine, was built at the foot of the Colborne Street on Lake Couchiching, with a lumber yard stretching to Mississaga Street. Employees worked from 6 a.m. to 6 p.m. for a dollar a day and Tait made sure they worked hard for that dollar. He built a mansion on Colborne Street that looked over all the others, and people said he could sit in his tower and watch workmen at his lumber

Andrew Tait and his wife, posing in front of their mansion Glenorma, began their lumber empire with one hand-powered shingle making machine. The house on Colborne Street between Matchedash and Peter Streets eventually became the Orillia House, and burned down in 1968. Lumber and its service industries provided the money to build many of the fine homes in Orillia's north ward.
Simcoe County Archives

It's said that Andrew Tait built a tower on his mansion so he could watch his workers at his sawmill nearby. The view from the tower to the west and north shows the grounds and in the distance, at the top right of the photograph, the side of the Orillia Opera House. The smokestack at the far left is likely the original Tudhope carriage works. This photograph was taken around the turn of the century.
Simcoe County Archives.

yard. Tait lived like a king. He thought dancing was sinful, so instead of a ballroom, he built a roller skating rink on the third floor of his mansion to keep his children amused and out of trouble. He played on Lake Couchiching on his own steam yacht, sharing the waters with another of Ontario's most successful lumber kings, John Thomson.

Born in Scotland, Thomson settled in Peterborough with his wife in 1855 and began dabbling in the lumber business there. The pine forests in Longford Township northeast of Lake Couchiching caught his interest, and he hired Rama native John Young to guide him through the area. On the month-long survey, Thomson calculated how much the lumber was worth. In 1860, the British-Canadian Land and Emigration Company paid the government about $181,000 for much of the land stretching from Longford Township east to Haliburton. But the emigration and settlement did not move quickly enough, so the company decided to sell its timber rights. Thomson headed to Toronto for the auction, armed with firsthand knowledge of the land. In the finery of the Queen's Hotel, Thomson bid against other Ontario and American lumbermen for the timber rights. It's likely no one knew the land as well as he did, and bidding moved slowly up to $10,000. Thomson started raising it by $1,000 a bid. When it reached $20,000, Thomson, tired of waiting, stunned the room by offering an astounding $30,000. Other lumbermen thought he must be mad, for it was expensive to move the timber out of the area down to southern mills. But Thomson had a plan to mill the lumber himself and ship it south.

First, he bought access to an unusual service operated by a pair of other local lumbermen, James Durham and Thompson Smith. The pair had timber rights near the Black River and mills on Lake Simcoe, but no easy way to get the timber to the mills. The Black River connected to Lake St. John by a creek too shallow for log drives. So Durham and Smith, with the financial backing of other lumbermen, dug a three-quarter-mile canal from the Black River to Lake St. John, and a steam-powered tramway from Lake St. John to Lake Couchiching. Spiked wheels drove a chain, which carried logs over the one-eighth-mile rise that separated the two lakes. The logs travelled about two miles an hour, and during peak times, workers put in twelve-hour days for 87 cents a day.

After gaining the timber rights to Longford Township at the Toronto auction, John Thomson built mills on Lake St. John. He brought the logs in by the new canal, milled them, then sent them to Lake Couchiching by his

John Thomson stunned other lumbermen in 1860 by paying a princely sum of $30,000 for the timber rights on land east of Lake Couchiching. The Longford Lumber Co. mill on Lake St. John cut about 20 million feet of lumber a year. Thomson also set up a shingle mill at the foot of Neywash Street in Orillia.

Sue Mulcahy Collection

own train tracks. From there, the lumber was towed to Lake Simcoe. Before the railroads arrived, Orillia's harbour was often clogged with lumber booms. Thomson's Longford Lumber Co. alone cut 5 million feet of pine in its first year of operation, 1869, and averaged 15 to 20 million feet a year after that. By the time the trees ran out, about 200 million feet of lumber had been milled.

Thomson's success brought him wealth, power, and independence. The Dominion Bank of Canada opened a branch in Orillia to serve the Thomson account. Apparently, the owners of the Northern Railway originally intended to run the railway up the west side of Lake Couchiching, but decided instead to cross The Narrows and run up the east side of the lake in order to gain Thomson's business. That northern extension was completed in 1873, a few months after the Midland reached Orillia. For

A panoramic view of Orillia's waterfront in 1872, taken when the Asylum that stood roughly where the Champlain monument in Couchiching Beach park stands today. The mill in the foreground is the Oliver and Sutherland mill. That company is credited with being the first in Orillia to establish regular working hours, 7 a.m. to 6 p.m., and pay the workmen regularly and in cash. The Midland Railway was a year away from running through Orillia.

mill, a large sash and door company, used a million feet of lumber a year and paid sixty people a total of $15,000 a year in wages. The Tudhope carriage factory — two large, three-storey buildings on West and Colborne streets — made 4,000 vehicles a year, using half a million feet of lumber and providing $30,000 in yearly wages for seventy-five people a year. Other carriage factories, planing mills, and a hub and spoke factory sprang up.

several years, Thomson used the rival Midland Railway to ship his lumber south. While the managers of the Northern stewed, he ignored their line just outside his doors. Finally, Colonel Fred Cumberland, the head of the railway, took a private train to Longford Mills. Cumberland was a powerful man who once threatened to turn the streets of Allandale to gold and Barrie to grass if Barrie did not support his railway. At Longford Mills, Cumberland told the conductor to tell Thomson he would like the lumber baron to visit him in his private car. Thomson refused, saying he did his business in his business office. Cumberland was not used to that kind of response, but the railway needed Thomson's business and eventually offered freight rates so attractive, Thomson started using the Northern line.

The lumber from mills like Thomson's and Tait's provided raw material for a growing number of Orillia businesses. J.R. Eaton's planing

The lumber mills sparked the growth of dozens of other businesses, such as the Ramsay Carriage Works (2) on the southeast corner of Coldwater Road and Albert Street, J.J. Hatley's butcher shop (1) on Mississaga Street Street, and the Victoria Foundry (3) and Machine Works, located on the northeast corner of Peter and King streets. The foundry is Orillia's oldest manufacturer, opened as machine shop in 1865 by William Bateman. By 1878, the shop was making machinery for the grist and saw mills springing up in the area. Robert Brammer bought the machine shop that year, and renamed it the Victoria Foundry & Machine Works. Brammer died in 1894, and his son-in-law, Erastus Long, eventually took over the business. It eventually became known as E. Long Manufacturing Company Ltd. By 1909, the company employed fifty men and was ready to move. The new plant on West and Queen streets cost about $30,000 to build. The town gave Long the new site for free, and a fixed tax assessment for ten years. The town also opened up Queen Street from West Street to Atherley Road, and extended a water main to the new building. Long died in 1916, just as the the production was at a peak. His wife, Sarah Long took over the operation of the 600-employee foundry until she died in 1933. After the First World War, the company focused on making mining equipment. It has changed names throughout the years — E. Long Ltd., Dorr-Oliver-Long Ltd., Dorcan, GL&V Inc. — but in one form or another has remained one of Orillia's largest employers.

Orillia Public Library

Dozens of companies supplied clothing, food, harnesses, and hundreds of other items for the camps.

Farm boys earned extra money working in the camps. About 80 per cent of local boys "went shantying" in the winter, estimated one logger. They worked hard for their money and lived in rough conditions. "Everybody got good strong stomachs," recalled Harold Overend in a panel discussion on lumbering hosted by the Orillia Historical Society in 1970.

There was rarely any fresh meat in the camps, but that was the least of their culinary worries, as Overend explained in his story about driving logs out of the bush one spring: "It was a pretty hot day and I walked down to see the cook and they had these old windows and he was baking and swearing, chewing tobacco and he wanted to spit it out the old open window. But the tobacco went in the dough. That spring I didn't eat anything else but canned tomatoes and boiled eggs.

It's no wonder some shantymen took to the taverns and the streets on their return to civilization. There were twenty-eight bars serving only 1,200 people in Orillia in 1871. Shantymen had been known to lose an entire winter's wage in one drinking bout, and villagers were often afraid to venture out in spring evenings when the shantymen returned from the bush.

The village's growth attracted newspapers, which added to the community's colour. The lone survivor from those days, The Packet & Times, had a birth fitting of the wild times. In 1867, Orillia's first year as a village, the publisher of the Lindsay Post, C. Blackett Robinson, sent a printing press and a young manager named Peter Murray to Orillia to begin a new paper. The Expositor first published on November 16, 1867 and prospered, although editing was done on a freelance basis, which made for varying degrees of quality from week to week. One mixup caused Murray a huge headache, while at the same time allowing him to buy the paper. Some campaign material that the Expositor had printed for the Liberals went out by mistake with the newspaper's masthead on it. The Conservatives in town were enraged by the paper's apparent endorsement of their rivals.

Publisher Robinson rushed to Orillia, and Murray, perhaps figuring this was the best way to get out of trouble, offered to buy the paper. Robinson agreed. Murray had little time to enjoy his monopoly in the growing village. The handsome and ambitious Doctor Robert Ramsay had returned to his hometown in 1868 after making a fortune in California. Ramsay wanted to get into Parliament and figured a newspaper provided the best platform for his views.

Ramsay let it leak out that he was going to launch a rival paper in Orillia. He waited a few days to make sure Murray was good and worried, then casually dropped by one day to see if it was true Murray was interested in selling the Expositor, rather than fight it out with a new paper. William Hale and his brother George were working for Murray at the time and urged him not to sell. But Murray, a restless man, sold the Expositor to Ramsay and moved back to Lindsay to try yet another paper. The Hales left too.

After a while, Ramsay changed the name of the paper to The Northern Light and made it a supporter of the Liberal Party. In 1870, two years after selling Ramsay the paper, Murray returned to Orillia to work with him, bringing George Hale along. William Hale was enjoying life editing Murray's other paper in Beaverton: "I was, therefore in no mood for a change when one day my employer, Peter Murray, again dropped in on me with a most amazing proposal. How any sane mind ever conceived a scheme so impossible one cannot imagine." The scheme was this. William Hale would move to Orillia to start a rival paper, supporting the Conservative Party, published out of the same office as the Liberal Northern Light. That way Ramsay could stop anyone else from starting up a Conservative paper. Such an idea, two rivals run by the same company, was unheard of, and Hale let Murray know what he thought of the plan with a "volley of ridicule." But Murray persisted, and Hale finally agreed, warning Murray the idea would float no better than a bar of iron in Lake Couchiching.

Ramsay was delighted, but he got more than he bargained for. When the Hales announced to the public they were starting a new paper in Orillia, Ramsay wrote an article in the Light ridiculing the upstart, called The Packet. The Packet's first issue, Thursday, November 16, 1870, launched a fierce counterattack, questioning Ramsay's credibility. Ramsay was astounded. He demanded Murray tell him who was writing the Packet's editorials.

"The boys are doing it themselves," said Murray, the "boys" being William and George Hale. The Hales intensified their attacks on the Light, the Liberals and Ramsay. A few weeks after The Packet started publishing, Ramsay announced he was running for reeve of the village. Much of the four-page December 7, 1870, issue of the Packet was taken up with accusations Ramsay was using his paper for political aims and that he made up quotes for his stories. Teetotalers and devout Christians, the Hales nonetheless knew how to throw around invective. Ramsay was no more than a drivelling, inconsistent, bad-tempered, public humiliation, they wrote.

It was getting to be too much for Ramsay, who was paying for the honor of having his name ridiculed. Six weeks after the start of his experiment, he told Murray to get rid of The Packet. William Hale turned to the local Conservative leader and the town's first reeve, James Quinn, and asked for a loan to keep The Packet going. With a small advance, Hale bought a press, rented an office and started publishing again.

For the next few years, the Light's Ramsay and The Packet's Hale boys waged an outrageous battle of words over each other's writing style, accuracy, and political stand. Ramsay called the small upstart "the Pamphlet", while the Hales called the established paper, which tried to please everyone on both sides of issues, "the Revolving Light." A fierce battle erupted over the railways. In 1871, two rival railroads raced to reach Orillia and its taxpayers' pocketbooks first. Extension of the Northern Railway from Toronto had stalled in 1853, after reaching Allandale, near Barrie. Legal battles and financial problems delayed the extension of the railway to Barrie until 1865. Four years later, a group of influential county and Orillia leaders incorporated to extend the line to Orillia and Muskoka. The new line was sometimes called the Toronto, Simcoe and Muskoka Railway, but was more commonly known as the Northern. Meanwhile, the Midland Railway had been built from Port Hope to Beaverton. At about the same time the Northern received permission from the province to extend north to Orillia, the Midland received permission to extend east to the same village. The race to reach the booming lumber town and a corner on its business had begun.

Railway companies demanded cash "bonuses" from municipalities before extending their lines. Rural residents especially were not always keen on handing over their money. Many county residents were still stinging from the high taxes paid out while the Northern was being built from Toronto to Allandale. Simcoe county historian Andrew Hunter calculated county residents paid about $1 million to build Northern rail lines in the 1800s. Trains also had a habit of killing livestock that wandered on to improperly fenced tracks and of rushing through hamlets had that expected to be important stops.

But Orillia leaders wanted the railways in order to ship lumber and other products out to bigger markets south and east. The Light and The Packet jumped aboard rival railways. Neither editor would oppose any railroad company outright - the importance of having any rail service in the village was too great - but in general the Northern Light favoured the Northern, while The Packet favoured the Midland. The reasons remain unclear. The Hales suggested in print that Ramsay and his newspaper, once the supporters of the Midland, had received favours from the directors of the Northern Railway in return for public support. Ramsay denied the charge. He wrote that the Northern would give Orillia access to the growing Toronto market. The Hales countered that the real market was to the east in Montreal.

Just how much Ontario communities wanted rail service can be seen in an incident that occurred in Orillia. Early in 1871, the managers of the Northern told the village council they had until January 30 to give the railroad company a $12,500 bonus or face delays in construction. If there was no bonus ready, the contract would lapse the railway delayed, warned Colonel Cumberland. Many councillors had won election on the promise the Northern would get the same bonus, $10,000, as promised earlier to the Midland, and weren't keen on the vagueness of the Northern's promises to build a station in the village. At a quickly called Saturday evening meeting, a stubborn council and Northern officials tried but failed to hammer out an agreement. Northern executives publicly expressed a great sadness at the decision. After all, said Cumberland, the company never thought to make one single cent out of the people of Orillia, but only needed help to defray the cost of running the line north through the village. On Sunday, a group of alarmed village residents signed a petition asking council to give the Northern its $12,500. At an emergency meeting Monday morning, January 30, council agreed to the bonus. The Light celebrated. The Packet never forgave the Northern Railway for "bullying" villagers and stepped up the campaign to ensure the Midland received a smooth path to Orillia.

In the spring of 1871, the Midland railway began making plans to reach Georgian Bay. In order to do that, the railway needed bonuses from Orillia and the surrounding townships. The Northern, fearing its fledgling monopoly would be broken, called the reeves of all the townships together and discussed what the Northern could do for them. Northern executives hinted that those municipalities that rejected the Midland bonuses might get new rail lines and even stations from their company. One by one that June, the townships voted on the Midland bonus.

A few of the townships refused to give Midland a bonus. Those refusals and problems inside the company ensured that the Midland would lose the race to Orillia. The Northern tracks reached Orillia first, on November 14, 1871. Residents celebrated and tried to get used to the Iron Horse in their lives. The Northern line came so close to Atherley Road, farmers and travellers on horseback had a hard time keeping their horses

Sir Samuel Steele (1851-1919) was born at Purbrook near Orillia. Joining the Royal Canadian Mounted Police in 1872, Steele soon earned legendary status as a strong yet diplomatic police officer who ensured peace during his command of the Yukon and British Columbia during the Klondike Gold Rush. Steele served in the Boer War in South Africa and was Major-General in command of the 2nd Canadian Division in the First World War. He was knighted for his service. He was inducted into the Orillia Hall of Fame posthumously in 1966.

Orillia Public Library

calm when trains went by. So the Northern built sheds at three points along the tracks, for horses to be driven into when a train came. Town residents learned to drive quickly from shed to shed if the trains were scheduled to arrive soon.

> In victory, the Light tried to be magnanimous. We do not wish here to allude to our Railway Policy; it has been severely criticized by friend and foe. We simply point now to those two locomotives shrieking at the Toronto, Simcoe and Muskoka Junction [Northern] Railway Station in our village. We are proud of the championship of that line who has been the first to enter our town.

A few days after the first Northern train reached Orillia, a three-car train consisting of two sleepers and the private car of the railway's managing director steamed into the village at 8 p.m. The crowd at the new station cheered and after a short greeting, the railway executives, provincial and national politicians, newspapermen from Toronto, Barrie, and Orillia papers and leading men of the village retired to a large freight shed for a banquet. The Northern Light described the celebration.

> The freight shed was handsomely decorated with flags and streamers. Around the room were the following mottoes in conspicuous characters: "Toronto and Orillia, "Our Government", "God Save the Queen, and protect her Dominions", "Long May the T.S. and M.J.R.R. flourish," "Hurrah for Cumberland and his Iron Horse". A streamer stretched across the middle of the building with a train of cars painted thereon, and the names of stations from Orillia to Fort Garry was a conspicuous feature of the decorations.

The Packet described the banquet at length as well, but refused to give up its allegiance to the Midland. In the same issue, a reporter noted how Midland surveyors were braving three-foot snowdrifts that week to extend the line to Orillia. The Northern's railway station was built at the bottom of Peter Street at King. When its tracks reached Orillia in 1873, the Midland built its station at the foot of Mississaga Street behind the present-day Champlain Hotel. The Grand Trunk Railroad eventually took over two routes, itself evolving into Canadian National Railway. Where those two rival railways crossed, called the diamond, CN built the present station, which is now the Chamber of Commerce building. The Canadian Pacific Railway built a track to Orillia in 1910, with a station, now the Royal Canadian Legion building, at the foot of Mississaga Street.

The Packet and the Light continued their fight for many years after the railways were settled. But the papers did more than feud. They gave a voice to the community, its dreams and fears. From debates over the shamelessness of young boys swimming off the public waterfront in front of strolling ladies to gossip about lovers spurned and grisly details of murders and drownings, the Northern Light and The Packet reflected the mundane and excitement of everyday life in the 1870s. Occasionally, the publishers even agreed on something. For much of the 1870s, for example, the rival papers led the way in pushing successive councils to improve fire protection. Fire could wipe out a village built of wood, such as Orillia, in hours. And a fire or two seemed to

Fires became a constant hazard in the hot summer months in the 1870s. When the village reached 2,000 people and became a town in 1875, council bought a lot at 27 Peter Street North and built a firehall. In 1896, the town rebuilt the hall on the lot. It featured a fifty-five-foot high bell tower, heated so the hoses could be hung and dried. The bell sounded the alarm and the time of day at 7 a.m., noon, 1 p.m. and 6 p.m. The fire brigade had one wagon with a thirty-five-foot extension ladder and pump operated by eight men. The horses, Pat and Barney, lived in the building and a special pulley system dropped the harnesses on them so they could be quickly hitched to the wagon. Pat and Barney earned their keep, helping to plow streets in the winter and pull a cistern of water to spray the same streets in the dusty, dry summer. The horses were also used to deliver wood to needy families in town. The fire department got its first truck in 1923. The department moved to new headquarters on West Street in 1971, but the hall remains, as do its legends. The late Allan Ironside, a volunteer at the station in the 1930s, liked to tell the story about the night the fire department set a hose on fire. In those days, the hydrants were filled at the top with kerosene, to prevent them from freezing in winter. Usually, firefighters flushed out the kerosene before they started spraying water from the hydrant onto a fire. One night, they forgot and sprayed the fire with about a gallon of kerosene. The hose itself was destroyed by fire.

Stephen Leacock Museum

take out a building or two each summer. A fire in May of 1872 burned a hardware store and part of the post office. The village's firefighters ran out of well water and had to bring some from the lake. The only thing that saved the rest of the village was the lack of wind. Luck saved the village again in August, when a fire that started in a bakery swept along Mississaga Street. Village residents stopped the fire by wetting the walls of a stucco building, using an engine borrowed from the Oliver Co. and throwing wet blankets on the roof.

"In many parts of the town, people had their goods packed and ready for removal, fearing that the conflagration would be the destruction of almost the entire village," wrote The Packet. Thieves made off with hundreds of dollars of goods and one-third of Mississaga Street was destroyed. The constant fires finally prompted Orillia to set up a waterworks system, a series of wooden pipes running from the springs in Victoria Park to cisterns located at the four corners of the downtown. When the village reached 2,000 people and became a town in 1875, council decided even more protection was needed. The town bought a lot at 27 Peter Street North and built a firehall with a fifty-five-foot-high bell tower, for ringing the alarm and sounding the time of day at 7 a.m., noon, 1 p.m. and 6 p.m. The fire brigade had one wagon with a thirty-five-foot extension ladder and pump operated by eight men.

That small force, even with the help of a privately-owned company fire engine, could do little to stop another major fire in 1879. It appeared an arsonist started a small fire behind a storehouse on Mississaga Street about 11:30 p.m. August 5. The flames caught the wooded buildings nearby and within minutes swept down the north side of the main street. Firefighters could do little more than try to stop the fire from spreading to the south side, which earned them criticism from businessmen on the north side of the street who watched their buildings burn without a fight. When the flames reached Peter Street, they raced down both sides to Colborne Street. Thirty buildings - a quarter of the town - were destroyed, and damage was estimated at $50,000. Fortunately, the wind died as quickly as it had risen, and firefighters gained control of the blaze. Town businessmen rebuilt their stores and warehouses out of limestone from quarries at Longford Mills. Many of those buildings on Mississaga Street remain standing today.

Lumber continued to support the town's growth for the next two decades. But the frame buildings of downtown Orillia, the symbol of the lumber years, were replaced by stone and brick, as new industries and new ideas took over.

THE COUCHICHING HOTEL

Soon after the Northern Railway was extended to Orillia in 1871, the directors of the company built the grandest hotel ever seen on Lake Couchiching. To the prominent politicians, generals, and statesmen, the Couchiching Hotel on Couchiching Point offered northern living at its finest. A graceful avenue leading through the woods greeted passengers when they stepped off the train at the special station built for the hotel. The 180-acre park was filled with flowers, shady walks, and croquet lawns. Pavilions, a summer house, and a "Fishing Temple" built out over the lake allowed guests to take in the fresh air in comfort. Guests could see the lake from three sides of the hotel and from all three floors.

The hotel quickly became fashionable and its guests over the years included Lord Dufferin, Canada's Governor General, a Civil War general and his battalion band, and Prime Minister Oliver Mowat. Couchiching Hotel is credited with beginning the tourism industry in Orillia. Its success was cut short by a fire in 1878, when flames escaped a defective flue in the reading room and raced through the wooden structure. It was never rebuilt. The land passed through the hands of many owners and was eventually subdivided into house lots. It took several years for Orillia to recover the tourism lost when the hotel burned.

The Couchiching Hotel on Couchiching Point promised fresh air in comfortable surroundings. The hotel started the tourism industry in Orillia, but its success was cut short by a fire in 1878.

Painted by E. Shrapnel, Orillia Public Library

THE DRY DAYS BEGIN

The new community of Orillia was only fifteen years old when several people decided it needed cleaning up. With whiskey at only 25 cents a gallon, settlers looking for a break from toil and retired military officers failing at farming headed into the village of Orillia for recreation and comfort. Worried citizens believed they were turning Orillia into a shambles.

A handful of Temperance supporters met July 14, 1854, at a school near Robertson's Corners, two miles outside of Rugby on the Orillia side. Delegates from the Barrie division of the Order of the Sons of Temperance helped the Orillians form the Orillia and Oro division of the Sons. The growing membership of the Orillia branch decided to build a hall for meetings, selling shares for $4 each. The Sons bought a site on Matchedash Street and built a twenty-five-foot by forty-five-foot wooden hall, with a platform at one end. Completed in the late 1850s, the Temperance Hall became the town hall of Orillia, hosting meetings of all kinds, concerts, church services, and weddings. The Temperance movement gathered support from churches, business leaders, and the village's two newspapers.

But the Temperance movement's initial success was flattened by the lumber boom. By now whiskey was 50 cents a gallon, but shantymen were making $1 a day in lumber camps, with no place to spend their savings until spring, when they landed in Orillia. And workers putting in the Northern and Midland Railways were making $1.25 a day, with Orillia hotels providing the best entertainment after a long day's work. By 1873, the village of 2,000 people had sixteen licensed hotels and eight shops that sold liquor. Citizens were afraid to go out on the streets on weekend nights because of the drunken revelry that spilled out of main street hotels.

Residents passed a bylaw in 1874 by a 144-3 vote to shut the liquor shops down. Bylaw 54 sparked more legal battles than anything else, partly because no one remembered to sign it. Liquor inspectors, appointed by council and later the province, faced deputations from Temperance supporters and rocks through their windows from liquor supporters no matter what they did. The hotels were still allowed to operate and got

around the laws about closing time by providing after-hours drinks to magistrates, bank managers and other community leaders. Teefy Mulcahy, an insurance broker and council member liked to tell the story about the time he and several other young men were caught drinking after hours in the Daly House by the town liquor inspector. All but one of the young men drinking slid down a chute from proprietor Jim Smith's backroom to his cellar, then scrambled outside. The last one down the chute was a rotund bank accountant whose bottom got him stuck at the chute's bottom. The liquor inspector discovered the accountant, or at least the front half of him, in the basement end of the chute and wrote him up in his black summons book. The next day, the inspector went to the bank to serve the summons. But the bank manager, an occasional customer at the Daly House, refused to let the inspector in. The inspector could not issue the summons as long as the accountant stayed in the bank. According to Mulcahy, the accountant lived in the bank for ten days until the inspector lost interest. (This tale, often told, was published first in the September 1967 issue of Maclean's Magazine in a article by Jack Batten.)

When the liquor shop bylaw was finally declared invalid by the courts in 1906, Temperance forces rallied to shut down both the stores and hotels. They immediately pressed town council for a new shop bylaw. In a stormy debate, the longest and warmest of the year according to newspaper accounts, the council considered putting a new bylaw out for public consideration. The anti-Temperance councillors called for a quick show of hands as soon as the bylaw was introduced and appeared to have won, when a councillor sitting on the fence asked for more discussion. The ensuing arguments grew so heated, council excused itself and went into a private session away from the public. A couple of council members said any prohibition interfered with the liberty of the people and encouraged people to lie and break the law to get liquor. But the Temperance movement was strong on council and in the town. In a 3-2 vote, the mayor and one councillor being absent, council put what was called a Local Option bylaw to the people. Both The Packet and the weekly Times urged residents to support the new bylaw.

"Are the people of this town retrograding morally? Many of the present electors have seen the ravages made by the drink habit...They have seen business concerns ruined, homes wrecked and worse than all, men destroyed through drink..." wrote the Times.

The Local Option bylaw passed easily. Breweries adapted. The law made it illegal to sell beer in Orillia, but it was not illegal to buy beer outside the town and have it delivered into town. The Orillia Brewery Company at Mississaga and Andrew streets found a way to obey the law and still stay in business. Every morning, the brewer loaded up his wagon and took the beer to a warehouse on the Fourth Concession of the old Orillia Township. The warehouse was a small shack with a door in the front and a door in the back. The driver unloaded the beer in the front door, then took the wagon to the back door. There he re-loaded the beer and returned to town. That beer, having been delivered from outside of town, was perfectly legal.

The year after closing liquor shops down, the voters of Orillia shut down all the bars and taverns as well. For the next four decades, officially at least, Orillia was dry.

CANADA'S FIRST MEDICAL PLAN

To his contemporaries, the P in J.P. Secord stood for parsimonious. The cash-conscious realtor and developer was always coming up with new ways to make and save money. None were more imaginative than the Red Cross Hospital and Convalescent Home and what may have been the first medical insurance plan in Canada.

The operators of the Red Cross Hospital tried to make money by selling medical insurance to shantymen. But the venture failed, and the hospital was turned into the Orchard Point Inn, shown in this photograph. The inn burned down in 1956.

Sometime in 1888, Secord and seven other leading men of Orillia got together to plan a hospital that would help the town, give it status, and perhaps make a little money. Early the next year they put up $10,000, incorporated the hospital and found a building on Orchard Point on Lake Simcoe near The Narrows. The plan was this: they would sell $5 certificates to anyone in good health. In return and if necessary, they would give that person free lodging, food, and medical and surgical care in the hospital for up to a year. Orillia doctors agreed to staff the hospital on a rotating basis.

The building and site were perfect for a hospital, the Orillia Times reported on October 11, 1889: "In summer, the lake breezes laden with ozone disperse the heat, afford sleep to the weary, vitality to the exhausted and health to all. In short, a better place for a hospital or sanatorium could not be found anywhere in Canada..."

With little fanfare but much optimism, the Red Cross Hospital was officially opened on November 6, 1889. J.P. and his partners had a plan to make sure the hospital thrived. They sent salesmen throughout lumber camps as far away as Whitney, Ontario, selling the certificates. Many of these men lived so far away, they would likely never collect on the $5 insurance. And those who did, were the better for it: "There are several Lumbermen, as well as some Ladies, now in the Hospital," read a hospital advertisement. "One of the former would have been fertilizing the daisies now if it had not been for the Red Cross Hospital."

At least one operation was performed at the hospital, the removal of a tumour from a North Orillia Township woman. But the hospital venture lasted only about three years. People who could afford the insurance did not go to hospitals, which they considered houses for the poor. And the poor could not afford the $5 for the Red Cross Hospital insurance. Lacking patients and their money, the hospital failed. The hospital was later turned into the Orchard Point Inn, which burned in 1956.

STEAMING INTO LEGEND

They carried dreams, pulled logs, and pushed romance. The steamers that plied Lakes Couchiching and Simcoe from 1845 to 1911 moved anything for the price of a ticket, from the first eager settlers to lumber, and after the railroads opened, young couples on church picnics. In brief and checkered careers that often ended in abandonment, the steamers caught the imagination of lakeside residents. They were immortalized by humourist Stephen Leacock, whose story of the sinking of the Mariposa Belle was not as fictional as steamer captains would care to admit.

It was only natural that as settlement stretched north of Toronto, some of the half-pay officers farming around Lake Simcoe decided to create a steamboat company. Their boat, the Sir John Colborne, made its maiden voyage in 1832, and the happiness of the settlers on the lake turned a day-long affair into a week-long celebration. The steamer had to stop at each landing for a bit of cheer. It's a wonder there were no accidents that maiden voyage. The Colborne could reach speeds of four knots, but drew so much water she kept getting stuck in shallow parts of Lake Simcoe. Converted into a schooner, she was eventually abandoned in the Holland River. Thus, she started three traditions on the lakes - steamboating, getting stuck, and meeting an unhappy end.

After the Colborne came the Simcoe, known also in her career as the Peter Robinson, the first to make it through The Narrows to Lake Couchiching, where it was eventually abandoned. Serious competition on the lakes began with the Beaver and the Morning. The two boats made regular stops in Orillia, the Beaver stopping in three times a week and offering weekend excursions around Lake Couchiching. The rivalry grew so intense that passengers were eventually riding for free, meals included. Naturally, such a situation could not last, and one man ended owning both boats. About then, the Northern Railway reached Allandale near Barrie. That put an end to the Beaver, which in a cruel irony ended up as landfill under the Allandale train station. The railway purchased the Morning and sent her to Orillia on Tuesdays, Thursdays, and Fridays. In the fall of 1862, the Morning was caught in a storm and swept on to a shoal in Lake Simcoe.

The ice trapped her before crews could free her and she ended up rotting near shore.

Lake Couchiching finally got its own steamers in 1864, as lumber camps and settlements began to thrive in the Canadian Shield country north

The Carriella and Ida Burton competed for business in the 1870s, racing to Washago and back six days a week.

Orillia Public Library

of the lake. Besides the big steamboats still remembered by name, dozens of smaller tugs worked the water between Orillia and Washago. Hardly a day went by without three or four steamers calling, reported the Orillia Expositor in June 1867. By 1870, two of the most famous steamers, the Ida Burton and the Carriella, competed for the business of transporting people and supplies to Washago. The fare from Orillia to Washago was 40 cents, to Longford 25 cents, and to Rama 20 cents. On its 1872 summer schedule, the Ida Burton left Orillia every morning but Sunday at 9, stopping briefly at Longford and staying a while in Washago. It left Washago at 1 p.m., stopped by Longford again, and reached Orillia by 4 p.m. — a fairly typical run on Lake Couchiching.

The Ida Burton was a bigger boat, but the Carriella was considered faster. One day, the captain of the Ida Burton, John Ferris Nelson, decided he'd had enough of watching the Carriella pass by. According to oldtimers' accounts, Nelson promised his fireman a bottle of Scotch whiskey if he could build up enough steam to get the Ida Burton to Washago first. The Ida Burton won the race and the fireman got his whiskey. But when Captain Nelson started unloading his freight, he noticed a few barrels of tallow destined for some northern tanneries were missing. The fireman had used the animal fat to give an extra boost to the fire. It's likely his prize had already been drunk. Competition between the two boats grew so intense, they collided September 15, 1870 off Four Mile Point in Lake Simcoe. The damaged boats returned to work soon after.

A year later, the Northern Railway reached Orillia and the workhorse days of the steamers ended. Lumber barons turned to the rails, not the water, for shipping lumber. The Ida Burton finished up as landfill for the Orillia railyards in 1876 and lies beneath the Royal Canadian Legion branch. Her rival, the Carriella, struggled by on a slim tourist trade until the 1887s, when she was stripped and beached at Couchiching Park. The remains of the graceful, single-screw steamboat lie under several feet of fill in the park, its bow pointing toward the old bandstand. From the 1880s on, several other steamers turned up on Lakes Couchiching and Simcoe to ply the excursion trade. The hardworking yet graceful Emily May was renamed Lady of the Lakes and ran until 1883, when she was left to rot at Bell Ewart. The only steamer built in Orillia, called naturally enough, the Orillia, proved popular in the 1880s, taking excursions to Strawberry Island in Lake Simcoe. The Orillia, later called the Islay, had quite a few mishaps — near-

This is the view of the foot of Mississaga Street from the deck of the steamboat Orillia in the 1880s.
Orillia Public Library

sinkings and lightning strikes — but it was her equally troubled rival, the Enterprise, which inspired Leacock's "The Sinking of the Mariposa Belle."

Of course, just about any steamer could have inspired the story, such as the Longford on its 1898 Thanksgiving Day excursion. The owner of the Longford Lumber Company, William Thomson, took the leading businessmen of the town out for an end-of-boating season excursion each Thanksgiving. The 1898 trip offered the usual nice scenery, the passing of a few bottles and, for no extra cost, two accidents on the same shoal. On their way to The Narrows near Ship Island, the passengers felt a sudden jar, as the Longford hit, then settled on Sanson's Shoal.

"With the first shock there was a general rush for life preservers," wrote a reporter for the *Orillia Times*, referring to the private flasks of whiskey gentlemen carried. *"Commodore Haywood never goes to sea without one of his own. As he reached for his hip pocket, he had several officers to assist him 'Blow' it."*

The embarrassed Captain Johnson lowered a lifeboat and took the Longford's anchor out a short distance, in an attempt to winch the boat off the shoal. That didn't work. A passing steam yacht took Thomson and some others back to Longford Mills, where they rigged up the schooner Curlew. The businessmen left the Longford steamboat and got aboard the Curlew for the trip back to Orillia. The Curlew had just got under way, when it too bumped the same shoal and ground to a halt. Everyone clambered aboard the Longford lifeboat, and, lighter now, the Curlew floated free. The excursion climbed aboard the Curlew and finally made it home. Another steamer pulled the Longford off the next day. The only loss in the accidents

In 1885, Captain Charles McInnes bought Strawberry Island in Lake Simcoe and built a hotel, cottages and picnic grounds. Then he built a boat, the Orillia, to carry excursionists to the island. In 1894, he rebuilt the Orillia and re-christened it the Islay. The 116-foot long Islay could carry 300 passengers, such as the employees of E. Long Ltd. in 1906. The Islay operated until 1914, when she was beached at Couchiching Beach Park, and used as a skating hut. Fire destroyed the vessel, the last passenger steamer on lakes Simcoe and Couchiching, in 1919.
Orillia Public Library

was a hat. And the shoal got a new name, after Captain Johnson hit it the second time.

"As he did so in gaelic, the reporter was unable to catch the title," said the Times story, "but it sounded like 'Howingehannadididothat'."

By the time Leacock immortalized steamboating on Lake Couchiching in 1912, the glory days of working and excursion steamers were over. The Orillia was converted into the Islay and ran excursions until 1914. The Longford's successor, the Geneva, ran excursions until 1911. Gasoline soon replaced steam and the people began buying their own boats. But you can't kill a good tradition in Orillia. Tourist boats, made up to look like steamboats, continue to take excursions around Lake Couchiching. And occasionally, they still get stuck on shoals.

ORILLIA CHURCHES

Church steeples have defined Orillia's skyline and much of its community life for more than 100 years. The four oldest trace their roots to the 1830s.

The Methodist Church (St. Paul's United) on the northeast corner of Peter and Coldwater streets, circa 1870 is in the foreground. Presbyterian St. Andrew's Church, on the corner of Peter Street and Neywash Avenue, is farther back on the

St. Paul's United

The Methodists were the first Christian missionaries to the area around present-day Orillia, setting up a school on Chiefs Island for Chief Yellowhead's band of Chippewas about 1828 and moving to the Indian Village in 1830 when the government re-settled the band. Methodist missionaries and teachers were among the first settlers, but the church itself suffered when the Chippewas were moved to Rama in 1839. Clergymen on horseback offered Methodist services in the 1840s. Reverend George McDougall settled in Orillia in the late 1850s and gathered a congregation large enough to warrant the construction of a frame church on the west side of Peter Street opposite the Sir Samuel Steele building, dedicated in 1859. When the congregation grew too large for the frame building, the Methodists built a brick church on the northeast corner of Peter and Coldwater streets, opened in 1870. The church has been enlarged and altered several times. Union with the Presbyterian Church in 1925 enlarged the congregation and the name was changed to St. Paul's United. The tower was eventually taken down.

St. James Anglican Church on the southeast corner of Peter and Coldwater streets in 1857.

St Andrew's Presbyterian

Some of the earliest settlers to Orillia were Presbyterians from Scotland, Ireland and England. They and Anglican setters urged the government in 1836 to help build a school house or church that both religions could use. Some may have attended Anglican services, which began in 1841, especially since the Anglican minister, Reverend John McIntyre, was a Highland Scot. A Presbyterian minister offered occasional services in the 1840s, and Reverend John Gray arrived in 1851 to conduct regular services. A frame church was built on the northwest corner of Peter Street and Neywash Avenue in 1852. As the congregation grew, the frame church was twice enlarged, then finally replaced by the present building in 1889. Orillia's churches were hardly dull places. In 1865, Presbyterians were divided over the use of music to bring people closer to God. An organ in the church upset some church-goers so much they carried it out. Church leaders referred to the Bible to convince them musical instruments could be used in worship. The Orillia Presbyterian Church voted 732-184 against union with the United Church in 1925. While some left to join the Methodist congregation at St. Paul's United, many more remained, ensuring the Presbyterian Church would continue to thrive.

St. James Anglican

The Society for Converting and Civilizing the Indians and Propagating the Gospel among the Destitute Settlers in Upper Canada sponsored the first Anglican services in the Indian Village as early as 1833. In October of that

year, Reverend Adam Elliot visited the village to conduct services for whites and natives. In 1841, after the natives were moved to Rama, Reverend John McIntyre formed the St. James Anglican parish, holding services in the old school house built for the Chippewas. A small stone church replaced the school house in 1857. The tower was completed early in the fall of 1863, but collapsed into the vestry. While it was being repaired, the nearby Presbyterian Church allowed the Anglicans to hold their services there. A larger brick church replaced the stone church in 1891. A fire on March 19, 1905 destroyed the church, and once again, the congregation had to take services elsewhere, this time in the Opera House. The rebuilt church opened only six months after the fire, and is the church that stands at the corner of Peter and Coldwater streets today. At the turn of the century and in the early 1900s, the church was led by Canon Richard Greene, well-loved and the inspiration for Stephen Leacock's Reverend Dean Drone in Sunshine Sketches of a Little Town.

Church of Angels Guardian, Orillia, Ont., Canada

A small cross atop the tower had to do until the landmark spire was added to Guardian Angels Church in 1927.

Marcel Rosseau Collection

was built and given the name, Angels Guardian. (The old log church was destroyed by fire four years later). The congregation and church grew, with a convent on Penetang Street added in 1903.

The church that looks over Orillia today was built in 1910 and 1911. Workers used horse-drawn sleds to drag limestone from the Longford quarries across frozen Lake Couchiching. No mishaps are reported in the transportation of the limestone or construction of the church, but the old steeple proved hard to dismantle, and when the ropes finally brought it down, it fell so hard it embedded itself six feet into the ground. The church's spire and lighted cross, a landmark in Orillia, was added in 1927.

Guardian Angels Catholic

Like many others, the first Catholic settlers to the area had to rely on travelling priests in the 1830s for services. Settler Peter Kenny bought 25 acres of land from Gerald Alley on the Coldwater Road in 1847, and offered his farm house for services. Seven years later, forty Catholic families each contributed one dollar for a one-and-a-half-plot on the south side of Coldwater Road, on the rise of land west of the city. The Catholic cemetery is located there now. The first Catholic Church, St. Michael's, was made of logs and built by members of the congregation. For a while, there were no pews or seats, and worshippers stood or knelt during Mass. Eventually, prosperous members bought their own pews. According to church stories, one parishioner grew angry that his pew was not in the front, and after Mass one Sunday, lifted his up and over the others, putting in in the front row. Other pew owners turned up for the next service with hammers and nails and nailed their pews to the floor, so they would not lose their positions. Masses were held sporadically by travelling priests and bishops for several years. Meanwhile, in 1872, a new brick church on West Street

THE ORILLIA SPIRIT

After the fire of 1879, Orillia's businesses were rebuilt with brick and stone. This view of Mississaga Street looking east toward the lake was taken from one of the towers of the Opera House about 1896.

Orillia Public Library

aylight Bill Frost woke up at the usual hour one Sunday morning in June 1912, thinking nothing was out of the ordinary. He dressed in his Sunday best, as befitted the mayor of the town of Orillia, and went to church. He arrived to find the congregation and minister already an hour into the service. Imagine his embarrassment. Not only was Frost late, but he had forced everyone else to arrive early. Daylight Bill had already forgotten his own revolutionary proclamation, that the clocks of Orillia be put ahead one hour at 10 the night before. His late

arrival gave an extra edge to the question asked by the pious around town: "Do you go on God's time or Bill Frost's time?"

For two weeks that summer, half the town went by one time and half by the other. Town bells rang at different hours, factory workers arrived late or too early for work, and boarding-house operators had to cook two sets of lunch and two sets of dinner each day for roomers. Daylight Bill had his good friend Charles Harold Hale to thank for mixing up him and the rest of the town. C. H. Hale had inherited the Packet from the "Hale boys" — father George and Uncle William - who had made life so difficult for their newspaper rival forty years ago. C.H. Hale was always looking for ways to make Orillia stand out from the crowd of Ontario's small towns. A few years earlier, Hale had become interested in the idea of daylight savings, first proposed in England. Turning the clocks ahead an hour in the summer would give working people, with a common shift from 7 a.m. to 6 p.m., an extra hour of sunlight in the evening. As president of the Orillia Board of Trade in 1911, Hale suggested the town try daylight savings, adopting the

Daylight Bill Frost, mayor, merchant and promoter of Orillia, forgot his own proclamation to move clocks ahead one hour and arrived late for church. Orillia experimented with daylight savings long before the rest of Canada, with chaotic results.

Orillia Public Library

49

slogan "The Town Ahead." The next year, Hale began a fifteen-year stint on council and with support from his colleagues, including William Frost, managed to get daylight savings a two-month trial in 1912.

The town greeted the idea with suspicion. Few people understood it. Some residents figured putting the clock ahead one hour meant they lost that hour permanently, every day, and would get less sleep. Others said it moved Saturday into Sunday, violating the Lord's Day Act. Daylight savings would force everyone to get up earlier and eat breakfast too early in the day, claimed some opponents. As the hour of daylight savings approached, 10 p.m. on June 22, fear grew. The Bricklayers Union voted against the proposal and petitions against it circulated through several factories. Some factory workers claimed daylight savings was a plot to make them work extra hours.
Hale tried to allay their fears in the Packet:

> The bone and sinew of the town, who work from 7 to 6, day in and day out, find it dark almost as soon as tea is over. Moving the clock one hour ahead would give these men an opportunity to enjoy another hour's daylight in the evening...Life will have a new zest... because they will sleep in the dark hours and have an hour more sunlight added to the waking period.

Hale tried to explain to people that the hours of a clock were set arbitrarily. Six o'clock came at the same time every morning because everyone agreed it was six o'clock. Putting the clock ahead did not mean you lost sleep, because you still went to bed at 10 and got up at 6. The controversy attracted the attention of newspapers across the country. Although Port Arthur, Ontario had already switched to daylight savings, Orillia was credited with trying a grand experiment.

"All eyes are on Orillia," The Packet proclaimed. "Manifest the Orillia Spirit."

At 10 o'clock on the evening of Saturday, June 22, the town bells rang to remind everyone to turn their clocks ahead one hour. Time and Orillia jumped ahead, sort of.

"The confusion was beyond belief," recalled Hale. "Some of the church bells were off time. The Town bell rang at six o'clock, daylight time, instead of seven. On Monday morning merchants who were meticulous in their arrival in the stores found themselves an hour late."

Some workers tried to take advantage of the confusion, Hale recalled. On the Monday morning, employees of the Hewitt Brothers trucking yard arrived at 7 a.m. daylight savings time, but sat around for another hour, waiting for standard time to catch up before starting work. Meanwhile, they teased other workers on their way to work at the proper time. At 8 a.m. daylight savings time, 7 a.m. standard time, they started work. The tables were turned when the town bell rang at noon. The employees of the Hewitt Brothers quit for lunch, but were told they still had another hour to work.

Some companies adopted daylight savings, but others rejected the plan. That caused a nightmare in everything from shipping schedules to baseball games. Employees working under the daylight savings time got off an hour before everyone else. As they wandered to the ball diamonds, they teased the men still at work, causing some bad feelings in town. Still other workers thought the new hours meant they had to go to work at 6 a.m. and waited for an hour for everyone else to show up. There were some advantages, however. Baseball teams could get a full nine innings in before darkness fell. Parents and their children attending the circus could go home when it was still light. But boarding-house keepers put pressure on town council to give up the experiment. With men going to work at different hours, boarding-house keepers had no idea when to serve meals. The confusion in boarding houses and the friction in town persuaded council to reluctantly repeal daylight savings time two weeks after it started.

Daylight Bill Frost suffered his nickname for years, and Hale felt badly about the ridiculing he had put his friend through. But when Canada adopted daylight savings several years later, Frost began wearing the nickname proudly. Orillia's daylight savings experiment turned out not to be a failure, but simply ahead of its time. And it was only one in a long line of brave attempts to make Orillia the best town in the province - not the richest or biggest perhaps, but the most spirited and innovative.

From 1880 to 1929, what is considered Orillia's first Golden Age, the town reached for and often seized greatness. Behind all achievements stood a group of young men who shared what they coined the Orillia Spirit. The dream to make something out of Orillia, and the energy and unity to realize that dream defined the Orillia Spirit. The dozen or so men who led the town in those forty-nine years called upon the Orillia Spirit to cajole Orillians into backing their schemes. The same names appear throughout those years as reeves, council members, board of trade presidents - Hale, Frost, the Tudhopes, Erastus Long - names that still carry the mark of honour in the city today. In the Golden Age, the town gave birth to one of the first Canadian automobile companies, the first successful medicare plan, the Champlain monument, the fairy-tale Orillia Opera House, the province-wide county battalion system, and the first long-distance hydro transmission system on the continent. The accomplishments came with drama, tragedy and comedy attached, none more so than the greatest - the Orillia power scheme.

Nothing less than province-wide ridicule, the near drowning of the mayor and council, a steamboat sinking, dozens of accidents, a midnight raid on the power plant, and a civil insurrection lay ahead when Orillia's leaders first contemplated tapping a distant river to bring electric power to

the town. After the fire of 1879 destroyed half of Mississaga Street, the town built more reservoirs, including one on the Peter Street hill on Benner Street, and in 1883 bought the private waterworks in Victoria Park for $3,330. As the town started to solve its water problem, the cry arose for the miracle of the century - electric lighting.

"Oh for the Electric Light," wrote the Orillia Times editor in May 1887. "When it is so dark that a man has to strike a match to see his way, it is getting pretty bad."

The town built an arc lighting plant that year. That first plant in Victoria Park used wood as fuel to drive the steam engines that provided electricity. The plant provided light for fifty lamps downtown. But the town was increasingly hungry for water and power. Over the next few years, townspeople argued over the best way to bring water to Orillia, a town on two lakes. The first time council proposed tapping the springs at Fittons Road and Stanton Drive, ratepayers voted down the $25,000 project, believing it impossible to do. More fires changed their minds and in the first recorded expropriation of private property in Orillia, the town bought seven acres of land from a reluctant H. W. Fitton for $2,000. An eight-inch cast iron pipe brought the water to the new steam pumping plant at the bottom of Jarvis Street. That plant, built in 1894, gave the town power for forty-five more street lights and 2,300 incandescent lamps that factories and private citizens could use.

This is what you saw standing at the intersection of Peter Street and Mississaga Street, looking toward West Street about 1890.

Orillia Public Library

In 1888, Oxford Street was just a pathway to building lots and beyond that, a few farms.

The world had seen nothing yet. As early as 1889, the town had considered schemes to purchase hydro-electric power from a mill in Marchmont or produce its own power at Wadsell Falls in Washago. Nine years later, Thomas H. Sheppard urged council to consider using Ragged Rapids on the Severn River. He ran for mayor in 1898 against J.P. Secord on the ticket of tapping the Severn River to provide cheap lighting and cheap power. Secord ran on a less glamorous ticket - opposing the move of the railway station a few blocks in town. Sheppard and a slate of power-scheme supporters won the election.

The new council wasted little time. After only a few days in office, on January 24, council, with a surveyor and reporters from The Packet and the Times travelled to Ragged Rapids. They rode as far as they could by sleigh, then snowshoed the remaining ten miles. Measurements showed the rapids had a fall of about thirty-five feet in less than a mile, enough to provide power. Buoyed by council's optimistic reports, town ratepayers voted in February by 399-61 to build the plant for $75,000. The little opposition there was came from people worried that the demand for wood would drop and hurt suppliers to steam plants. The idea was ridiculed in the provincial legislature, but in Orillia, support rarely dropped, even during all the misadventures surrounding the power scheme.

And there were plenty. Council dropped the first contractor, the Buffalo Construction Company, because it soon appeared to have financial difficulties. The contract was handed over to P.H. Patriache, a Toronto builder. The Times rejoiced, "There is no doubt about the work being pushed to a speedy conclusion now that it is in Mr. Patriache's hands," and predicted the plant would be running by the fall of that year, 1899. A journalist's visit to the site in the fall revealed 115 men working eleven hours a day were busy erecting the dam. Yet the men were hampered because there was no way to get steam-operated equipment to Ragged Rapids. Trips to the site invited disaster. Boats hit rocks and dumped workers into the icy waters of the Severn. A scow carrying council members on one inspection trip was cut by ice and started to sink. The passengers saved the boat by shifting bags of cement to the stern to lift the sliced bow out of the water.

Early in 1900, anxious to see how work was progressing, council members, their wives, and other dignitaries, including a Scottish minister, Reverend George Grant, took a trip to Ragged Rapids. Their return on Patriache's steamer, the Syesta, took them through the Sparrow Lake Chutes, where the waters of Sparrow Lake plunged seven feet down through a narrow, 100-yard-long chasm of churning water. A crew on shore had to pull the Syesta over the rapids with a rope and windlass. Most of the party got off the boat before the rapids and walked along shore. Eight men stayed with the Syesta. J.B. Tudhope, now the mayor, and Councillor Robert Curran sat in two of the small rowboats being towed behind. Somehow the men on shore running the windlass allowed the rope to slacken and the steamer turned broadside to the rushing water. In seconds the current flipped the hull on to its side and water poured in. A reporter on the trip described the sinking: "You can hear the snarling of the fire as the water strikes the boiler and then she strikes a rock and straightens up on an even keel for an instant. A second later she is borne down again, careens over on her side and with one rush the water fills her and sucks her down."

The engineer and one man jumped out and swam to shore. Another man struggled through the twenty-foot-deep stream to Tudhope's rowboat, and taking hold of it, almost tipped it over. The man swam off to Councillor Curran's rowboat, and Tudhope managed to row himself to shore. Curran's rowboat was still attached to the steamer, but someone cut the rope just as the steamer sank. With a man clinging to each side of his boat, Curran rowed to shore. As the horrified party on shore watched, the last man in the water, Frank Evans, struggled to another boat. He couldn't cut the rope to the steamer in time and the sinking Syesta took the rowboat with it. A couple of paddlers in a nearby canoe quickly rescued him.

"It is little less than a miracle that all escaped alive," wrote the reporter. Councillor Crawford Miller led the group in singing "Praise God From Whom All Blessings Flow." (The blessings didn't flow far enough for Grant. He watched his valuable picnic silverware go down with the boat. Grant sent town council a claim for the silverware, but council rejected it. It's not known whether Grant ever picnicked on the Severn again.)

Council's visit did nothing to speed up construction. Patriache had trouble paying his men and his suppliers. Acting on behalf of the town in the winter of 1900, Patriache bought some hydraulic equipment from the Jenokes Machine Company of Sherbrooke, Quebec, for $8,000. He was supposed to pay for the equipment, which was being stored in Severn Bridge. By June, the company had received little of its money, so it sent a private train and crew to Severn Bridge. At midnight one Sunday in June, the crew sneaked into the storage shed and loaded the equipment on to a rail car, then headed back to Quebec. The theft was so bizarre, Mayor Tudhope refused to believe rumours about it the next morning. But two councillors rushed to Atherley, just in time to see the train pull out. Police stopped the train in Lindsay, and Orillia council won possession of the equipment through a special provincial order.

Patriache himself soon ran afoul of the law. He had bought another steamboat, Queen, and was taking it through Lake Couchiching to the Severn River. He had stopped in Orillia to do some repairs. In the meantime, there was a mix-up over his payments on the boat and the Orillia police had been notified. While Patriache was away from the steamboat trying to settle the payment problem, an Orillia constable tied the boat to the Orillia dock to prevent it from leaving. Patriache settled the financial problems, finished his repairs, untied the boat, and headed to Washago. Knowing nothing about the settlement, the angry constable raced to Washago. Meanwhile, Patriache's repairs had come undone and the boat began to sink. He had to beach the boat near the railway bridge in Washago. While wandering through Washago, Patriache felt a hand on his shoulder and heard the words of an angry constable, "You are my prisoner."

"For unexpected developments, downright hard luck, continued bungling and amusing incidents, Orillia's power scheme takes the cake," concluded The Packet after the arrest.

That matter was settled, but breaks in the dam, trouble transporting equipment, and inexperience delayed work on the dam. By 1902, taxpayers and council were reaching the limits of patience over the delays and rising costs of the power plant. Tudhope won his third term by acclamation as mayor, and Frost was returned to council. But in a bitterly fought election, three council members, including tanner Crawford Miller, a strong supporter of the power scheme, were defeated. Tudhope vowed to push Patriache to complete the dam and start sending power to Orillia, even if the town had to take the plant over itself. The dam was completed on January 16, 1902, and townspeople were told power would be transmitted the next day. It didn't come the next day or for several days after that. Patriache began lighting the town to test the plant, but the town waited and waited for full power. Early in March, Patriache got the plant running to full capacity, but threatened to shut it down if he wasn't paid for providing the town light for the past few months. He showed no intention of completing the plant to council's

satisfaction or turning the plant over to the town. Late in March, council gave Patriache a forty-eight-hour deadline to get the plant up and running. He ignored the deadline. On Saturday, March 22, council met and secretly planned the next step. A clause in the contract gave the town the right to take over the plant if contractors were moving too slowly, said the town lawyer, F. B. Johnson. Patriache was in Toronto trying to sell that city on another power scheme, so council launched its attack. First, a town worker cut the phone lines to the Ragged Rapids plant, then council notified Patriache the town was forced to take the plant over. Patriache tried Monday afternoon to call the plant and warn the workers there to defend it, but of course, he could not get through. At noon that Monday, three police constables, town engineer Peter Ritchie, and two other town employees started the march to Ragged Rapids. They reached the plant by 10 p.m. and took the workers by surprise. An anxious council received word by wire that night that victory was theirs. But it appeared victory would be short-lived. William Wagner, the foreman ousted by the town's force, began gathering men in Severn Bridge for a counterattack.

"Is it Civil War?" The Packet asked. Rumours spread through Orillia that an army of men was launching a counterattack on the Ragged Rapids plant. Mayor Tudhope instructed the power plant force to provision itself for a siege. By the Wednesday after the Monday takeover, Wagner had gathered a troop of eight men at nearby McLean's Bay. He promised them $10 each to help him take back the power plant. They were ready to march, until some residents told the men they'd be foolish to get in the middle of a fight between the town and Patriache, and the most of the so-called soldiers deserted. The next day two men, claiming they were sightseers, appeared at the plant and started to make fun of Patriache. The suspicious constables at the plant refused to allow them in for a tour. One of the men showed up with the ex-foreman, Wagner, the next day, and admitted he had been paid $5 to get into the plant. Outside the plant, Wagner ridiculed the men inside the plant who had given up the plant without a fight. He demanded to get in to take an inventory. The constables refused, and Wagner attempted unsuccessfully to push his way in. The persistent foreman - and one has to hope he was well paid by Patriache - next tried to get a judge to issue a warrant of arrest against the town's men in the plant. When that didn't work, he apparently asked another magistrate to issue a warrant to arrest the entire town of Orillia. That didn't work either, so Wagner went back to Severn

Bridge and Gravenhurst to again hire men to retake the plant, but found few interested. He returned to Toronto on the Saturday, finally defeated.

Orillia at last had power - thanks to Patriache's delays a little more expensive than planned, but still less expensive than in most places. Industrial and commercial users bought 600 of the 800 horsepower produced by the plant, with the town using the rest for the water-pumping station and lights. But neither Patriache nor his dam were through with the town yet. He sued the town, seeking $1,075 for his costs in running the plant from January 25 to March 24, and $12,000 for equipment seized in the March raid. Patriache tried to make a deal with the town. If it sold the plant back to him, he would guarantee low rates. Town council told him to forget it. The courts awarded Patriache $250 for expenses and $1,000 for equipment. It was likely more than he deserved for on April 7, 1904, Patriache's dam burst plunging the town into darkness and stopping factory engines. Town engineers discovered the Ragged Rapids dam was not built on solid granite, as promised, but on loose rocks. The steam plant on Jarvis Street was put back into use, and factories had to rely again on their own wood-powered steam plants. A temporary replacement dam was built at Ragged Rapids in 1905 and a new, permanent dam in 1908. The permanent dam cost the town about $11,000 more than expected, and also caused trouble. Lights and power went out again January 19, 1911, when a flume burst and flooded the power house. Two men in the power house narrowly escaped death by clambering up through an opening in the dam.

By now town council had had enough and decided to build a new dam a few miles down river. About the same time, the federal government announced plans to complete the Trent-Severn canal system, and town council eventually worked out a deal with the federal government to build on a different location. The Swift Rapids plant was the result. It was completed in 1917 and is still operating today.

In spite of the early problems, the electricity from the Severn River gave Orillia a jump start over other towns in the early 1900s. In 1909, the town's factories employed 1,048 people, paying $344,850 in wages and producing about $1.2 million in goods. By 1912, those figures had jumped to 1,488 employees earning $802,650 in wages, producing $4.6 million in goods. Orillia had twenty-nine factories in 1901, but forty by 1911. In the same period, Barrie gained two factories. In 1911, Orillia finally topped Barrie's population: 6,828 to 6,420.

The Tudhope Carriage Company, ORILLIA, ONT.

MR. JAMES B. TUDHOPE, Manager.

THE TUDHOPE Carriage Co.'s Factory is the largest in Canada, and has a floor space of over two acres. Output, over 5,000 vehicles annually.

THE TUDHOPE CARRIAGE CO.'S FACTORY, ORILLIA.

James Brockett Tudhope, always dashing and always thinking, built up one of Canada's first automobile plants. He served as mayor, member of the legislature and member of parliament, but he will best be remembered as the man who almost made Orillia a Detroit of the north.

Orillia Public Library

Electric power inspired the creativity of many great industrialists in Orillia in the early 1900s, but none continue to tease the imagination like James Brockett 'J.B.' Tudhope. What's left of his former factory on Colborne and West streets still takes up a city block. The old brick smokestack, TUDHOPE spelled out in 4½-foot-high letters, stands out in the city's skyline as prominently as the church steeples and Opera House spires. The question "What if?" always simmers beneath the city residents' casual interest in Tudhope. What if he had done it? What if Tudhope had succeeded in building an automobile empire in Orillia? He had a good car, made in Canada for the Canadian climate, an innovative staff, the best production plant. If the Tudhope automobile had driven into everyone's garage like the Ford or Chrysler, Orillia could have become Detroit north, and Canada would have its own car industry dependent on no other country. But the Tudhope did not become the Ford, and one of Orillia's chances at industrial greatness slipped away. Tudhope remains a legend, though, for his vision and daring.

Tragedy struck the Tudhope family as soon as they arrived in Canada in the 1800s, and forced independence on the first generation born here. James Tudhope and his eldest son, George, sailed from Scotland in 1831 and settled on Concession 11 in Oro Township to clear the land and make a home for the rest of the family. After two years of hard work, clearing the land and sowing crops, James sent for his wife, Christian, and eight other children. He had never seen the youngest, William. As his wife and children were sailing over, eager to reunite the family, James suddenly died. Christian was met only by her son when she arrived. She died two years later, and George, twenty-three, was forced to raise the rest of the family. In 1835 George became clerk of Oro Township, starting a 134-year Tudhope dynasty in that position.

The youngest of the Tudhopes, William, grew up after losing his mother when he was four and without ever seeing his father. That may account for the slight stammer and the fierce strength of mind he carried all his life. Mechanically inclined, William learned the blacksmith trade. He tried to open a shop in Orillia in 1864 and failed, then tried once again a few years later. In a small wheelwright shop and smithy on the southwest corner of Colborne and West streets, William Tudhope began fixing carriage and wagon wheels. His second attempt succeeded. As Tudhope began to build wheels, then entire carriages, the business expanded east on Colborne Street. Son J.B. joined the company in 1880. As William grew less active in the business, J.B. took on more responsibility.

The dashing J.B. Tudhope built an empire over the next three decades — the Canadian Wood Specialty Co. Ltd., the Dominion Wheel Co. Ltd., the Orillia Furniture Co. Ltd., Standard Chemical Co. Ltd. in Longford Mills, all carried his stamp. But the base for all his enterprises became the Tudhope Carriage Company Ltd., formed in 1897 when brothers William and Hugh joined. The firm leapt the boundaries of local prominence in the 1900s, forming a partnership with Harry Anderson of Winnipeg to sell wagons and other equipment to the farmers in the booming west.

Although the carriage company continued to grow, Tudhope noticed that the latest invention, the automobile, was taking a piece of his market. With the typical straight ahead spirit of the Tudhopes, he decided to build automobiles in Orillia. Tudhope sent his son, Bill, and another man to the United States to arrange a deal to buy engines. The two talked for a while with a young man in Michigan named David Buick, but Buick's car didn't

In the leather shop of Tudhope Carriages, workers assembled the canopies for cars and carriages.

Orillia Public Library

have enough financial backing to satisfy Tudhope so he went with another firm and engine, McIntyre. (Buick eventually got out of early financial difficulties by merging with Chevrolet and Oldsmobile into General Motors.) The first Tudhope-McIntyre, a two-cylinder, air-cooled horseless carriage, with hard, rubber buggy tires, drove out of the plant in 1907. It sold for $550, more than a Ford Model T, partly because it was tougher. Included was a horn and three lamps. Its top speed was thirty miles per hour.

But the Tudhope-McIntyre met an early doom. About ten of the cars sat in the factory on a hot Saturday afternoon, August 22, 1909, awaiting shipment to the automotive show at the Canadian National Exhibition. A few men were working in the the four-storey, brick factory, one part of the Tudhope compound that took up the entire blocked bounded by West, Colborne, and Andrew streets, and Barrie Road. Most workers got Saturday afternoon off, but some had to stay behind to put the finishing touches on the automobiles heading to Toronto. Many of the Tudhopes, including J.B., were working in the offices. Suddenly a shout rang through the building.

The 1906 Tudhope-McIntyre motor buggy, not much more than a Tudhope carriage with a motor, sold for $550.

A fire in 1909 destroyed the Tudhope Carriage company, threatening to put hundreds of people out of work. Tudhope was courted by 19 other municipalities, but decided to stick with Orillia. His new plant, with the most modern assembly lines, was built in record time. One can see the Orillia Opera House in the background of the photograph taken of the factory ruins the day after the fire.

Stephen Leacock Museum

"The factory is on fire!" Workers rushed out of the paint shop as flames leapt into the plant. Tudhope's brothers, William and Hugh, sounded the alarm and scrambled to close the fire doors between the various buildings. They managed to get a few shut but the fierce heat and flames drove them and the others outside.

By the time firefighters arrived, smoke was pouring from the upper windows of the car plant and carriage factory. Flames shot 150 feet into the sky with the roar of a giant furnace. The four-storey front wall collapsed in half an hour. Within an hour the building lay in ruins. Townspeople fought to save nearby foundries and homes for another two hours. Housewives on nearby streets formed bucket brigades in an attempt to save their homes. Workers at the J.R. Eaton Planing Mill across the road sprayed the flames from the roof, as they watched the large letters on the wall of their building melt off. The town wired to Barrie, which sent up a steam fire engine. The flames burned through one hose, and firefighters could only watch helplessly as the fire hydrant remained opened, sucking the pressure from the rest of their hoses.

By the time it was over, the fire had claimed the twelve buildings of the factory, ten houses, a bakery, and scores of outbuildings in back yards. Ten automobiles and 2,000 cutters were destroyed. About 150 carriage wheels, some auto frames, and a few files remained. The losses totalled $500,000. Worse, the town had lost its largest employer and 200 men had been thrown out of work.

J.B Tudhope refused to say publicly if he would rebuild. Town residents demanded council do something, while nineteen other municipalities across Ontario tried to tempt Tudhope away from Orillia. One offered him a grant of $50,000, a free factory site, a tax exemption, and a dock site. Orillia council, at a quickly called meeting, could offer Tudhope only an interest free loan of $50,000 to stay. In return, Tudhope had to buy $1,600 a year in power, light, and water and pay at least $50,000 a year in wages, which was no hardship since the payroll averaged $100,000 a year. To loud cheers, Tudhope told council and residents he wanted to stay in

Orillia. "From the Atlantic to the Pacific there was not another town like it," he said. Based on the support shown at that meeting, he would begin building immediately, Tudhope concluded.

The agreement had to be ratified by plebiscite. Town leaders left nothing to chance, and through the newspapers urged supporters to get out and vote for Tudhope. The vote carried 763-22, one of the largest majorities in any vote on any subject in Orillia's history.

By 1912, the Tudhope was a made-in-Canada automobile. Former Simcoe East MPP and Justice of the Peace Gordon Smith, shown in this photograph from 1965, bought and restored this 1912 Tudhope, the last of its kind. The car was purchased by the Orillia Heritage Foundation in the 1980s and continues to make regular appearances in Orillia. This Tudhope was driven by an Owen Sound dentist from 1912 to about 1920.

Courtesy of Gordon Smith.

Tudhope must have been pleased, but all along, he had no intention of leaving. Perhaps he was waiting to see what the town would offer, or how much Orillia Spirit he could count on. For Tudhope, never one to move slowly or cautiously, had decided the evening after the fire to rebuild a bigger and better plant on the site of the destroyed one. That evening, sitting

with his family, Tudhope asked his daughter for a large piece of paper. On it he sketched the rough plans for a huge plant. Work on the factory's foundation started September 18. 1909. The factory was finished on December 6, seventy-nine days later. The contractor boasted his crew had set a record for building in Canada.

Tudhope formed the Tudhope Motor Company the next year and built an addition to the new plant. He bought the rights to build the Everitt-30, or Tudhope-Everitt, a four-cylinder car that sold for $1,200 to $1,500. The Orillia plant purchased the tires, radiators, and lights, but built the rest of the car, including the engines. Tudhope wasn't happy just to produce another man's design or compete with just the ordinary old Ford. The Tudhope cars were sold with a two-year warranty against mechanical defects, a rarity in those days. Tudhope modified the design for Canadian customers, adding a primitive shock absorber. The car eventually dropped the name Everitt and became known as the Tudhope. The price had risen to about $1,600 by 1912.

The Canadian Pacific Railway (CPR) gave Orillia its third railway line in 1910, running on fill along the waterfront roughly parallel to the Grand Trunk Railway lines (which became the Canadian National Railway). The CPR changed Orillia's shoreline dramatically, cutting off commercial and private boathouses. The town forced CPR to build new boathouses, and eventually the land between the rail line and shoreline was filled in.

Orillia Public Library

His car was good and his factory used the latest mass-production equipment and techniques, yet Tudhope did not have the network of dealers, in Ontario especially, to sell his product. At the same time, Tudhope had sunk a lot of money into his modern production line. By 1913, the Tudhope Motor Company was in serious financial difficulty. Two industrialists, one named Fisher, helped reorganize the company as the Fisher Motor Company Ltd. Tudhope retained some control over the company and auto production continued.

The First World War, beginning in 1914, gave a boost to the troubled Tudhope factory and the rest of the city's growing industries. During the war, Orillia foundries worked around the clock to make ammunition. It was estimated three of the biggest manufacturers, E. Long Ltd., National Hardware, and Fisher Motors made $1 million in gross revenue in 1915 just on shell production. The munitions factories employed 1,200 to 1,500 men. The Orillia Times boasted in 1917 that fifteen large factories and a dozen or so smaller ones employed about 2,500 people. The largest, Fisher Motor Company Ltd., had 650 people working mainly in munitions. The five companies, including Fisher, that Tudhope controlled employed 1,360 people. That same year, Orillia turned on a new power plant at Swift Rapids, which replaced the troublesome Ragged Rapids plant.

In an August, 1914 parade troops bound for the First World War marched confidently down Mississaga Street. A local tanner promised to tan the Kaiser's hide if anyone brought it home.

Orillia Public Library

Orillia entered the First World War with its municipal spirit inflamed with national fervour, much like many other towns and cities across the province. But the town continued to keep a step ahead. A local committee charged with recruiting men for the army decided to raise not a mere company of town boys, but a complete battalion of companies from Simcoe County. Midland, Collingwood, Barrie, and county council got behind Orillia's idea. The federal government, sceptical that a county could form an entire battalion, gave its approval. Within ten weeks the Simcoe County battalion, complete with officers and equipment, was raised out of headquarters in Barrie. The county battalion system spread like wildfire throughout the province, becoming one of the most effective recruiting methods in the First World War. Rallies were held throughout the war to raise money and recruit men. Orillia gave her best. On August 15, 1915 at one of the first Orillia rallies, about sixty young men, including the entire championship hockey team ,signed up and $15,000 was raised for seven machine guns, two ambulances, seven field kitchens, and a complete set of band equipment for the Simcoe battalion.

By the time the war was over, about 1,000 young men from Orillia and the surrounding regions had signed up. The sons of Orillia went across the sea to fight the Kaiser with all the parades and bands and optimism a small town can muster. Tanner John Miller told the first group to leave he would tan the Kaiser's hide for free if anyone brought it home. The YMCA, the local Red Cross, church auxiliaries, and other charities sent reminders of home to the servicemen in the form of clothing, baked goods, and local newspapers. Patriotic drives raised about $265,000 during the war to help soldiers overseas, to provide for their families, and to help pay for ammunition and hospital ships.

The newspapers brought the war to Orillia, in reports of battles, and in the revealing letters from soldiers to home. In the early letters, the men are stoic, and casual in the description of injuries and battles.

"The wound bled rather too freely during the operation," wrote Private Walter Dunham to his mother in Orillia in May 1916, after he was shot in the cheek. "...I have to undergo another operation tomorrow to get a piece of fractured bone out, which has made my face swell again. I don't relish the thought of more chloroform."

But the despair faced by soldiers in muddy trenches, fighting for months over inches of land, began to show through in later letters.

After four and a half months in hospital, Dunham returned to battle. His last letter to his mother, September 10, 1916, shows little of his earlier confidence.

"Listen to me. I cannot see the sense in attempting the impossible under the present circumstances - trying to make one believe that things are not what they really and obviously are. Facts are facts and you know, and I know thoroughly (God knows I ought to know, it is not the first time I've been here) exactly what I'm up against, that I may go down very shortly." Dunham, 25, was killed a month later.

These three young men, all about 18, shared a few laughs the day in 1914 when they were photographed on the shore of Lake Couchiching in Orillia. From left to right, Harold Deans, Crawford Miller, and Fred Bailley, were all killed in the First World War. Orillia and neighbouring communities lost about 150 of its young men in the war.

Orillia lost about 150 of its young men in the war, and each week the papers were full of lists of the dead and wounded. At home, the war took its toll on everyday life. In 1917, the town launched a Thrift and Production campaign to encourage everyone to grow more food for the war effort and waste less. At rallies, speakers urged homeowners to use every square inch of yard to grow food. "While our boys are conquering the enemy, let us conquer the soil," urged one speaker.

Everyone had a role. High school students were to work the fields in the summer. Stable owners were urged to sell manure at reasonable prices to town gardeners. Smite the weeds! A potato in every plot! went the rallying cries in newspapers. One editorial writer for the Orillia Times even suggested all dogs not used for work be killed, because they ate too much meat. The Board of Trade and churches encouraged manufacturers to spare workers who could help in seeding and harvest. The board set up teams of workers to help on the farms.

Captain Merton Plunkett brought fame to his hometown of Orillia by bringing laughter to troops around the world. Merton and his brothers Albert and Morley founded the comedy troupe, the Dumbells, in the First World War. Many letters from Orillia soldiers during the war mention Captain Merton, who had been working for the YMCA in Toronto when the war began. He was posted as an entertainment promoter for the troops. After the war, Merton took the Dumbells on tour and played to full houses in England and the United States.

In the photograph above, Merton sits in the centre of the middle row, surrounded by "women".

As the war continued, measures became more extreme, In February 1918, the town's factories and businesses shut down for three "Heatless Days," under the order of the federal Fuel Controller, to save on coal and wood. By then, the first wave of soldiers had returned home. The fanfare that greeted some could not hide the scars others carried.

Bright and cheery George Bradbury had heard someone shouting about the war on August 5, 1914 while driving his delivery wagon up Mississaga Street. He stopped his team, jumped down and rushed to the telephone. Get someone here to take the team, he told his employer, the Canadian Express Co. Then he ran to the enlistment office to sign up. Nine days later, Bradbury was among the first men to leave Orillia for training.

Twenty-six months in the trenches in France destroyed more than his early enthusiasm. In those 26 weeks, he had only two seven-day leaves. He was slightly injured once and rose to corporal. But he returned to Canada broken emotionally and mentally.

"Let George Bradbury slip in very quietly," a YMCA worker wrote to C.H. Hale in June 1917 while travelling from Halifax on a hospital train.

"George is nervous, and subject to attacks. Something the same as hysteria and I am told by the other men that he was a fearless fellow and a fine soldier," the letter to Hale reads. "George is sensitive, so do not say anything about his condition."

A second letter, written from Quebec City, warns against any large homecoming for Bradbury. "He had a bad attack on the train last night and I sounded him this morning by saying, 'Well George, they'll be glad to see you back at the old town and I'd like to be there for the reception.' His reply was a wish that there would be nothing of the kind for fear he could not stand it and collapse again." Bradbury eventually recovered enough to take part in an August ceremony welcoming the boys back home.

But he was never the same. Family and friends looked after him when he was not in hospital. He returned to England under the care of a friend, but was soon admitted to hospital, where he died in October, 1922.

Hale dealt with the suffering in a typical way: he tried to think of some way the town could lessen it. One night in the middle of the war, he lay awake, wondering how the town should best honor the fallen. His thoughts settled on the town's hospital, an over-crowded building of thirty-five beds. "Why not build a new or additional hospital and make it a memorial to the Orillians who have fallen?" he asked himself. Hale didn't

By 1908, the 35-bed Queen Mary Hospital on Dunedin Street had become overcrowded.

The Packet & Times

C.H. Hale led the creation of Soldiers' Memorial Hospital, completed in 1922. It provided free medical service for veterans of the First and Second World Wars. The new hospital fronted on Colborne Street. Highway 11 ran through town along Colborne Street, and that is why there is a direction sign at the corner of the hospital lot.

The Packet & Times

just want to tag the hospital with the word Memorial and leave it at that. "How can we make it a real memorial?" he asked. His answer, drafted before he fell asleep that night, created a unique hospital. In those days, people paid for their hospital stays. There was no medicare plan. Hale wanted to change that, for the soldiers at least. He proposed building an entire hospital to honour soldiers, with plaques remembering the dead and free medical care helping the living for as long as they lived. The leading doctors in town, Arthur Ardagh and A.R. Harvie, liked the idea and had no trouble convincing other doctors with hospital privileges to give free treatment to war veterans. A committee was struck, with J.B Tudhope a member, naturally, and money raised from canvassing. The town gave $25,000, but only one township, Orillia, accepted the offer to join the deal, paying $10,000. It was just as well, recalled Hale later, because the doctors probably could not have handled too many more patients.

The hospital was completed in 1922 at a cost of $100,000. At first, many soldiers did not like the idea. Some said they would have preferred a cenotaph instead. Hale and other hospital builders figured 1,000 men deserved the certificates for free medical help, yet could get details on only 150 for the opening ceremonies. Only half of those 150 soldiers accepted the initial offer. But as word spread and the plan began to work, more veterans joined the free medical plan. Hale remembered one Orillia veteran coming from his new home of Halifax for an operation. The money he saved by having the operation done at Soldiers' Memorial Hospital paid his way to come home and see his family. (Eventually, a cenotaph was built. Benefits were extended to the Second World War veterans, and sadly, the memorials to the fallen has grown).

The town greeted the official end of the war on November 11, 1918, with a seventeen-hour celebration of noise, prayer, tears, and laughter. Mayor Robert Curran learned about the armistice at 3 a.m. and called up the town's leaders. All the church bells rang and all the factory whistles blew at 7 a.m. to announce the news and kept ringing and whistling for half an hour. Thousands gathered in the market square at 9 a.m. for a thanksgiving service. So many bands and soldiers and impromptu floats and decorated motor cars took part in the afternoon parade, the first units reached the lake before the last left the market square. Clowns, a kazoo band, tin horn brigades, and politicians dressed in wild costumes that "would have created a furore even in Paris itself" marched before thousands on Mississaga Street, reported The Packet.

One effigy of the Kaiser was dragged behind a car, and another was suspended from a gallows while a veteran stabbed it with a fifteen-inch butcher knife. That evening downtown, residents built a huge bonfire and burned yet another effigy of the Kaiser, cheering as it dropped into the flames. Fireworks lit up the sky and a second bonfire in the market square burned until midnight.

The First World War claimed more than people as its victims. It also ended the Victorian Era its ideals, occasionally practised, of gentility and restraint. The 1920s across North America and Europe were marked by an initial depression, followed by rapid growth, good times, and cynicism. Orillia reacted in a typical way, with a mixture of retreat and advancement.

The retreat came in the automobile industry. When the First World War broke out, Tudhope's carriage and auto plants were converted to munitions production. After the war, Tudhope chose not to carry on with automobile production, but concentrated on the carriage business. It was a strange decision, given that automobiles were well on their way to replacing horse-drawn carriages. But the car business had not been making him much money before the war. Tudhope merged three other carriage manufacturers and continued to produce carriages and car bodies until 1924. For a time, the firm was the largest carriage maker in the world. The Fisher Motor Company faded into a minor supplier of car accessories until it too died in 1928. The Tudhopes remained involved in metal and appliance factories until 1966, but never returned to making automobiles.

After the war, the Board of Trade found it difficult to attract new industries to Orillia for several reasons. A lack of suitable buildings to rent kept four manufacturers away in 1923. Other companies looking to expand refused to move too far from growing Toronto. Even the will of the town to bring in new industries seemed to be fading. The board refused in 1927 to even consider giving a rubber factory and textile mill $50,000 bonuses to move to Orillia. Before the war, the board's annual reports and most of its efforts focused on industry, with a little footnote about the importance of tourism thrown in almost as an afterthought.

It's not as if the town's leaders had ignored tourism. In 1898, the town's young business leaders took over the defunct Board of Trade and at the same time as it began encouraging industry, it began promoting tourism. To make up for the shortage of accommodation, the board persuaded sixty homeowners in Orillia to take in summer visitors. The board began promoting

Orillia in the American South, by convincing the Grand Trunk Railway to publish and distribute 20,000 illustrated brochures advertising Orillia throughout the Southern States, convinced people there would want to head to the cooler north in the summer. The good response from that campaign inspired some board members to buy the defunct Red Cross Hospital on Orchard Point and turn it into the Orchard Point Inn. In 1901, advertising took off. The board made a deal with the Grand Trunk Railroad, which had merged the Northern and Midland lines, to distribute 20,000 brochures advertising the town. Each year the board promoted Orillia, and each year more people arrived for fishing, canoeing, sailing, steamboat excursions, and picnics in Couchiching Park. More and more, the economy of the town became tied to tourism. By 1906, seven hotels with a total of 225 rooms stood in the downtown core. When the Grand Trunk Railroad went on strike during tourist season in 1910, the Board of Trade and town newspapers urged a speedy end. Leaders embarked on a new campaign to clean up residential yards and fix up houses to impress tourists. Yet through all the tourism campaigns, industry remained the board's priority.

The first Board of Trade report after the war shows that trend was reversed for good. The efforts to increase tourism led off the reports, with the industrial promotion now relegated to secondary status. Where once the construction of the motor car carried the hopes of Orillia, now simply getting them here with ease occupied town leaders. Throughout the 1920s, business leaders urged the provincial government to improve roads so tourists could drive to Orillia quickly and comfortably. The completion of the Trent-Severn Waterway in 1920 added boat traffic to automobile visits. So busy was the town in the 1920s, more homeowners were urged to open up rooms for tourists. And so important was tourism by 1928, the board asked the Canadian National Exhibition in Toronto to change its start date so it always opened in September. When the CNE opened in August, it killed the tourist trade before summer ended, the board complained. That same year, the board contacted thirty-four industries looking to relocate, but managed to persuade only one to move to Orillia.

After the First World War, the Orillia Board of Trade shifted its focus from attracting industry to attracting motor tourists. This photograph looks west along Mississaga Street from just east of the Peter Street intersection, and shows one of the first automobiles on Orillia's main street.

Marcel Rosseau Collection

Orillia produced many heroes in its first Golden Age, from about 1880 to 1929. Jacob Gill "Jake" Gaudaur (1858-1937) learned to row on The Narrows and used his skills to win the double sculls championship of the world, with F. Hosmer, in 1890 on Lake Couchiching and the world single's sculling championship in 1896 on the Thames River. The bridge over The Narrows is named after him. He was inducted into the Orillia Hall of Fame posthumously in 1966.

Stephen Leacock Museum

Since the 1920s, tourism and industry have been the main pistons driving Orillia's economy. At different times, the community's leaders and residents seem to favor one over the other. The arguments over which is better for Orillia are not really about money - both tourism and industry are important and co-exist quite nicely - but, as usual, about image. Should Orillia maintain its small-town image, an image that as a fringe benefit attracts tourists? Or should it seek large new industries, more jobs and growth, at the risk of losing its small-town appeal? The argument over the community's image, sparked first by alcohol in the 1850s, became a permanent fixture in Orillia with the publication of a gentle satire on small-town life in 1912.

Of all the projects, schemes, and dreams that marked Orillia's Golden Age, none has had a bigger impact on the community than the small collection of stories written by Stephen Leacock titled Sunshine Sketches of a Little Town. The book immortalized Orillia as Mariposa, and its characters were based on the residents Leacock knew. The writer lived on Brewery Bay on Lake Couchiching from 1908 until his death at age seventy-four in 1944. He loved the town and made good, long-lasting friends here. Many of the characters and incidents in Sunshine Sketches were easily recognized by Orillia residents. Some Orillians never forgave Leacock, first for having the nerve to be a writer and a drinker, and second, for lampooning their town. Ironically, those conservative Orillians benefited the most from Leacock. His sunshine image of Orillia stuck and Mariposa became, for some, the ideal Orillia. In yet another irony, which he would surely enjoy, many who liked Leacock the man grew sick of Leacock the image. Attempts to spur growth in Orillia have often been blocked by the invocation of the Mariposa image. In the 1970s especially, certain development lagged because many Orillians decided it did not fit the Mariposa image. Today, Leacock and the image he created for Orillia comforts, encourages, annoys, and frustrates its citizens.

The complex relationship between Leacock and Orillia would take an entire book to explain. Yet no one doubts the veracity of Leacock's view of Orillians. Eccentric characters continued to spring up long after Sunshine Sketches was published, none more colourful than the man who would lead the town through the depression, J. Benjamin Johnston.

Walter Knox (1878-1952) needed all his legendary strength just to wear all his medals. Knox moved to Orillia at 15 and practised track and field with other boys near their homes on Gill Street. From a home-made jumping pit and forty-yard sprinting track, Knox graduated to Canadian and world championship track and field meets. He competed in running, shot putting, discus throwing, high jumping, pole-vaulting, the 105-pound hammer throw and broad jumping. In a twenty-year career that began in 1900, he broke numerous records. He was inducted into the Orillia Hall of Fame posthumously in 1966.
Orillia Public Library

The Group of Seven led a revolution in the arts in Canada, painting with techniques that rebelled against European styles and better reflected this country's wilderness. Orillian Franklin Carmichael (1890–1945) was one of the Group of Seven and is remembered as one of Canada's greatest artists. He was inducted posthumously into the Orillia Hall of Fame in 1966.

HALE AND HEARTY

A lot of people have good ideas, but few act on them as often as Charles Harold Hale did. The gentlemanly, scholarly publisher of The Packet & Times accomplished so much for the city he became known as Mr. Orillia. The efforts sometimes left him exhausted, as he was in 1912 after working in the 1911 federal election. Hale spent a few weeks in bed, then took a trip to Quebec City and Saint John, New Brunswick. It struck him as odd that these two cities had wonderful monuments to Samuel de Champlain, but Orillia did not. If it occurred to Hale that Quebec City and Saint John were many times the size of Orillia, it likely didn't matter. Hale immediately set out to build a monument to Champlain in Orillia.

C.H. Hale, shown in the 1950s, had many good ideas. One of his greatest was the Champlain monument, a landmark on the waterfront erected to create harmony between the English and French.

As he often did, Hale first proposed the idea to people of influence, in this case the Orillia Canadian Club (which he had also formed) and several provincial leaders, including Ontario's chief archivist, Alex Fraser. Hale knew whom to tap for ideas and support, and he always gave them more credit than himself. He originally planned to spend $10,000 for a modest statue. But Fraser told him to dream bigger and try for $20,000 and

a statue unlike anything else in the country. Luck visited the monument committee when it travelled to Ottawa to ask the federal government for money, Hale recalled. The committee was supposed to meet Prime Minister Robert Borden, a cold, practical, and unromantic man unlikely to hand over a lot of money for the arts and culture. But Borden was busy debating in the House of Commons, and the committee was forced to meet Sir Thomas White, the minister of finance. A poet, art lover, and amateur historian, White was only too happy to give the committee not only the amount requested, $10,000, but an additional $2,500 when expenses increased.

A competition for design attracted twenty-two entries from France, England, and Canada. The committee had been advised that many top sculptors did not like to enter competitions, but a brilliant young artist from England named Vernon March should be urged to submit an entry. The jury made an unanimous choice from the anonymous entries, learning later young March, twenty, had won the competition.

Before the statue was raised to its pedestal, sculptor Vernon March, far right, gave it a final going over.

The Champlain monument was supposed to be built by August 1915, to mark the three-hundredth anniversary of the explorer's visit to

Huronia. But the First World War delayed work on the sculpture and the opening was replaced by a recruiting rally. The delay caused by the war also increased expenses, although March and his family of sculptors refused to raise their own fees. If there were any complaints about the cost, finally set at $35,000, or delays, they were drowned out by the celebration when the Champlain monument was unveiled. For public extravaganzas, the July 1, 1925, gathering in Couchiching Park has few equals in Orillia.

About 250 men, women and children painted and dressed as Chippewa re-enacted the landing of Samuel de Champlain on the shores of Lake Couchiching during the elaborate celebration unveiling the Champlain monument, July 1, 1925. Roughly 10,000 people crowded into Couchiching Park to watch the unveiling. The monument is considered a masterpiece, and its sculptor, Vernon March, later created the War Memorial in Ottawa.

About 18,000 people, more than twice the population of the town itself, crowded into Couchiching Beach Park to watch a historical re-enactment of Champlain's visit. That re-enactment "must be placed in the front rank of historical reproductions ever attempted in Canada," wrote the not-entirely objective publicity chairman in a souvenir booklet. More than 250 men, women, and children dressed up in Huron costumes. The loafing braves, busy squaws and playing children were first frightened when Champlain showed up. Their fright turned quickly to curiosity then joy. The squaws sang and the braves danced a welcome. Nothing was said of the unfortunate circumstances that befell the natives because of Champlain's visit. And the statue itself, still magnificent, puts natives in a clearly servile position. The twelve-foot-high bronze Champlain, dressed in full court attire and cloak blowing in the breeze, stands alone. Plumed hat in hand, he looks not across Lake Couchiching but down, as if in thought. Below him on one side, symbolizing Christianity, a robed priest holds the cross high above the wonder-struck natives at his feet. On the other side of Champlain,

symbolizing Commerce, a fur trader examines a pelt brought to him by two natives, also at his feet.

Native rights were hardly in fashion in 1925 and the world was still the whites' for the taking. Yet the speech of Rodolphe Lemieux, the speaker of the House of Commons, made it clear what the Champlain monument was to represent - a country based on different nations, with each person having the right to worship God in his or her own way, and speak freely his or her ancestral language. In the heartland of conservative Ontario, where distrust of Quebec has a strong foothold, the 100-ton monument stands not only as a remarkable physical achievement but as a persistent and not always welcome reminder of other cultures. The monument has also come to symbolize not only Champlain's vision, but the vision of C.H. Hale.

The Champlain monument.

A MOTORING ADVENTURE

Muddy roads and ruts that seemed deep enough to swallow cars whole awaited the first drivers of J.B. Tudhope's automobiles.

In 1909, Bell Telephone employee A.W. Robinson was instructed to pick up the company's first truck and deliver it from Orillia to London, via Toronto. Bell Telephone had decided to try the automobile as an experimental replacement of horses. Tudhope workers gave Robinson and other company officials a quick tour of the factory and brief instructions on how to drive the car.

That first day, Robinson, two Bell officials, and a Tudhope worker on his way to Toronto to demonstrate the car to Toronto Hydro drove the thirty miles to Barrie in two and a half hours, scaring horses and startling spectators on the way. The next day they picked up two more company officials and enough mud to build their own road. The car got stuck in the mud once, and Robinson had to get a farmer to pull it out, while frightened company officials in their patent leather shoes stayed in the car.

"The weather was really nasty when we reached the Yonge Street road leading to Aurora," Robinson recalled. "The mud was flying in all directions (there were no mud guards or canopy on the car). When we stopped in Aurora at noon for lunch the mud was spread on us pretty thickly and it took us about twenty minutes to wash up."

It had taken about ninety minutes to travel about fifteen miles from Newmarket to Aurora. One company official elected to take the train from Aurora to Toronto, but the other five stuck with the Tudhope. On the way, they noticed that the railroad tracks appeared the same width as the Tudhope's steel-rimmed, rubber tires. So they tried the car on the railroad tracks.

"We opened the throttle wide and must have been making about twenty miles an hour," recalled Robinson, "when the section man flagged us down. He told us to get the hell off the track and stay off."

The group arrived in downtown Toronto covered in mud, but triumphant in making the last thirty miles in three and a half hours.

A FAIRY-TALE ENDING

In the very heart of Orillia sits a fairy-tale building, and inside the building, legends are born. For a hundred years the city has dreamed, laughed, wept, and fought inside the Orillia Opera House. Many of the city's defining moments have taken place under its landmark twin spires. Politicians and political hopefuls have sweated under its stage lights and the heckling of voters. But if it weren't for politicians, the place might be nothing more than a shed today.

Not long after Orillia became a village, residents began to think about moving the market from its location near the waterfront. After a few years of debate, a landowner named Goldwin Smith agreed to donate a half-acre lot on the northwest corner of Mississaga and West streets. In return, the village had to clear Mississaga Street West of stumps so Smith could subdivide another parcel of his land up the street. (Smith also donated the three acres that became Victoria Park and built the Grange in Toronto, which he donated to the Art Gallery of Ontario.)

Beside the Opera House stood the market, with sheds for farmers' displays. Farmers drove their livestock to and from the market along Mississaga Street, seen here at the intersection of West Street looking west.

Stephen Leacock Museum

The market square grew especially crowded on days when Massey Harris sold farm implements. This photograph, taken in 1897, looks toward West Street and the back of the old town hall and lockup, which were demolished in the 1960s.

Sue Mulcahy Collection

The original Opera House, built in 1895, looked even more castle-like than usual when plank sidewalks were set over the mud, like bridges over a moat. The Opera House included a tower at the rear of the building along Mississaga Street.

Orillia Public Library

Some people in the village wanted nothing more than a good, large shed and a few stalls put up in the market for farmers. But the village councillors wanted a new town hall to replace the Temperance Hall and a proper lock-up for the rowdies that plagued the lumbering town. Arguments over the building of the hall delayed its opening, but council finally had its first meeting in the new hall August 7, 1874. That town hall and lock-up served well from 1874 to 1877. But council again decided something grander was needed for both the shed and town hall, and after a few false starts, the Opera House was completed in 1895. It cost taxpayers $25,000 and held the council chambers, auditorium, city hall offices, market stalls, and eventually the lock-up.

The Opera House, described as "the finest building for corporation purposes of any town in Ontario," became an immediate source of pride for Orillia, an example of the Orillia Spirit.

Of course, pride has a pricetag, and Orillians would pay only so much for it. A fire broke out in the Opera House in July, 1915, sparking rumours Kaiser Wilhelm's Germans had attacked Orillia and destroyed much of the building. The last of the debentures for the building had just been paid, and Orillians did not want to pay much more for a new theatre. The town had to get the taxpayers' approval to borrow large amounts of money in those days. Council and the Board of Trade pushed for a bylaw authorizing a $50,000 debenture to rebuild the Opera House, but residents voted it down. It was too much to spend on a theatre in times of war. The next year's council tried for a smaller plan, costing taxpayer $35,000, and it was approved. The official opening March 1, 1917, featured the English pantomime Aladdin and His Wonderful Lamp and cost from sixty cents to a dollar admission.

Orillians at first blamed the Kaiser for the fire of 1915, which destroyed much of the Opera House. The view in this photograph is from Mississaga Street, looking toward West Street. After arguments about the cost of rebuilding, the tower at the back was not replaced.

Orillia Public Library

That is the kind of legend the Opera House inspires. Stories about secret tunnels under the building have burrowed into the city's mythology. It is said one tunnel was dug from the Opera House to a store basement on the other side of Mississaga Street, where politicians and their cronies could head unseen and enjoy the company of women and liquor. No one can prove anything, as mysterious doorways in the foundation of the Opera House were covered up long ago.

The grand old lady has shown her age over the years, and at times lost her popularity. Parts of the building were allowed to deteriorate. In the 1980s, the city began restoring the building. By the time the Opera House celebrated its 100th birthday in 1995, it had regained its former glory, drawing thousands of Orillians and tourists each year, a fairy-tale ending to a story about a simple shed.

For many years, the Opera House hosted politicians upstairs and criminals down, with the politicians generally causing more ruckus than the criminals. The jail was eventually moved, but the council chambers remained. Great battles have been fought in those chambers over subjects as diverse as the liquor trade and incinerating waste. Residents have crowded in the gallery to jeer and cheer their villains and heroes on city council. Federal, provincial, and municipal candidates have all sweated on the Opera House stage during election debates. The acoustics of the auditorium have drawn the greats, such as Oscar Peterson and Gordon Lightfoot, and the would-be greats, such as high school bands and community theatre groups. One of the most legendary performances was witnessed by an audience of one. Opera House technician Terry Rideout drove by one night in the 1970s and noticed someone was in the auditorium. He slipped inside and heard someone playing the piano on stage, beautiful notes rising clear in the cold, darkened auditorium. In a heavy coat and gloves on the dark stage, Glenn Gould played for nothing but the joy of the music. Rideout turned up the lights for him and for half an hour enjoyed a private concert by one of the world's greatest pianists.

KING BEN

Mayor Ben Johnston was looking for government handouts to help build a sidewalk. He asked the county, federal, provincial and township governments for grants. When he was done, one of his rivals pointed out that Johnston had been so stupid as to collect 125 per cent of the grants, more than necessary. To that, Johnston replied, "Usually when I am behind something, I am behind it 100 per cent." This time, he was just adding an extra 25 per cent to his usual effort. John Benjamin Johnston, auctioneer, farmer, pedlar, and politician - and just plain Ben to friends and enemies - often gave a little extra, and for his efforts, sometimes took a little extra.

For five one-year terms in the Depression - 1929, 1930, 1931, 1935, and 1936 - Ben Johnston held court as mayor of Orillia. He created his own rules and his own money. He offered hope to the unemployed, despair to the democratic, and a welcome mat to the bootleggers. The truth never impaired Johnston's vision, nor reality his mission. Mixing a sharp temper with a sharp wit, he out-shouted, out-insulted and outraged his real and imagined enemies. Scandals plagued his administrations and council meetings routinely drew a full house of spectators primed for fireworks. Johnston was the focus of people's dreams, frustrations and anger. His rise and fall, and rise and fall again, helped define Orillia in the Depression.

His long reign began quietly, with few signs of the storm ahead. In the fall of 1928, six incumbent council members, including the mayor, dropped out of the election race. The door was wide open and Johnston stepped in. Born in 1878 in Leaksdale Ontario, he moved with his family to Orillia in 1893. He worked off and on as an auctioneer and pedlar. For three years he farmed near Brechin, then moved to town because he couldn't stand the loneliness of rural life.

"I wanted somebody to talk to," he told reporters. What he always dreamed, said Johnston, was to some day become mayor. He had served on council in the early 1900s, twice lost the race for mayor and sat as East Simcoe MPP in 1920. In the fall of 1928, Johnston promised voters he would do more to bring factories to town and wanted to take Orillia out of the county to save money - nothing really too controversial. The bigger issue that year was a bylaw authorizing council to spend $58,000 on a new sewer system. The spring thaw and yearly rains had been forcing sewage up

Tom Hill's unique hotdog stand and gas station at 80 Colborne St. E. served up inexpensive food and a feast for the eyes. Hill built the stand in 1926 out of bricks, mortar, broken glass, pop bottles and marbles. Local children were happy to donate the marbles and broken pop bottles. At that time, Highway 11 ran through town along Colborne Street and Hill captured tourists by providing information and a "last chance" for gas and food. The building was demolished in 1975.

Sue Mulcahy Collection

through the manholes and into the streets. Sewage overflowed the ditches at the pumping station and ran into Lake Couchiching three-quarters of a mile from the pipes that sucked in the town's drinking water. A bad snowstorm January 7, 1929 kept voters at home and Johnston squeaked to victory, 670-573. In the same election, voters defeated the bylaw to repair the old sewage system. Perhaps it was an appropriate omen. There was about to be a lot more muck and a lot more raking of it.

The year the Depression started, 1929, began calmly for Orillia. Johnston and C.H. Hale, publisher of The Packet & Times, engaged in a respectful debate about the town's sewer bylaw, which was defeated in yet another vote that year. Hale maintained that taxpayers voted down the sewer bylaw because they wanted the system run by the Water, Light and Power Commission, not the town. Johnston disagreed, saying taxpayers simply didn't want any more taxes. When The Packet & Times and the Board of Trade offered to hold a third vote on the bylaw, free of charge to the town, Johnston called them "fanatics", perhaps the first sign that year of what was to come.

Hale sparked the war that would rage between him and Johnston for the next seven years. Over the summer, the town had worked out a scheme with Simcoe County to pave several major town roads, Coldwater Road, Coldwater Street and Barrie Road. It was a complicated deal, but Hale discovered the bottom line meant town taxpayers would be paying to pave a county road - the portion of Coldwater Road from the town's limit at Emily Street to the Fourth Concession. The sewer system would have cost taxpayers about $3,700 a year to build, while the paving was to cost $5,600 a year. Not only that, said Hale, but the deal was probably illegal. After the story ran, several taxpayers had the Supreme Court of Ontario issue an injunction against any work until the issue was sorted out. The Department of Public Highways investigated and told the town and county to forget any such deal. The deal " was the most improvident and ill-digested scheme that has ever been entered into, or even considered, by the council of the town of Orillia...," Hale concluded. Johnston had more in store for Hale. A few months later, Johnston suggested the town sell the Orillia Water, Light and Power utility to Ontario Hydro. "Having failed to get his way cutting a paving melon, Mayor Johnston, like a petulant child, is now intent on smashing the china," wrote Hale.

Hale stepped up his attacks throughout the fall of 1929, as the impact of the October stockmarket crash reached Orillia. He accused Johnston of running up a $3,500 deficit, after starting his first term as mayor with a $747 surplus. Johnston seized on his battle with the erudite Hale as reason enough for people to vote him in as mayor for a second time.

"This journal is liked canned eggs. It hits you and run. If the editor can't have a council he can can, he proposes to can the council he can't can," quipped Johnston in his fiery election speeches. In the style of any good populist, Johnston appealed to the working man's sense he wasn't getting a fair shake from the intellectuals in power, such as Hale. And like any good populist, Johnston promised to clean up city hall, although he had

The opening of the simple hot dog stand near the waterfront has long been the herald of summer, just as the shutting of its windows each fall leaves no doubt winter is coming. George French, handicapped and looking for a way to support his family, obtained a lease in 1920 to open up a hotdog stand on the waterfront. Business at French's Stand boomed when excursion trains ran from Toronto to Couchiching Park, sometimes as many as twenty a day. In the Depression, business dropped, but French's still fixed up a boathouse and heated it during winter so children had a skating hut. Over the years, thousands of people have taken a break at the stand, including Stephen Leacock. As the lake was filled in, the stand lost its spot on the water, but not its place in Orillia's heart.

Marcel Rosseau Collection

been in charge of it himself for a year already, and get good jobs for all. That was enough to win him a second term as mayor, for 1930.

Meanwhile, the Depression had taken root. That winter, tramps and hoboes began riding the rails to town. Lying between the cities to the south and north, Orillia gathered in displaced young men, cold, dirty, and begging police chief Lew Church to let them sleep a night in the cells.

"The cities, and even the villages are full of men out of work, starving, desperate," said one town policeman. "It's not the spineless old guard, the old hobo who took things lying down that make up their numbers. It's young, able-bodied men, eager for work, self-respecting, courageous and desperate because of the raw deal life is handing them."

The federal, provincial and municipal governments began a system of relief payments. Indirect relief went to help municipalities hire men for public works projects. Direct relief went for food, fuel and clothes for the worst-off families. In Orillia, the combination of relief and growing unpaid

Couchiching Beach Park, Orillia, Ont., Canada.

At least Orillians could swim and canoe for free during the Depression. Bathing pavilions were set up along the water's edge so swimmers could change discreetly before cooling off.

Marcel Rosseau Collection

taxes made money - the pursuit and spending of it - the key issues for the ten years of the Depression. Johnston was a freewheeling spender, but even better at hiding his spending behind lengthy speeches, and confusing bookkeeping.

Hale's claims that Johnston had rung up a deficit in 1929 sparked the first of many battles between Johnston and his 1930 council. The wrangling over the auditor's report for 1929 took weeks for the 1930 council to resolve. So angry was Johnston over claims of a deficit, he stomped out of a March meeting when aldermen tried to pass the auditor's report and threatened to pass an injunction declaring council's business invalid if it did anything after he left. He did leave, but came back and displayed the oratorical style that came to typify his debates.

"You're out of order, anything you say is out of order," he shouted to Alderman Teefy Mulcahy, an insurance broker and one of Johnston's chief opponents. (The auditor's report, showing a $2,960.10 operating deficit, was accepted at a later meeting). Johnston continued to make up new rules for running council meetings. He accused the deputy reeve of taking a kickback, a charge later proven wrong. When Alderman Mulcahy asked for a written report on the charge, Johnston made up a new power of the mayor's office.

"When I say it out loud, it's a written report," he said.

So rambunctious were the council meetings in 1930, newspapers made special mention of the first calm meeting of the year, held July 7. The calm lasted one week. At the July 14 meeting, a reporter found the spectators had taken all the chairs and asked a man in the crowd to get him one so he wouldn't miss any of the debate. As the man got up, Mayor Johnston shouted at him to sit down. The reporter asked again for the chair. The man went to get the chair. "Them guys should be made to stand up!" Johnston shouted. "Them guys think they can run this place."

With relief money in one hand and the other raised against the forces of evil, Johnston won the race for mayor for the third straight time in the fall of 1930. His popularity was at a peak, and he thumped his opponent in not only the working class south and middle-class west wards, but the conservative and old-money north ward. Almost twice as many voters, about 2,300, turned out for the election as the year before, with the heaviest voting in the south ward.

Johnston truly dug himself a place in Orillia history that winter. A third vote on the sewage system had taken place a year ago, and, just as

Hale had predicted, ratepayers approved the plan as long as the trusted Orillia Water, Light and Power Commission operated the system. As part of the sewage plan, council approved the construction of a storm-water pumping station at West and James streets. The station would drain the swampy land in the southwest area of the town and pump it into Lake Simcoe. Over the summer of 1930, Johnston had suggested the town build a long canal from south of Barrie Road just east of West Street to Lake Simcoe, in order to do much the same thing as the pumping station. Nothing came of his idea, or so everyone thought. That December, after his big election win, Johnston hired teams of men to begin digging the canal. Shocked council members read about the digging first in Hale's Packet & Times. Ever one to notice the bottom line, Hale pointed out that Johnston's canal bypassed the new $6,000 pumping station, making it useless.

Seven angry council members forced Johnston to call a council meeting late in December. They tried to get three motions passed; one that the drainage work follow the original plan; two, that the canal work be stopped; and three, that a county judge investigate the mushrooming relief payments Johnston had been authorizing. They wondered why Johnston was paying men to dig the canal, when digging machinery owned by the town was sitting idle.

Johnston packed the Opera House council chambers with supporters from the south ward and stonewalled the council members. He refused to allow any aldermen to speak, threatened to have one alderman thrown out, then ordered a constable to throw out another, Teefy Mulcahy. The constable refused. Johnston ruled every motion made by council out of order, and after several hours, a frustrated Mulcahy asked him, "What makes a motion out of order?"

"Being out of order," the mayor replied.

Playing to the crowd, so noisy it was heard outside the Opera House, Johnston accused his rivals of sitting on the relief money to starve the unemployed into taking less money per hour next spring. As for the success of the canal, "I don't need engineers to tell me water will run down hill," said Johnston. Nothing could be accomplished at that meeting, so council met in a private session in January, 1931 to consider the canal. After several hours behind closed doors, council agreed to a compromise between the original plan and Johnston's. The town would spend about $8,000 of its own and other government's relief money to have a canal dug from Mount

Slaven Creek to Lake Simcoe. The pump house would be used to drain swampy land into a series of ditches that connected to the canal.

Johnston predicted his four-foot deep, 20-foot wide canal would become a resort-like area of fine houses. The canal never did reach the size or grandeur Johnston planned. It does not wind through an area of beautiful homes, but some fields and wetlands. However, the canal did provide work for several men on relief, and it did become a helpful drainage ditch. It's also one of the few things named after Johnston, still known as Ben's Ditch.

Johnston's popularity rose. After the canal debate, about 300 people met in the South Ward Community Hall to start a boycott of The Packet & Times and its advertisers "should any further intimidation of his Worship, the Mayor occur."

Johnston showed up to lend his support. "I don't know the purpose of this meeting, but I am always willing to address a meeting of the ratepayers of Orillia," he said, before launching a fierce attack on Hale and The Packet. Of the man who created Soldiers' Memorial Hospital and the

Motorists driving to Orillia in the 1930s and 1940s often had to wait for boat traffic through The Narrows. A worker in the tower made sure both cars had stopped before he swung the bridge open.

Marcel Rosseau Collection

Champlain Monument, Johnston said, "In thirty-five years as a resident here, I have yet to see anything in The Packet & Times that brought anything in the way of industries or work to the town."

"Ben is Ben to us all," said one man at the meeting. "There is no high-hatting at the Mayor's office nowadays."

Johnston kept up his attacks on the powerful in town. Attending court as a spectator at one spring session, he ran afoul of a police court magistrate for opening up and discussing a document while court was in session. The magistrate told him to put the document away.

"I didn't know you wanted to make a Methodist Sunday School out of the proceedings," Johnston told the magistrate.

The magistrate ordered police chief Church to remove Johnston. A couple of years earlier, Johnston had accused Church of getting confessions by promising criminals leniency and of misusing a free railroad pass. None of the charges were proven. In court that day, Church smiled when the magistrate ordered him to remove the mayor. As Church guided Johnston out of court, he assured him, "It is only in compliance with my orders."

"I'll go out quietly but this won't be my last word," Johnston shouted. Later that spring, council gave the magistrate a pay raise, as required by the province. Johnston refused to sign the paycheque. His tirades fell on deaf ears, and council simply passed a motion giving an alderman the right to sign the cheques.

Johnston's appeal to the frustrations of south-warders might have kept him in power for several more terms. But his increasingly embarrassing personal battles and questions about the way he handed out relief began to turn public sentiment in the summer and fall of 1931. It became apparent he was not always the friend of the worker. When the town clerk asked to reduce the hours the office was open, so she would not have to balance the books after 6 p.m. every day, Johnston replied he would rather fire her and hire a man.

Aldermen began pushing for more control over the town's money, especially relief payments, which were handled mainly by the mayor. In the fall of 1931, they put several plans in motion which should have guaranteed a good fall and winter. The town's bank account was thinning out, and it would be a month before the province promised more money for relief. At the same time, relief work was about to stop for the winter, leaving men without a paycheque for several months. So council decided to hold back half the wages for men working on relief. The men would work a full day now and get half of the 20 to 30 cents-an-hour pay immediately. The rest would come December 15. This way the town could save money until December 15 and the men would have money over the winter. Men with special circumstances could ask to get the full pay immediately. At first, the unemployed men in town agreed to the plan. And in October, town council came away from a meeting with provincial officials confident of getting a request for $171,000 in relief projects approved.

The optimism crashed a few weeks later. The province told Orillia council it would have to make do with $50,000 in relief projects, with half coming from the town. There was worse news. Expecting more money from the province, the town had already spent all but $13,000 of the $50,000 promised. Meanwhile, the unemployed in town, about 575 men and women, began getting restless and started organizing. The full-day for half-pay plan had some men working from dawn until dusk with little to show for it. At an October 6, 1931 meeting at the United Workers Hall, 300 men agreed to ask council for an eight-hour day, 35 cents an hour pay instead of the 20 cents paid, no more contract work, and no holding back of the money. Contract work was especially galling to the men. The town paid relief to certain contractors, who then hired the men. The contractors were getting rich on relief, many of the men charged. It was no longer enough to stand on street corners and shout, said organizers. Workers had to unite and demand council listen.

"The trouble is that the working men are afraid to approach the lion in his den," club president Terry Jackson told the crowd.

At later meetings that November, workers wondered aloud why Mayor Johnston took so many trips to Toronto on taxpayers' money. They approved a slate of candidates for the next election that did not include Johnston, but several of his rivals, like Teefy Mulcahy. Meeting chairman A.E. "Paddy" Ball told workers they should vote in a new administration, and ran for office himself. At an uproarious nomination meeting in the Opera House that fall, Johnston attacked Ball, calling into question his war record and accusing him of never paying taxes.

"Where were you during the war, Mr. Johnston?" shouted someone.

"Here at home in Orillia, doing my work and supporting my family," a flustered Johnston replied, to more boos than cheers.

Johnston attacked another labour candidate for having a police court record.

"You were in court yourself, Ben!" shouted someone.

When Johnston called the workers who opposed him "canned heat agitators" he was roundly booed. His opponent for mayor, Robert Curran, pointed out that Orillia paid its contractors twice as much for relief projects as other towns, suggesting someone was getting rich from the taxpayers. Other candidates wondered aloud how much money was getting into the pockets of working men.

Johnston tried his best to win back the favor of the town's unemployed. On the Saturday before the Monday, December 7 election, Johnston opened up the till. He got together all the men who had been working on relief. A week before the town was supposed to, Johnston paid the men the rest of their wages, about $4,000 in total. It didn't help him. Curran won the mayor's race 1,488-1,380, and four other men backed by the United Workers Club also won.

Johnston wasn't through yet. The new council discovered to its horror later January, 1932, that Johnston had gone on a spending spree after the election. "Not one dollar of relief money, direct or indirect...is in the treasury," announced new mayor Curran. In the six weeks between the December 7, 1931 election, and the sitting of the new council in January, the "spiteful, selfish and small-minded" Johnston had spent the rest of the town's relief money, which was supposed to last all winter, said Curran. In the last week of December alone, $4,500 was spent for relief, with 320 men on the public payroll even though the public works construction had stopped.

"It is a cruel thing to the people who had looked to these huge sums to ensure them employment and livelihood during the severe winter months," said Curran.

The town started 1931 with $11,000 credit in the bank, but now had a $31,000 overdraft. When Johnston first came to power, the town had an operating surplus of $1,411. After his three terms, it had an operating deficit of $46,500. On the assets and liabilities balance sheet, the town went from a $49,000 surplus three years earlier to a $38,000 deficit. The Dominion Government sent a representative to town to examine the relief payments. The government worker criticized Orillia's handling of relief payments, which were not supposed to be paid to contractors. The town had to borrow $100,000 instead of the usual $50,000 to tide it over the winter. A volunteer Citizens Relief Association sprang up to help the town raise money for relief. Teachers and other town employees were the first to contribute five per cent of their wages to the fund.

Over the next three years, Johnston-free councils tried to whittle down its operating deficit and the debt that had piled up. The cost of relief and unpaid taxes forced the town to cut all but essential services. The unemployed continued to meet. Some spoke of violence, but nothing came of it. Town council created a public welfare board to handle relief more properly, and the Depression settled in. Several large companies, such as J.R. Eaton and Sons and Tudhope-Anderson, fell into ruin. But there was some good news. The banks sent up Ross W. Phelps to see what, if anything, of Tudhope-Anderson could be sold or salvaged. In 1935, after talking things over with town officials, Phelps decided to keep the company going. He asked council for a fixed tax assessment of $15,000 for 10 years. Council agreed and put the bylaw giving the fixed assessment to a vote of ratepayers. The bylaw lost by a few votes. Phelps was upset, but agreed not to do anything until council checked into matters. A recount gave the bylaw victory, and what was to become one of Orillia's largest industries – Otaco – was born.

Another of the town's largest employers came to town during the Depression. A group of businessmen in Toronto, under the name Ventures Alloys, were ready in 1935 to take advantage of the soon to be booming metal industry. They had several patents but little money. When National Locks Ltd. on Barrie Road in Orillia went under in 1935, Ventures Alloys jumped at the chance to get a large, if ramshackle, building for only $50 a month. Inexpensive power offered by the town's utility and a fixed assessment of $3,500 a year from the town sealed the deal. Fahralloy Canada Ltd. started off small. When the sirens screamed to signal the molten metal about to flow, office workers scrambled into the foundry to help out, recalled Alex Wilson, an original employee and later president in the 1970s, for The Packet & Times in 1985. That first year, Fahralloy employed eleven men producing stainless steel parts. At its peak in 1970, the company employed 500 people. In the midst of the Depression, with companies such as Fahralloy and Otaco demanding more power, Orillia built a new power plant at Minden. With inexpensive labor and government help, the bold move turned into a wise one.

It also allowed Ben Johnston to get back into the mayor's office. A local firm had lost the tender for the construction of the plant. That was all

Johnston needed to make himself the friend of the working man again. He won election for the 1935 term, and soon town residents had a source of inexpensive entertainment. Early in the year, Johnston tried to have the town's only high school, Orillia Collegiate, shut down because it was costing too much money. The world didn't need intellectuals; it needed workers, said Johnston.

The Packet's Hale served up Johnston's plan with relish to its readers. "Our only criticism is that is so intensely practical. The plan lacks the true imaginative touch that is the mark of true genius," wrote Hale in a March 21, 1935 editorial. Hale suggested, "Orillia should be transferred, holus bolus, to the Moon." There would be no taxes, no worries about the Depression or another war, and no school to trouble children. On the moon, the mayor would have no Huey Long, the controversial governor of Louisiana, to compete for space on page one of the newspapers. "There will be the question of who shall make the first trip," concluded Hale. "We are willing to toss with the Mayor for that honor."

The Toronto newspapers loved reporting on the rumors that buzzed around Johnston's administration that year. Reports that gangs of workers were being forced at gunpoint to work on the Minden power plant, and that young girls of thirteen and fourteen were getting drunk after hours in the town's restaurants found their way into the Star and Telegram in 1935.

But Johnston kept taxes down, partly by borrowing money from the bank, ensuring his popularity. Given his popularity, Johnston wondered aloud why he wasn't more respected. A mayor of his standing should be acclaimed for the 1936 term, Johnston told reporters. When he had to run a campaign, Johnston blamed the elite in town for spreading lies and rumours about him. He would get them, vowed Johnston. He would keep on running for mayor until someday he was acclaimed.

"I am going to contest the Mayoralty until I am seventy-five until I am treated as well as anyone else would be," he said.

He won the mayor's race that fall by only 39 votes, but entered 1936 as confident and controversial as ever. It was one of the wildest terms of office in Orillia's history. Johnston was accused of drinking with bootleggers, running up his expense account on personal business and selling a town car then pocketing the money himself. But what was money to Johnston? As mayor, he could make his own, he figured. So he did. His inspiration came from Kitchener, Ontario, where scrip had been used for

three years. That city received money for relief from other government levels and borrowed from the bank, just like Orillia. Instead of handing that money over to people on relief, however, Kitchener paid the relief in special vouchers. The people on relief could use the vouchers at Kitchener stores. When a Kitchener merchant brought the relief vouchers to city hall, he was paid 97 cents on the dollar. That gave Kitchener three cents on each relief dollar it had originally received, to pay off the interest on the money borrowed from the bank, or build up a surplus. The merchants might have complained, but without relief, there was little money coming into their stores.

Johnston thought the vouchers, or scrip, was a great idea for Orillia. So did Reeve Wilbur Cramp, later a mayor modelled on Ben's style. The scrip "would be as good as a U.S. dollar," he predicted. Some of their colleagues on the 1936 council were less enthusiastic, and in a stormy

Mayor Ben Johnston's scrip looked good enough to replace real money for a few weeks in the fall of 1936. It was redeemable, although merchants disliked the idea of subsidizing relief. The scrip and Johnson were equally popular in the election of that year and Johnston lost. He would not be mayor again, although he did not give up trying.

Orillia Public Library

meeting in September, a council committee voted the idea down. Johnston brought the issue up a week later. When an alderman pointed out the vote had already been taken, Johnson ruled the matter still had to come to council. Protests about order got aldermen nowhere. "Well, this is my ruling," said Johnston, and ordered the clerk to read the proposed bylaw.

A name-calling session erupted, with Johnston calling one alderman a "yapper", and the alderman comparing the mayor to something found under a rock. Council passed the scrip bylaw by one vote. The town prepared $30,000 in denominations of 1, 5, 10, 25, and 50 cents and $1. The system was different than Kitchener's. Merchants had to use the scrip and buy one-cent stamps from the town to put on the vouchers. Each time the dollar scrip was used, the merchant or bill collector was to stick one stamp on it. Only when four stamps had been placed on the voucher, could the merchant take it to city hall or a bank and get it redeemed for 99 cents on the dollar. The town made that penny, plus the four other cents in stamps the merchant had to buy to get the scrip redeemed. Bylaw 1356 approving the scrip plan allowed the mayor and treasurer "to make such other arrangements as may be found necessary to have the said Voucher or Scrip as perfectly made as possible."

And perfectly made it was. The scrip looked so authentic, Johnston slapped a one-dollar voucher on the counter of a Cleveland hotel, just as a joke, to buy five cigars. The clerk put the voucher in the till and gave Johnston 50 cents in good American silver. Johnston let the clerk in on the joke later, but he had proved Cramp right in predicting the money's worth. On one side of each "Co-operative Purchasing Relief Scrip", under the fancy scroll work, stood the imposing figure of the Champlain monument and the signatures of Johnston and town treasurer Carrie Johnston (no relation). On the other was a picture of the Swift Rapids power plant on the Severn River. Above the picture were the words, "Orillia-Pioneers in municipally owned electric development."

Ironically and in spite of the free advertising, the Orillia Water, Light and Power Commission refused to accept the scrip for payment. The Commission believed it would become a clearing house for scrip from merchants looking to pay their heat and hydro. Merchants reluctantly accepted the scrip, because they had to. But they complained about the nuisance of the stamps, and council repealed that part of the bylaw. The scrip did not catch on. The first week, city hall released $1,150 in scrip.

About $700 was redeemed. After the city paid off interest to the bank, it was left with $35. The scrip never did make much money, costing almost as much to print and administer as it brought in. During that fall's election campaign, Johnston offered to repeal the scrip if that's what council wanted. Voters refused the offer, electing rival John Good instead. At the first meeting of the new council, January 11, 1937, council took only fifteen minutes to abolish the scrip. Many Orillians held on to the scrip as souvenirs. In 1956, $159.45 was still held in city hall reserves to redeem any leftover scrip. At that time, council gave up holding on to the money and put in the surplus account.

Rumours had plagued Johnston's administration throughout 1936, but the extent of the scandals did not become fully public until 1937. The new town council, tired of problems and rumours in its police force, demoted Chief Lew Church to constable. An angry Church issued a report suggesting the problems lay not with the force, but with council. Some council members tried to interfere with police business, he charged. In the fall of 1936, Mayor Johnston told a constable to drop two Liquor Act charges against some of his friends, Church said. Johnston denied Church's claims, and Church eventually apologized. But council investigated the incident and discovered the interference charge was true. Not only that, but Johnston had written the letter of apology and with the help of an alderman, forced Church to sign it to cool things down.

The past continued to catch up to Johnston in 1937. A muckraking weekly newspaper called The Saturday Night had run a series of articles in 1936 and early 1937 accusing Johnston of several crimes and unseemly acts: engaging in wild drinking parties at an Orillia hotel; selling a car seized by town officials and pocketing the money himself; lowering the tax assessment on property he owned; falsifying information about a shirt factory coming to town in order to get elected; and generally fattening himself at the taxpayer's expense.

"...relief has been made a racket by cheap chiselling politicians who have been waxing fat while others are on the verge of starvation," wrote Saturday Night editor George Bryan Curran, trying to live up to the motto on his little paper, which read "Print the Truth" and "Condensed but Dynamic".

When Johnston sued for libel in 1937, detailed allegations against his administration came out in the preliminary hearings that April, covered by newspapers. Johnston admitted he charged the town for taking taxis, often four a day, but said he was always doing town business.

"You have cost the Town $300 to $400 a year for cars," said lawyer Hugh Grant, defending Curran against the libel charges.

"I was a cheap man even at that. You are not worth $5," Johnston retorted. "All you have done this year is criticize."

Johnston maintained throughout the preliminary hearings that his business was always the town's business.

"I can't separate myself," he said. "The Mayor and J.B. Johnston were the same person."

The stories about the seized car were harder for Johnston to defend. Three people from Windsor drove through town in a car in rough shape. The police stopped the car and fined the three because the car did not have proper lights or brakes. The three did not have enough money to pay the fine, so Mayor Johnston intervened and ordered police to buy the three people train tickets back to Windsor and seize the car. While the car was being held by the town, about $14 in repairs were done. The town paid for the repairs. Meanwhile, Johnston found out a Windsor company was owed money on the car. He paid that company $20 for the car, paid the outstanding fines of $29, then sold it for $80, making a nice $31 profit. He never did pay the town back for the repairs made.

Each day the hearing drew a crowded house, especially when court heard allegations Johnston had been drinking in the mayor's office and at a bootlegger's house. Three lacrosse players testified that while hosting a convention of postmasters, a drunken mayor Johnston and Reeve Wib Cramp ended up at a female bootlegger's house on Front Street. Johnston drank so much there he fell into a storage room, fell on to the floor, and finally passed out on the bootlegger's bed, where he was the object of passing interest until he woke up about 8 a.m. the next day. Johnston admitted he had a few beers that day before going to the bootlegger's house, where he lay down to rest and woke up the next morning. There were no postmasters with him, he added.

After three days of hearings, the judge decided the libel suit should go to trial. Before the matter came to trial, Curran issued an apology, accepted by Johnston that read: "I apologize to you for and retract any such statements which may have unfavorably reflected on you personally."

It wasn't much of a victory for Johnston. George Bryan Curran and Johnston both ran for mayor in the fall of 1937. Curran insisted his apology was only for the slights against Johnston's character.

"The charges concerning town affairs have not been disproved," insisted the publisher.

Neither man won, and for the rest of the Depression, life in Orillia calmed down. There was even a movement to have the 1937 council acclaimed to run the town in 1938, to acknowledge its steady work and to save the $400 cost of running an election. Johnston decided to run, ruining the chance of acclamation. He suffered his worst defeat at the polls. He ran for mayor four more times and threatened to keep running until he won by acclamation. Johnston died in 1942, before his threat could be carried out. He was hauling a load of hay down Laclie Street near his home at the corner of Borland Street, when a spring pole holding the unbaled hay down sprang loose. The pole struck him on the head and knocked him between the horse hoofs and wagon wheels. His death was mourned by many, friend and adversary alike.

By then, the Depression that had handed and taken away his career had been overtaken by war. Orillia was already getting its affairs in order as trouble broke out in Europe. At end of 1938, the town had an operating surplus of about $4,600 and the debt down under a $1 million, signs things were finally looking up. The Second World War turned everything around. There were more jobs than Orillia had ever seen.

In 1936, Otaco had 11 employees. Three years later, it was running three shifts of 1,600 people turning out undercarriages for Mosquito bombers. As it did in many other towns and cities, the Second World War turned Orillia's industry around. E. Long Ltd supplied cartridge case machinery for manufacturers throughout North America. Hunter Boats Limited produced the Fairmile submarine chaser.

And just as they did twenty-five years ago, Orillia sent its youth overseas to fight. Many of them trained at Camp 29, where Park Street Collegiate stands today. At the outset of the war, a soldier would join a specific regiment, but later on, he would attend Camp 29 to determine the outfit he was best suited for. Soldiers trained from 6 a.m. to 5 p.m., then walked into town for a bit of relaxation, most often at the Maple Leaf Club. From June 1942 to February 1946, the club, nicknamed the Hostess Club, gave soldiers a taste of romance and home in the vestry of St. James

Orillia's Maple Leaf Club provided soldiers with a home away from home. They could get their clothes mended, or blow off some steam dancing with local girls in the vestry of St. James Anglican Church.

Orillia Public Library

Anglican Church. Soldiers could visit the Writing Room, Games Room, Reading Room, Lounge, Canteen, Table Tennis Room, or Mend-it Corner, where volunteers fixed their clothing. The Writing Room proved the most popular. Soldiers and members of the Canadian Women Army Corps posted letters from the Writing Room, as many as 300 a night, 33,000 a year. Town organizations, such as council, the Orillia Water, Light and Power Commission, the Lion's Club, Board of Trade, Y's Men Club, and factories, donated money to keep the busy club going.

The Maple Leaf Club was one of the busiest of its kind, making about 3,000 meals a month. The canteen began with fifty-four workers and had to expand only a year later to 100 workers.

About 200 patriotic local girls volunteered to spin around the floor of the main hall on dance nights, allowing the young soldiers to let off a little steam while obeying the strict rules of the dance. "It is a patriotic duty to help keep the soldiers happy, thereby you help to win the war," read one rule. Keeping them happy did not involve, however, dancing too long with one soldier, or leaving with a soldier unless you were his guest.

"Develop excellent topics for conversation," stated the Dance Night Rules. "The Supervisors should be pleased to supply excellent subjects for conversation..." Occasionally, a girl broke the rules. Recalled one volunteer for a newspaper article in 1995, "Quoting from the Good Old Church of England prayer book, 'I hope I will be forgiven the things I did which I should not have done, and for things which I left undone which I should have.'"

The soldiers appreciated whatever was done. In 1944, members of the Champlain Barracks of Camp 29 wrote, "Many is the man, now overseas who will carry with him memories of Orillia as their home away from home, and many is the man on his way over who will carry him over rough spots."

Marriage ceremonies for soldiers were eventually performed at the Club. The first was the marriage of Corporal Katherine Lillian Smith, member of the CWAC at Camp 29 in Orillia, and Lance Corporal Nyk Katarynych, of the same camp, on August 17, 1944. The Maple Leaf Club was the cheapest place they could find for the service. An unexpected wedding gift was the announcement of a change of orders the following day. At the wedding ceremony, they were each presented with a new stripe.

Like other towns and cities, Orillia got behind the war in countless other ways, raising money for armour, sending care packages home through the Red Cross, and suffering shortages of wood and coal and rationing of other everyday supplies. In 1941, the Orillia War Committee was asked to raise $13,500 a month for the rest of the war to build two armoured carriers and two universal carriers. The campaign began with the tolling of church bells and blowing of factory whistles, a schoolchildren's march down Mississaga Street, and a fundraising dinner at the YMCA. The war did not make ordinary people rich, and by the end of the first month, Orillia's 9,400 residents had raised only three-quarters of the amount needed for one carrier.

Life at home wasn't easy either. Suppliers ran out of coal in the winter of 1943. The few men around to cut wood had trouble getting in the bush because of heavy snows. Housewives were used to seeing up to seventy-five loads of wood a week for sale at the Farmers' Market, but one week in March 1943, only one farmer arrived with only one load - just under a cord of wood. It was quickly snapped up.

The news that the war ended came at 11 a.m. May 7, 1945, with the sound of factory whistles and church bells ringing in the cool, Monday morning air. VE-Day was not officially announced until the following day, but Orillians were impatient to celebrate. Orillia's VE-Day committee, assembled several months earlier, could not decide to begin the festivities on the Monday or wait for the official announcement scheduled for the following day. The committee members quickly decided to celebrate immediately. Factories shut down, and merchants closed their stores. Factory workers rushed out of town to get liquor as Orillia, being dry, had neither liquor stores nor taverns. An official parade was to be held the next day, but the Orillia Newsletter reported an impromptu march "led by a soldier playing a bagpipe, accompanied by make shift drums of garbage lids and old scrub brushes for drumsticks." That night Mississaga Street was roped off and a crowd danced to Andrews' Orchestra until the early morning hours.

The HMCS Orillia, a corvette commissioned in 1941, escorted supply ships from Newfoundland to Iceland, and back again for four years. It was a dangerous job, and her crew had to worry about "wolfpacks" of German submarines and the sickening "sealeg roll" that corvettes were famous for. The corvettes would often climb the wall of wave, hang on a 50 degree list, then slide down the wave like a surfer, say those who sailed on them. The HMCS Orillia played a key role in several battles and rescues. After a convoy was attacked in August, 1941, the Orillia rescued ninety-five men from three ships. The Orillia crew towed a damaged oil tanker, the Tahchee, back to Iceland, falling behind the convoy and putting themselves at risk to save the valuable tanker. The Orillia was de-commissioned in 1945 and sold for scrap.

The Packet & Times

The Second World War gave a boost to Orillia's factories, but the town was still small in geographic size. Easily recognizable in this 1945 photograph are the old Eplett's Arena and Opera House on West Street. Continuing down West Street are the Tudhope block and just past Barrie Road, Canada Electric Castings Ltd., which closed in 1964 and became the site of Canadian Tire. Farther down West Street are E. Long Ltd. and Otaco.

The next day at the Lion's Oval, thousands listened to an amplified radio broadcast of King George VI's VE address, then paraded down Mississaga Street to Couchiching Beach Park. An effigy of Adolf Hitler received the same treatment the Kaiser had two decades ago. Reported the Newsletter: "While the scarlet-uniformed mounties stood rigid at attention, the torch was applied to the gasoline-soaked effigy [of Hitler] as a roar of cheers broke from thousands who lined the park."

Later in the day, "the blazing effigy of Hitler was drawn through the streets on a trailer behind Howard Thiffault's car to the din of motor horns and shouting children. They finally came to a stop in front of veteran Dorm Raymond's residence. More fuel was added to the blazing torso and flames rose high in the air in their eagerness to wipe out every sign of the once deadly enemy."

According to Royal Canadian Legion records, Orillia lost seventy-eight soldiers in the war. Many more were injured. Wives lost husbands, children their fathers, sisters their brothers. However, through ten years of the Depression and five years of the war, Orillia had survived, its spirit intact.

"ALL MUSSED UP"

Laughter was sometimes all people had in the Depression. The late Allan Ironside, a city historian and storyteller, once recalled for the Packet & Times what life was like in Orillia during the Depression.

Orillia in the 30's was large enough to provide for one's interests but small enough to escape the stress of the city life. It offered religion, culture, sports, recreation, politics at all levels, clubs and fraternity societies and much more. It welcomed participation and support. It was a good-natured society, ready to amuse or be amused.

The hard times forced Orillians to trade by barter, to trust customers with long lines of credit, and to present gap-toothed smiles to the world because it was cheaper to get a tooth pulled than repaired. Those lucky enough to work in the factories earned $7.68 for a forty-eight-hour week in a time when it was estimated the average family needed $18.66 a week just for food, clothing, rent, and heat. Two-income families were rare, as it was still the custom for a woman to resign from her job once she got married. Banks allowed women to work, but they were so underpaid they were forced to live with their parents. The relief system was overwhelmed and often ran out of money.

The town's businessmen tried to bring in more tourists, creating in the summer of 1933 and 1934 the "Week of Sports". One of the events held in the summer of 1934 was exhibition wrestling, not the spectacle it is now. Phil Lawson (who later became Whipper Billy Watson's trainer and manager) brought his wrestlers from Toronto's YMCA Wrestling Club. The matches took place at Eplett's Arena at the corner of West Street and Coldwater Road - the current site of city hall. The main bout featured Lawson as the "good" guy and a much bigger man named Ben Engblom as the "bad" guy. It was refereed by Pete Stover, the owner of the popular Stover's Tea Room and chairman of the Week of Sports Committee.

Stover, an expert wrestler in his youth, expected to referee a professional and clean match. But the outcome was already planned. At the end of the match, bad guy Engblom was to swing at the referee, who would duck the punch. Lawson would then dive over the referee and pin Ben to the mat. Good would triumph over evil.

When he heard the match was fixed, Stover grew reluctant to take part. Ironside was persuaded to take over as referee. As an organizer and host, Ironside was dressed in his finest suit. Before he entered the ring, a rowdy friend forced a swig of whiskey down his throat. Hot, distracted by the match, and head starting to swim with whiskey, Ironside forgot to duck.

This untimely lapse earned me the full force of Ben's ham-sized fist in my mouth. With blood streaming from my cut lips, I charged straight at Ben who, with masterful showmanship, allowed me to knock him to his knees. Phil was equally alert to opportunities and landed on both of us. Before we were untangled one of the ring posts was knocked down, some of the crowd entered the fray, the police were rushing to quell the miniature riot, and my clean cream flannels were red with my blood and dirty from the grime of the mats.

Few forgot that show. Ironside overheard a farmer from Oro Township on the way out.

I always wanted to see one of these here 'rasslin' matches," said the farmer, "but the part I like best was when the feller in them white pants got all mussed up."

ICE INDUSTRY

At least Orillia still had winter in the Depression.

A frozen Lake Couchiching supplied ice for much of Ontario in the days before refrigerators. A story in the Packet & Times, dated January 26, 1933, notes that last season, 350 carloads of ice had been shipped by train to points across the province. From $4,000 to $5,000 was paid in wages, a helpful addition to the town's depressed economy.

THE FINEST POSITION IN THE DOMINION

Some people thought seriously about Mayor Ben Johnston's suggestion during the Depression that Orillia shut down its high school to save money.

Support for publicly funded schools had never been unanimous in Orillia. Some thought that they encouraged undesirable mixing of different social classes. Others feared teaching children how to read and write would only lead to an increase in the crime of forgery. And in the last century, as in this one, parents questioned and criticized the decisions of trustees and the methods of teachers.

Orillia's first high school got off to a rocky start. The first headmaster, a resident of Campbellford, shipped his wife off to Montreal to visit friends, then eloped with an eighteen-year-old. Before he even arrived in Orillia he telegraphed his resignation from Detroit, where presumably, he was enjoying his honeymoon.

In spite of the incident and delays in building, the high school sitting atop the hill at Borland and West Streets garnered praise from the Orillia Times on November 9, 1876. From the school's tower, "....not only Couchiching, but the whole of Lake Simcoe with its bays and headlands is visible...and the country in all directions for miles and miles around can be seen...it occupies the finest position of all the High Schools in the Dominion."

Built for $4,606, the Orillia High School opened with 57 students on January 8, 1877. It had four classrooms, an assembly hall and gymnasium. That school lasted until 1898. Weeks after the board decided against a higher insurance policy, the school burned to the ground. For two years after that October 14, 1898 fire, students attended classes in another building on the town's main street.

In 1898 trustees decided not to increase the high school's fire insurance and the school promptly burned to the ground. The new high school above opened in 1900.

Orillia's first high school on the hill at West and Borland streets occupied "the finest position of all the high schools in the Dominion" wrote the Orillia Times in the fall of 1876, a few months before the school was opened.

Simcoe County Archives

From its opening in 1900 to today, Orillia and District Collegiate Vocational Institute has undergone several major renovations. The last of the old wings was demolished in 1979. Park Street Collegiate Institute opened in 1961 and Twin Lakes Secondary School opened in 1973. A separate school, Patrick Fogarty, opened in 1985.

The city's elementary schools have an even longer history. In 1833, pioneer James Dallas converted a stable on his property on Barrie Road into a schoolhouse. (That school burned down in 1920) His wife and two daughters taught children free of charge. The first proper school, a one-storey log building, was built on the south side of Coldwater Street. The log school gave way to frame and brick buildings on the other side of the street. In the early days, parents and school officials objected to hiring female teachers, believing women could not maintain discipline or teach boys how to be proper men. By 1861, the first female teacher was hired. Elizabeth Rawson received about $120 a year for her troubles. The school's other teacher, William Jupp, made $320 a year.

Education was not free, and families paid a small charge, about 20 cents a month per child. That practice ended in 1866, but not without some protest. Orillia's population grew quickly during the lumber boom of the late 1800s, and soon 391 students were taking classes in three locations. The board decided to build one large school for all elementary age students. The two-storey Central School on Coldwater Street, located just west of the earlier school site, was completed in 1882 for about $12,000. It was followed by West Ward School and South Ward School, both built before 1897. West Ward School burned down in 1968 and the site is now the front parking lot of Soldiers' Memorial Hospital. Details on the South Ward School are sketchy. It appears a fire damaged the school on King Street in 1934, and it was rebuilt on the same site. The South Ward School was closed about 1970, and has changed hands several times. Central School was closed in 1985 but still serves as a pre-school.

By the turn of the century, three large elementary schools, shown in the postcard above, served Orillia's young. The Central School building on Coldwater Street and South Ward School building on King Street near Laclie Street remain standing, but are no longer used as elementary schools. West Ward School on Mississaga Street burned to the ground in 1968.

Orillia Public Library

Catholic students used a log building, the first church, as their school in the 1850s. Increased enrolment led to the building of St. Mary's in 1879, beside the new brick church, The Angels Guardian, on West Street. Both church and school adopted the name Guardian Angels over the years. The school was enlarged in 1957, but replaced in 1970 by a new school. The old school was torn down and the space used for the new school's playground. This photograph was taken about 1889.

Ontario Public Archives Acc. 2625 #32

CHASING RUM-RUNNERS AND NAZIS

Al Hunter was only on board to make sure the new owners of the Ditchburn patrol boat were satisfied with its performance. As the supervisor of mechanical and electrical operations for the Orillia plant, Hunter had travelled on the boat up the St. Lawrence as far as Quebec City. The new owners, the Royal Canadian Mounted Police, seemed satisfied. The captain seemed satisfied, except that suddenly he began shouting at a boat speeding across the St. Lawrence. The boat had a machine gun on board, but not a full crew. So Hunter, who knew something about guns, volunteered to fire a few warning shots across the bow of the rum-runner. He fired the shots and the rum-runner raced to shore. The Ditchburn patrol boat caught it, forced it to beach, and arrested the men on board. Rumour had it the captain's niece was kidnapped in retaliation and never seen again. Al Hunter returned safely to Orillia, more convinced than ever that his boats could do the job.

The J.H. Ross Canoe and Boat company began operations in the 1870s. Ross sailboats won races all across Ontario.

He was only the latest in a long line of Orillia boat builders. For about a century, boat builders turned out racing craft, pleasure boats, rum-runner chasers and war boats in Orillia.

The J.H. Ross Canoe and Boat Company and Deans Boats were the first to begin selling craft on the waterfront, both in the 1870s. According to Don Hunter, an Orillia historian and boat builder himself, Ross built fine sailboats that won races throughout Ontario and what was likely one of the first motorboats on Lake Couchiching. The third generation of the family was still building boats in 1964, in the same location just north of the town dock. John Dean began building canoes on the other side of the dock, designing the famous Sunnyside racing canoe that was shipped all over the world. Those two boat building operations were mainly family affairs, but later manufacturers, Ditchburn Boats Limited and Hunter Boats turned into large operations.

The Ditchburns could trace their boat building ancestry back to the builders of iron-clad battle ships for the 19th century British Navy. Herbert Ditchburn represented the fifth generation, and he was the one who put the family name on the Orillia waterfront at the foot of Elgin Street about 1924, so the company's 100-foot cruisers could be shipped down the Trent system to the sea. Newspaper accounts of the day state that Ditchburn was an unsung nautical genius. In crude experiments with single planks of wood, he saw firsthand how water resistance and vacuums created by moving boats slowed those boats down. His racing boats, Rainbow III and IV, won international competitions in 1923 and 1924 and forced design changes in other racing boats. Ditchburn boats set a world record, travelling 1,218 miles in twenty-four hours on Lake Rosseau in Muskoka in 1924. Movie-makers filmed that feat and showed it in theatres around the world. Rainbow VII, built in 1927, had 1,100 horsepower and could supposedly reach seventy-two miles per hour - faster than most boats on the water today.

The speed of Ditchburn's boats caught the attention of the Canadian government. For the government, he built thirty-eight-foot, 290-horsepower boats with top speeds of thirty-three miles per hour, cabin space for three men, and a mount for a machine gun. The government tried it out on the Atlantic and quickly ordered five more to chase rum-runners and smugglers off the coast. The most powerful politicians, financiers and industrialists of North America, from the Eaton family of *department store fame to the president of Imperial Oil, ordered custom-built Ditchburn boats. At the company's peak in 1928, about forty men worked in the Orillia plant with 100 in the Gravenhurst factory. The company did about $300,000 in business that year, with one cruiser alone going for $60,000. The year 1929 began with expansion plans and predictions Ditchburn would compete with the largest boat-builders in the British Empire. But its millionaire customers ran out of money after the stockmarket crash of 1929, and Ditchburn closed its doors two years later.*

In 1941, Hunter Boats produced the first Canadian Fairmile, 112-feet long, heavily armed, capable of reaching thirty-two knots and hunting submarines in shallow waters. Named the Mariposa Belle in honor of Stephen Leacock and Orillia, she made her way down the Trent Waterway and to the coast of Canada. The boats featured double planking and brass rivets. The earlier models' two 850-horsepower engines were later replaced by 1,150-horsepower models because the German submarines were getting faster.

In 1899, Frank Rolland's Palace Boat Livery offered canoes with shade covers for rent.

Hunter Boats, located north of the town dock, built seven Fairmile patrol boats during the Second World War. The first two, each 112-feet long, were shipped through the Kirkfield lift locks in the fall of 1941. Work on the boats was completed in Trenton. The boat on the left, the Q-060, was the only one to be named. Hunter named it Mariposa Belle, in honour of Orillia.

In 1932, Al Hunter bought the Ditchburn boat-yard from the city. He began a much smaller operation, building canoes in one of the small shops that was heated by an oil drum converted into a stove. The Second World War changed Hunter's operation overnight. In a hurry to sink German submarines, the Allies commissioned several boatworks in Ontario to build the Fairmile, a small and fast coastal patrol boat. Hunter's small canoe shop turned into a boatyard with 120 men scurrying through the original Ditchburn buildings and a new one that Hunter built.

The seventh and final Fairmile produced at Hunter Boats almost blew up the entire lakefront Oct. 13, 1943. That night three workers boarded the Fairmile Q-116 after supper to do some final work before its test run the next day. The boat was moored to the docks and its tanks had been filled with fuel earlier in the day. Gas had leaked through a loose coupling. The three men, Reginald Bradley, Howard Brohm and Harold Ariss, heard a dripping sound from the engine room and began to look for the cause. Under one engine they discovered an oil pan filled with gasoline. They turned off the gasoline at once and were about to go ashore to shut off the electricity when a spark ignited built-up gasoline fumes. The explosion burned them, injured six others and killed 16-year-old Stanley Peacock, an electrician's helper. He had been looking into a hatch, when the ship exploded and blew him 100 yards into the water. Badly burned, he drowned. Don Hunter, Al's son, ran to the waterfront. As he and others rescued the badly burned workers, they tried not to think about the thousands of gallons of gasoline 100 feet away in the Imperial Oil depot.

The final Fairmile to be built almost blew up Orillia's waterfront. The explosion of the Fairmile Q-116 on October 13, 1943 killed one man and injured several others. A tangle of wood and metal greeted workers the next day.

"Boy, I can tell you there were some anxious moments," Hunter told reporters many years later. The fuel tanks were made of bullet-proof steel, preventing the 2,000 gallons of gasoline in them from igniting and starting a chain reaction of explosions along the waterfront. The explosion sheered the deck off the Q-116, but it was rebuilt and put into service.

After the war, Hunter Boats returned to building pleasure-craft, enjoying popularity during the 1950s and 1960s. Tired of boat-building, Don Hunter closed down manufacturing in 1965, although the service department stayed open until 1976. His was the last boatworks on the waterfront. The Ross boatworks caught on fire in 1964, burning the Miss Orillia pleasure boat, and part of a neighboring boat livery, Rollands. Deans boatworks, by then a livery, sat out on the water and collapsed from the shifting ice in 1964. By then ice had damaged the couple of dozen private boathouses that lined the waterfront almost without interruption from the town dock to French's fast-food stand at the foot of Tecumseh Street. Those boathouses had been built when the CPR filled in the waterfront in 1910, to replace the private boathouses suddenly landlocked by the railway. The city ended the leases and had the boathouses torn down to create Centennial Drive and Centennial Park. Hunter Boats caught fire in 1990 and again in 1993. The city tore down the remaining buildings to create a waterfront park.

After the war, Hunter Boats built pleasure cruisers in a variety of sizes for both day sailing and overnight trips.

ANYTHING WAS POSSIBLE

an a man make a cloud dissipate and vanish simply by willing it to do so? Does the human mind possess some strange force which, if recognized and harnessed, can alter the entire destiny of the human race?"

These two questions, slightly more cosmic than the usual posed by reporters, led off the front-page story in The Packet & Times on September 10, 1954. The answer brought readers down to earth, in Orillia no less. "To both of these questions Dr. Rolf Alexander of 15 Whitney Avenue answers 'Yes'."

For twenty years after the Second World War, anything, even cloud busting, seemed possible in Orillia. The 1950s and 1960s are sometimes called the second Golden Age of Orillia, when industry boomed, politics sparked, and ordinary people built a community centre, started a national folk festival, and came within an inch of red tape of building a university. Yet the second Golden Age shone with a different light than the first. The debate over moving ahead and keeping things the same intensified, as some of the players changed sides. The company owners and industrialists lost the mantle of heroes they wore in the early 1900s as they moved the town ahead. Ordinary people began to see these leaders as a clique determined to keep things the same for their own benefit. The owners of the large industries were accused of keeping out new companies and the accompanying unions and higher wages. New blood infused the Orillia Spirit. Anyone could give anything a try - from factory workers and housewives to a newcomer who predicted he could destroy clouds at will.

Dr. Rolf Alexander was born in a 1891 to a Scottish physician and his wife, on a ship bound for New Zealand. He spent much of his life travelling, and studying other cultures. After graduating in medicine from the University of Prague in 1912, Alexander lived and studied with Tibetan lamas, Buddhist monks, Hopi Indians, North African medicine men, and West Indies sorcerers.

After decades of study and experimentation, Alexander was ready to write the book that would change the world. Something drew him to Orillia. The tall, white-thatched man with pale blue eyes settled in the small town with his wife and young son. He began recording weekly broadcasts at CFOR radio station for another station in Port Arthur, where a devotee paid for the air time. Young Orillia broadcaster Pete McGarvey taped the material and grew fascinated with Alexander.

The two became friends. The idea that man's mind was a powerful force was not new, but Alexander's arguments were more lucid and reasonable than most. Alexander was not content to spread the message by radio. He had something bigger in mind, and he invited McGarvey over to his house one day in August 1954. Alexander told McGarvey he would have a book called Creative Realism published in October, explaining how psychic energy could influence both animate and inanimate objects. To prove his point, he would wipe clouds out of the sky right then and there. A surprised McGarvey followed Alexander outside.

"Pick a cloud, any cloud," Alexander told him. McGarvey did, and to his surprise, the cloud disappeared. Several experiments with equal success fuelled McGarvey's amazement, and when Alexander asked if he would help publicize the book and a public demonstration of cloud busting, the radio broadcaster agreed.

In the days before the experiment, Alexander explained to newspaper readers and CFOR listeners that a strange power lay in the subconscious mind, rising to the surface in the form of daydreams and fantasies. He had learned how to release that power at will, said Alexander. "This cloud busting is not a unique power I alone hold. Anyone can learn to do it," he said. Cloud busting was only a device to prove the existence of the power. The power itself would free men and women to tap their own creativity. It strengthened the mind.

Jesus Christ understood this power and described it in His own words, said Alexander. The Russians were already using some of the power, he added.

"I have spent a lifetime studying this subject. And I believe this force must be brought to the attention of science in so concrete a form that the necessary expensive research into it will be undertaken," Alexander said. "This can be one of the biggest ideas in twenty centuries if we can get it accepted." Alexander told reporters he chose cloud busting to prove the existence of the power because no one could accuse him of falsifying results.

Conditions for the experiment were ideal the afternoon of Sunday, Sept 12, 1954. A bank of cumulus clouds had settled over Lake Couchiching.

2:09 P.M.   2:11 P.M.

2:14 P.M.   2:17 P.M.

The Packet & Times recorded Dr. Rolf Alexander's experiments in cloud busting in September, 1954. The doctor, wearing a cap in this series of photographs, made clouds disappear several times before an astonished audience at Couchiching Beach Park.

The Packet & Times

About 300 people gathered at Couchiching Beach Park. Just after 2 p.m., Alexander arrived at the mound behind the ball diamond, where McGarvey introduced him to Mayor John MacIsaac and reporters. Alexander spoke briefly, then invited the mayor to pick a cloud, any cloud. The mayor, perhaps being polite, picked a small one. After a few minutes, the cloud disappeared. Twice Alexander did this, while nearby clouds remained unmoved. The crowd murmured. Then a newspaperman stepped forward, and politeness be damned, chose a large cloud. This was the real test, and the reporter recorded the events by the minute. At exactly 2:09 p.m., the experiment began. Alexander took a deep breath and concentrated on the cloud. It enlarged slightly, then began to twitch. At 2:11, it showed unmistakable signs of thinning. At 2:14, it had been reduced to wisps. By 2:17 p.m., the cloud was gone. Observers applauded. Alexander repeated the experiment several times, and each time, the cloud disappeared while adjacent ones remained intact. A few observers claimed Alexander knew which clouds were going to disappear, but that did not explain how he wiped away clouds others had chosen. One enterprising reporter contacted the Weather Bureau later. A dry front moving in likely broke up the clouds, said a weather forecaster, but he doubted anyone could predict which clouds would break up and when.

An exhausted Alexander quit after about an hour, but the news spread through Orillia the next day. Reporters from Toronto, then across North America picked up on the story as interest in his experiment and book grew. Unfortunately for the Alexanders, the radio interviews and magazine articles drew the attention of the federal immigration department. Government officials checked out Alexander and found his visitor's visa had expired. He and his family were forced to move to England, and he eventually died in Florida.

Alexander's experiments were the strangest but not the only sign things were a little different in Orillia after the war. The industries that boomed during the war continued to thrive. The leading companies were still owned by the founding families, the Longs at E. Long Ltd., the Tudhopes at Tudhope Metal Specialties, for example. Other owners had run their plants since the 1930s. But the men who returned from overseas soon learned the boom gave them jobs, but not necessarily a fair wage. They were ripe for unions, and the Canadian Congress of Labour responded, sending the tough George Brough to town in early April 1949 to organize six to eight of the leading factories. Brough found willing workers at the Heywood-Wakefield plant on northwest corner of Forest Avenue at Atherley Road, where founder Jim Lloyd oversaw about 110 employees making the Lloyd Baby Carriage. Workers like Kenneth Howes were making 65 cents an hour to chrome-plate carriage handles. That seemed like good pay at first, recalled Howes in an interview for this book But after a while, workers realized others in Barrie or on provincial highway contracts were making $1.25 an hour for similar work. Within a month, Brough signed up about seventy employees of Heywood-Wakefield to the Orillia General Workers Union. Lloyd gathered his workers together and told them he didn't mind if they joined a union. Then he laid off eighteen employees, most of them with long service, and all but one a union member.

"We put two and two together," remembered Howes. Without Brough's knowledge, a group of workers met Sunday, May 1, 1949 and voted that night to strike. About seventy employees walked off the job Monday, circling the plant and blocking the main entrance off Forest Avenue. With handmade signs, they began marching twenty-four hours a day in Orillia's first large-scale industrial strike.

The strikers gained immediate sympathy throughout Orillia. In the first week, construction workers at a nearby housing site raised $40 for the strike fund. Merchants sent over free ice cream and pop to keep up the strikers' spirits. Tempers flared occasionally that first week. One striker opened the car door of a worker driving into the plant and punched his colleague in the head. A truck refused to stop for the picket line and carried a couple of strikers for a short but slow ride on its fender. One cab company that drove non-striking employees across the picket line the first day was plagued the next day by dozens of phony requests for cabs. After sending cabs all over the city for phantom passengers, that company, like others, refused to go near the lines again. Orillia's frustrated factory workers, seeing a sign of hope for better pay, joined in. The Canadian Congress of Labour organized a parade and speeches on the Saturday after the strike began. Several hundred workers gathered in the Oddfellows Hall, where fiery labour leader Henry Rhodes of the Congress urged them to fight the family-run factories in Orillia that kept wages low.

The speeches worked. Monday's picket lines drew 200 angry workers, many from other factories, waiting for the cars of non-strikers to come in before rushing off to begin their own work days. One car of non-striking workers came up Forest Avenue too fast for the pickets' liking. The pickets forced the car to stop, then rolled it, with its five occupants still inside, into a ditch. No one was hurt. But the five town constables were powerless to stop

the rollover or the fights that broke out all morning. The strikers even stopped Lloyd's car and let the air out of his tires. Town council met that night and gave Mayor W.M. Seymour and the police committee the power to call in the Ontario Provincial Police for help if necessary. Tuesday was relatively quiet. Strikers and their sympathizers bounced a few cars up and down, bending the licence plates. And a factory foreman returned from a lodge meeting that night to discover strikers had splattered red paint on his car and put paint into his gas tank. By now only foremen, a nurse, maintenance staff, and office workers were getting into the building. Lloyd maintained throughout the strike that employee relations had always been good, and that the strike was illegal, as the union had not been certified. Some of his points were valid, but he lost support in the community when he sent notices to all the striking workers telling them they had "fired themselves" and were out of jobs.

The strike grew violent again that second week. Wednesday morning some pickets tried to overturn a car. The mayor called in twenty OPP officers to handle the strike. He and council members stressed they would not take sides, but would not tolerate violence. Council tried several times, with the help of the Department of Labour, to get the two sides to compromise. But Brough wanted his workers to get their jobs back before ending the strike, and Lloyd refused to hire any one back. Meanwhile, the strike was inspiring other factory workers to sign union cards, and more businesses were offering the strikers money, groceries, and other goods. The support of the town's

CFOR reporter Pete McGarvey, left, interviewed union leader George Brough after striking workers at Heywood-Wakefield overturned a car carrying non-striking employees.

Courtesy of Pete McGarvey

merchants was understandable. It was the town's workers, not the factory owners, who bought the groceries and the paper supplies and the ice cream every week. Support for the strikers was hardly unanimous and the picket lines divided the town. Yet as the strike finished its second week, the anger seemed to lessen. On the Monday night fifteen days after the start of the strike, the Department of Labour announced the strike was over. Management and Labor Congress officials reached a compromise — all strikers would be hired back, except for the eighteen laid off. A county court judge would determine if dismissal of the eighteen was justified. His decision would be considered final.

The judge's hearing, like the strike itself, made front-page news for several weeks. Union and company lawyers clashed over the reasons Lloyd

had laid off the eighteen workers. The judge eventually ruled that all but two workers should be taken back. Kenneth Howes didn't bother to return, as he was offered an unskilled job, not the job he had held before the strike. In his parting speech, Labour Congress leader Rhodes took a shot at all Orillia manufacturers. Orillia could no longer be an anti-union town run by a few factory owners, Rhodes warned. When the fifteen-day strike was over, Orillia had become, if not a union town, at least a town with unions in it.

Unions never gained the power in Orillia they did in other towns. But the working class in Orillia had gained new self-respect and showed signs it was a potent force. Any doubts about that were destroyed the year after the strike. A working man's hero, in his own mind at least, rose to power and began another colourful reign at city hall. Wilbur Cramp was his name, Wib to just about everyone. A local seed merchant and comrade of the late Mayor Ben Johnston, Wib Cramp styled himself the protector of the poor, friend of the labourer, and enemy of the "minority interests" running the town. In style and even looks, he was another Huey Long, the populist governor of Louisiana in the 1930s. Cramp himself first tasted power in those days, running a campaign for council in 1932 with the slogan "Fair play for the taxpayer and square deal for the unemployed," finishing fourth in a field of thirteen. In his first term as

The wives of 215 striking workers at Otaco in 1960 were as determined as the men on the picket lines. They defied police orders and set up tents and telephones so their husbands could seek shelter from the sun and rain, and keep in touch with their families. When a company official tried to film a clash between strikers and the police, the wives used their hand mirrors to reflect the sun into his eyes and forced him to stop. The strike began June 1 and lasted seven weeks, ending the day after 58 workers ignored a court injunction and swelled the numbers on the picket line. Union and company officials were worried about more violence and settled July 19. The deal raised the average salary to about $1.26 an hour, but did not allow the United Steelworkers Union to force employees to sign union cards. It was the third major strike since the 1949 strike at the Heywood-Wakefield plant, which sparked a round of union drives in Orillia. Employees at E. Long Ltd. had gone on strike in 1952.

Seed merchant, friend of the liquor trade, and fiery defender of the working class, Wilbur Cramp led the councils of the 1950s, just as Ben Johnston had in the 1930s. Cramp rode dissatisfaction with Orillia's elite to the mayor's chair four times.

The Packet & Times

alderman, Cramp co-sponsored a motion calling on all municipal bureaucrats earning $1,000 a year to take a 10 per cent cut in pay, with the money going into relief funds. Council amended the motion to a 15 per cent cut for four months. Only a few years later, as reeve, Cramp tried to get council members a pay raise of $50. After that and a second motion of his were defeated, a petulant Cramp donned his coat and hat and left the council meeting. Council tried to get him back, in order to have enough members present to vote on two bylaws. Mayor Ben Johnston asked a reporter to telephone Cramp at his seed store across the road from the Opera House. Cramp told the reporter to tell council to find a proper messenger. Two aldermen then called, but Cramp's reply was that things had gone "from bad to worse." Finally a third alderman convinced Cramp to return, in exchange for re-introducing one of his motions. His association with Mayor Johnston and that administration's scandals only improved his popularity. Cramp presented himself as an outsider fighting "the hush-hush tactics of council", although he was on that council as often as anyone. He served four times in the 1930s, two as reeve, and three times in the 1940s.

But it was in the 1950s that Wib Cramp truly earned his legendary status. Like Johnston in the depression, Cramp galvanized the discontented in Orillia. His dreams were their dreams. His anger was their anger. He wanted what they wanted — for one thing, a good drink. In 1950, a group of businessmen in town formed the Orillia Volunteer Workers to bring a liquor store and brewery warehouse to the town. Too many Orillia people were driving to Barrie or Bracebridge to shop because they could pick up beer and liquor there, argued the businessmen. Making the sale of liquor legal would wipe out the bootleg trade, they said. Temperance supporters, naturally enough, argued liquor was evil and its sale should be discouraged. On radio and in the press, the two sides battled in the fall of 1950. The Temperance supporters called on voters to respect the opinions of their church leaders. Mayor Austin Cook, speaking as a private citizen, argued on the radio against the rowdyism liquor brought to a town. Cramp led the other side, countering that special interest groups such as the church ministers were trying to interfere in the town's life and business. The liquor fight turned nasty when someone threw a brick carrying a death threat through the window of Cramp's apartment at Mississaga and Andrew streets. Crudely written in ink and lipstick, made to look like blood but less hard on the writer, the note told Cramp to "get out of town in 24 hours or you die."

Each side collected the names of supporters, either new in town or not enumerated before, to add to the voting list. The Temperance supporters added 450 names, the liquor store backers more than 1,000. Still, many expected the Temperance forces to win, as they had done several times since 1907, when prohibition had settled on Orillia. Besides a long tradition and the town's sunshine image, the Temperance forces had thrift on their side. The liquor supporters needed a 60 per cent majority to win. But many of the twenty-one-year-old men in town, new to voting, refused to put their names on any list because they would be subject to a $5 poll tax. Wisdom had it the liquor forces needed those young men to carry the vote, but it seemed a lot of people in Orillia were tired of driving out of town just to get a beer. Times had changed and it was time to be progressive. The voting November 28 drew one of the largest turnouts in the town's history. Sixty-one per cent of the voters agreed the town should allow a government liquor store and brewery warehouse. There would still be no beverage rooms in Orillia for another seventeen years, but the vote was the first crack in the Temperance wall.

Cramp rode the success of the liquor vote into the 1950 election campaign for mayor. He stepped up his attacks on the "Minority Pressure Group" that ran the town — the industrial leaders and old-money Orillians who wanted to keep wages low and life the same. "Who is it that keeps new industries out of Town?" asked Cramp in his election ads. His speeches were confrontational, though much less concise than his ads. The town was run by "a fascist-like group who don't believe in democracy to such an extent they won't even let you talk or think as you like if you don't agree with their views," Cramp charged, to cheering audiences. He accused incumbent Cook, a manufacturing executive, of being the front man for the so-called pressure group. In the best Joe McCarthy style of the era, Cramp held up a piece of paper during a debate at the South Ward Community Hall and said it contained proof that two workers had been fired because they were talking to a union organizer. "Is that the kind of democracy you want?" Cramp asked the crowd. Challenged to name the company, Cramp refused to answer publicly, saying he would not embarrass the firm, but would give the name to anyone who asked privately.

Cook was heavily favoured to win the 1950 election. A good sportsman, member of St. Paul's United Church male quartet, and an active member of an influential service club, Cook represented the best of old Orillia. He could be as tough as Cramp in an argument, but was not as showy. But

Cramp surprised the political wisemen with a big win at the polls in December, 1950.

Thus began one of the strangest reigns at city hall. Only five months into his first term as mayor, Cramp took on one of his favorite targets, the police, and all hell broke loose. The police arrested an acquaintance of Cramp's, a chain store manager, for a minor infraction of the Liquor Control Act after finding him with a Coca-Cola bottle full of liquor in his possession. Cramp had long complained about police "harassment" over minor liquor infractions and somehow found out his friend had been arrested early in the morning of April 20, 1951. Cramp called the station to find out what was going on and got Corporal Everett Lynn on the phone. When Lynn told Cramp he was going to charge the man, Cramp said, "We'll see about that" and rushed to the station. There are two versions of what happened when Cramp reached the station, at about 4 a.m. Cramp claimed he had heard many complaints about the police and wanted to see if they were true. Learning the accused had gone home, he started to leave too, when Constable Murray Robinson charged him at the counter and said he would tramp him into the floor. His own hand might have brushed the constable's tunic as he raised it in self-defence, Cramp admitted, but nothing else happened.

Constable Robinson told a different story. In Robinson's version, Cramp argued with police, pounding the counter and shouting, "I will not stand back and see my friends persecuted." The mayor swore at Robinson and grabbed his tunic. Robinson said he knocked Cramp's hand aside, then took off his hat, belt, and holster. "If you lay a hand on me again I'll tramp you into the floor," he told Cramp. The mayor left the office.

The police charged Cramp with assault, and Cramp retaliated by calling a special meeting of council April 25, 1951 to demand the resignation of Chief William Carson. No other council members showed up, saying through a statement to the press that the matter was before the courts. But 130 people crowded into the council chambers and 1,000 more listened to the mayor's attack on the police through loudspeakers on the market square. Cramp said the police went after him only because he opposed a $100 raise for them and had stopped paying for the phones in officers' homes. He raised the spectre of police department corruption and offered a convenient excuse to avoid proving his claims. Because he had been summoned to court on the assault charge, he could not reveal what he had learned, Cramp told the crowd. Cramp had Stephen Leacock Jr., the author's son, to help him craft his speeches. The mayor and the eccentric and imaginative Leacock Jr. had formed a friendship based equally on the appreciation of a good time and a dislike of authority other than their own.

"On numerous occasions I have tried to impress upon Councils that a reign of terror exists and has existed within many years due to the oppressive, high-handed and vindictive actions of our police," Cramp told the crowd that April night in the council chambers. The chief was in his office off the council chambers that very minute, "skulking in the dim light of his office listening with one ear to the door while a stenographer took down my speech in shorthand", Cramp charged.

After an hour-long tirade, Cramp announced he would ask the attorney general to investigate. "Do you believe that I should continue my crusade on behalf of your personal liberties and democratic rights?" Cramp asked the crowd. The crowd cheered and those parked in the market square honked car horns in the market square.

Cramp's dislike of the police likely started about the same time he began enjoying the services of bootleggers. And there were always some questions about the force. For example, the Orillia police routinely refused to allow an arrested person to make a telephone call to family until they were through dealing with him. In the middle of the Cramp's war on the police, council's police committee changed that rule. But council refused to do anything else with Cramp's complaints about the police chief.

Cramp countered that council was in the pockets of the mysterious minority pressure group that had opposed his election in the first place. In court on May 16, 1951, Cramp was found guilty of assault and fined $10. It came down to Robinson's word against Cramp. The constable had made no notes that night, but scribbled some down the next night. His colleague on duty, Corporal Everett Lynn, did the same thing and confirmed the incident took place just as Robinson had said. Cramp's lawyers pointed out a few minor inconsistencies in the officers' testimony, but it was hardly enough to change the judge's mind.

His pockets lightened of $10, Cramp continued his attack on the police force all summer long, suspending Chief Carson in July until an investigation into the police force was launched and completed. The town lawyer told an upset council that the mayor had the right to suspend the chief. But a week later, the lawyer learned the province had just rescinded the part of the police act giving mayors that right. A rebellious council voted unanimously to declare the suspension illegal and the investigation dead before it even started.

Support for Cramp's crusade had started off strong, but his constant attacks aroused the fears of many Orillians that the town's valuable image was suffering. So vitriolic were Cramp's charges against the police, they attracted the attention of the Toronto media. Orillia's sunshine image suddenly fell into shadow. And that upset a lot of the merchants who depended on the tourist trade. Led by businessman and Orillia, Water, Light and Power commissioner Frank Tissington Jr., Cramp's enemies formed the Citizens Committee for Civic Betterment to counterattack the lies that had made Orillia a "laughing stock throughout the province." Things had turned so bad, Toronto reporters mentioned Orillia in the same breath as the perennially troublesome Crystal Beach, said committee members.

To Cramp, the Betterment Committee was nothing more than the official front for the "mysterious pressure group." But more than a minority were tired of Cramp's tirades. Tissington, running again for the power commission and former mayor Cook, trying to win his seat back, focused on Cramp's feud with the police and the tarnished image of Orillia in the 1951 fall election campaign.

"It is hard to convince outsiders that something has not gone wrong with Orillia and Orillians," Tissington told election crowds.

"During the past 11 months, Orillia has taken it on the chin," said Cook, who usually campaigned in a quieter style.

Cramp deflected some of that criticism by charging that Tissington, Cook, and the rest of the minority that ran the town tried to keep power rates low for industrial users. Tissington owned the Tools and Hardware plant, and Cramp charged him with a conflict of interest. But Orillians had been stung by Cramp's feuds and voted him out.

Cramp's political career was hardly over. He won the mayor's race for the 1953, 1956, and 1957 councils and served as reeve in 1959. He made headlines again in 1965 when he was found not guilty of three charges of municipal corruption. Nine years earlier, Cramp had accepted free shares from the Northern Ontario Natural Gas company and had coincidentally promoted that company's quest to gain the franchise to serve Orillia. The court ruled Cramp did get the shares for free but did not promote the company any more than he normally would have. Cramp returned to politics the next decade, serving as a councillor from 1973 to 1979, when a stroke ended his career.

Cramp died in 1985, and his shenanigans have taken on legendary status. To those who served with him, Cramp remains a darker figure, a dangerous would-be demagogue who lied to get his way and had no real interest in the average man.

Whether Cramp really was always the friend of the working man remains open to debate. There were other mayors more or equally effective in the 1950s, but Cramp remains a telling figure of that decade because he focused the dissatisfaction many Orillians had with the powerful men guiding the town. In most of the yearly elections for council in the 1950s, Cramp won overwhelming support in the working class south ward, while losing heavily in

Orillia in the 1950s and 1960s was an industrial town, with several large factories employing hundreds. The Big Three, Dorr-Oliver-Long, Otaco and Fahralloy Canada Limited, employed more than 1,300 people in 1964, with Dorr-Oliver-Long alone employing about 615. By the 1990s, the successors of those three industries employed about 610.

In its industrial heyday, Orillia made its mark around the world. Above, Otaco built toys, trailers, and twenty-ton sleds for the United States Navy's exploration of Antarctica. In 1958, the company received the Navy's Certificate of Merit, the first time the honour had been awarded outside of the United States.

The Packet & Times.

Orillia-born Leslie Frost, son of Mayor William "Daylight Bill" Frost, led the province as premier from 1949 to 1961. "Old Man Ontario" displayed a folksy image to the public, but maintained a firm control over the legislature and the province. During his Conservative administration, the province introduced a hospital insurance plan and a law against discrimination in housing and employment. Frost also embarked on a massive road building program and oversaw Ontario's post-war economic boom. He died in 1973 at age 77.

Letherby, right

Rynard, centre

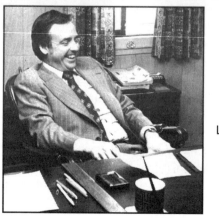

Lewis

the more well-off, established north ward. When he struck a chord among merchants, clerks, and foremen alike, he won election by gaining the votes of the relatively middle-class west ward. When his bombast grew too much to handle, the west ward removed him from council for a year or two. Each of his elections races was marked by Crampian complaints against the secrecy of the Orillia Water, Light and Power Commission (OWLP) and the powerful elite of industrialists running the town.

No one has been able to prove a collusion of industrialists kept wages low in Orillia, although today it is an accepted fact among many Orillians. There were plenty of other reasons why new industries did not come to Orillia in the 1950s - a lack of available land, especially on Highway 11, and high assessments are two. Don Hunter, a former member of the Orillia Industrial Associates, a group of industrial leaders that met frequently in the 1950s, said there is no truth to rumours industrialists colluded to keep industry out or wages low.

But it is clear some business leaders preferred the status quo over large-scale growth in the 1950s. At a dinner in April 1950, some business leaders suggested Orillia did not necessarily need more factories or more jobs. Things were fine just the way they were. The Orillia Junior Chamber of Commerce fired off a counterattack in a letter to the newspapers a few weeks later. The town needed to grow to provide jobs, the junior members said. No

McLean, right

Orillia's Conservative legacy stretched back to the 1930s and the men who ran for the party often had reason to celebrate on election night. The provincial riding of Simcoe East has elected a Conservative since the mid-1937s. John McPhee, Lloyd Letherby, Gordon E. Smith all won four times during the streak. Al McLean, had won five times by the time he was chosen Speaker of the House in 1995. The federal riding, Simcoe North, was Conservative from 1957 to 1994, with Dr. P.B. Rynard winning seven times, followed by lawyer Doug Lewis' streak, which began in 1979. Lewis held several cabinet posts, including Minister of Transport, Minister of Justice, and Minister of the Solicitor-General.

Highway 11 used to run through Orillia along Colborne Street, then along Laclie Street north. Summer traffic clogged the streets of Orillia and after driving through town on the August Civic Holiday weekend in 1953, Premier Leslie Frost vowed to build a bypass. That he did in 1954, but Orillians were in no mood to thank him. While Barrie received stop lights and overpasses where its major roads met the bypass, Orillia received only stop signs. Town politicians warned the province the bypass was an accident waiting to happen. The bypass opened June 30 and thirty-six hours later, two people were killed trying to drive across the highway at Coldwater Road, part of Highway 12. After a second accident, town council protested to the province and The Packet & Times ran a front-page letter of appeal to Premier Frost, who was visiting town on another matter. Frost promised to look into the bypass. Stoplights soon went up, above, but it took two more years for Orillia to get overpasses.

The Packet & Times

unemployment? the letter writers asked. Tell that to the 508 people looking for work in the city. More industry might bring Orillia's wages back up. The Junior Chamber pointed out that a provincial study divided Ontario into eighteen areas, and only one of those had lower wages than Orillia. More factories would provide competition for skilled labourers, thereby increasing wages. Higher wages would inspire more spending and create even more jobs. The letter concluded — and this was no populist mayor or union leader writing, but the Junior Chamber of Commerce: "Until these new industries come to Orillia then we might as well accept the fact that this is an industrially controlled town. As long as the industries control the wage scale, they control the buying power and through it they control Orillia."

Trust in their leaders, Temperance - many of the standards of the early 1900s fell in the 1950s. None symbolized the change in Orillia as clearly as the 1953 vote on the OWLP's bid for a new power plant. The town's public utility, and one of the most innovative examples of the original Orillia Spirit, had grown considerably since the early 1900s.

Industry, business, and residences all consumed more power, with demand doubling in the period from 1925 to 1945. The OWLP commission had built another power plant in 1935, this one on the Gull River near Minden, and one more in 1950 at the Matthias Falls on the Muskoka River. It seemed obvious Orillia would need even more power as it grew.

About that time, Ontario Hydro renewed its efforts to get Orillia's power utility into its system. Packet publisher and former OWLP commissioner C.H. Hale had tangled for years with Ontario Hydro officials, charging they longed to get Orillia to join the Ontario Hydro grid. Ontario Hydro looked at the OWLP as a rival because its low rates sparked Ontario

The landmark Shangri-La Gardens sign was erected in 1959. For years it served as beacon to boaters and motorists alike. When it was taken down in the 1990s, Orillians mourned the end of an era.

The Packet & Times

Hydro customers to question their own rates, said Hale. Sir Adam Beck, the founder of Ontario Hydro, had failed in 1916 to persuade Orillia voters to join Ontario Hydro. The provincial utility had a better chance in the 1950s, when Orillia faced building a plant at Horseshoe Falls. Ontario Hydro officials suggested Orillia join their grid, rather than build a new and expensive power plant.

The question became two-fold. Should Orillia build a new plant, or join Ontario Hydro? It divided the OWLP, council, and the town. The OWLP's new engineer and a Montreal consulting firm recommended Orillia join Ontario Hydro. The town's engineer for the past twenty years recommended against joining the provincial utility. Each side threw a barrage of facts and figures at the public. Some of the industrialists favoured joining Ontario Hydro so they would be guaranteed power at rates that were equal to all plants. Others, like Clarence Long of E. Long Ltd. asked publicly how anyone could make a decision with the conflicting numbers and many questions still in the air. OWLP commissioners in favour of affiliation said the new plant would cost more than estimated and not produce as much power as calculated. The idea that industries came to Orillia because of low power rates was ridiculous, said the manager of Fahralloy, which had started up in the 1930s. Some rates paid by the company were just as high as those charged by Ontario Hydro, he said.

Supporters of the new plant and the OWLP's independence argued that controlling its own power would continue to guarantee Orillia low rates. The Horseshoe plant would provide plenty of power, and the OWLP had three more sites on the Severn River for future expansion. Besides, said supporters, the $1.2 million debt and the extra $900,000 debenture would not be repaid by taxpayers, but out of OWLP revenues. The complex battle threw people on to unexpected sides. Mayor Cramp, a constant critic of the OWLP, argued against joining Ontario Hydro. The confusing question came to voters September 14, 1953, and even though the OWLP won the vote, it lost the war. Orillians voted 996 to 911 for the new plant, but that did not come close to the 60 per cent needed. The new plant was lost, and affiliation with Ontario Hydro came soon after.

Newspaper writers at the time wondered why the town was willing to give up its independence so easily. It's likely the huge debt remaining from the building of the Matthias plant in 1950 and the fact household rates differed little from Ontario Hydro rates dampened the enthusiasm for a new plant, wrote the Orillia Newsletter.

"It has been a heartbreak of my old age to see...Orillia's future as an industrial centre thrown away," wrote C. H. Hale in his book, Reminiscences. The result of that decision was clear, he wrote. After forty-five years of the lowest electrical rates in Canada, it took only ten years of affiliation with Ontario Hydro to put Orillia's rates above those in Barrie, Midland, Coldwater, and Gravenhurst, said Hale. Today, the OWLP still produces power at a lower cost than Ontario Hydro, but must buy about 70 per cent of the city's power at the higher rate from the provincial utility.

Hale saw the vote over the OWLP as a battle between Old Orillians with pride in their power plant and newcomers who had no such loyalty and were backed by Ontario Hydro's Barrie office. It was likely not that simple, for in the shifting debate over Orillia's future, it has often been newcomers who try to maintain the community's link to the past. It was a newcomer, young radio announcer Pete McGarvey, who led the fight to buy and restore Stephen Leacock's summer home on Old Brewery Bay (see "A Leacockian Tale"). The ending of the OWLP's independence symbolized the end of the trust in industrial leadership of the early 1900s, but it hardly marked the end of a spirit determined to make Orillia unique.

Gordon Smith opened radio station CFOR in 1945 above the Loblaws grocery store on Mississaga Street. With 250 watts of power and a home-made transmitter tower, CFOR struggled along for five years. In 1950, CFOR increased its power to 1,000 watts and four years later, moved to new studios on West Street. In 1957, comedian Bob Hope was persuaded to visit Orillia to officially turn on the switch to boost CFOR's power to 10,000 watts. Thousands of people crowded into the station's parking lot across from Orillia and District Collegiate and Vocational Institute to watch the ceremony, hosted by broadcaster Pete McGarvey, whose back is to the photographer. The station earned its FM licence in the 1990s and has since offered both country music and easy rock.

Courtesy of Pete McGarvey

LIKE WHEAT BEFORE THE SCYTHE

The 1950s ended in Orillia with a bang, a stopover by Queen Elizabeth and Prince Philip on their 1959 tour of Canada. The Royal couple arrived by train in the afternoon of July 5 and thousands watched the two in a motorcade parade through town to Couchiching Beach Park. The Queen and Prince chatted with politicians and organizers as an official guest book was signed. A child patient of the Ontario Hospital School presented the Queen with a bouquet of flowers and Peter McGarvey Jr. presented her with a special copy of Leacock's Sunshine Sketches that included a forward by C.H. Hale.

Many residents avoided Orillia that day, preferring to go swimming in Bass Lake or to head to northern fishing holes, reported The Packet & Times. Some merchants complained that the tourists spent hardly any money. The crowds were slightly smaller than expected, but still large and enthusiastic. And no writer could beat The Packet's for overwhelming its loyal, conservative readers with a parade of superlatives in coverage of the great day. Before the Queen's charm, and wit, "the hearts of Orillians went down like wheat before a scythe and long before the Royal farewells had been waved from the rear platform of the train Orillia was theirs forever."

Orillia said goodbye to the 1950s by saying hello to Queen Elizabeth and Prince Philip. The Royal couple made a stop in the town during its 1959 tour of Canada. Children crowded into Couchiching Beach Park to get a glimpse of the popular Queen signing the official guest register.

The Packet & Times

A LEACOCKIAN TALE

Were it not for the backroom politics of an Orillia outsider, Stephen Leacock's graceful home on Lake Couchiching would likely have been demolished a long time ago.

Stephen Leacock spent many of his summers and vacations on Brewery Bay in Orillia. Mornings were spent writing in the boathouse, and afternoons visiting with friends and family, sailing, playing cricket and reading. Behind Leacock and son Stephen Jr. is Brewery Bay and one of Leacock's sailboats.

Stephen Leacock Museum

Fans and friends of Leacock tried to gain possession of the home but ran afoul of Stephen Jr. None other than C.H. Hale - the champion of Soldiers' Memorial Hospital and the Champlain monument - continued to press for public ownership of the home in the early 1950s. He gathered a group of like-minded Leacock boosters, including young alderman and radio broadcaster Pete McGarvey. For several years, the committee fought council indifference, even hostility, and the whims Stephen Jr. in its efforts to buy the home. The committee's best chance came in 1956. Toronto developer and publisher Louis Ruby bought the property, and, after a little persuading, agreed to give the Leacock Home Committee a year to find $25,000 to buy the home and a surrounding 1.4 acres. Town council again refused to spend any money on an old, falling-down summer home. Premier Leslie Frost, though born and bred in Orillia, offered little help. There is speculation the Frost family, devout Temperance supporters, did not appreciate Leacock's thirst for alcohol.

Determined to devote his time to the purchase of the Leacock Home, McGarvey told fellow aldermen he would not be running for the 1957 council. To their horror, they realized McGarvey's withdrawal would result in acclamation of council. One of the only six people left in the race was a town eccentric who promised to make council's life miserable. The incumbent councillors pressured McGarvey to stay in the race and keep the eccentric out. McGarvey made them a deal. If he ran on a single-platform, the saving of the Leacock Home, and won a lot of votes, they would have to back him in buying the property.

McGarvey collected the second-highest vote count, and the rest of council kept its part of the bargain. The town purchased the Stephen Leacock Home in 1957. Alive with tourists and community groups, the home has become a memento to Leacock's grace and hospitality.

Information from Pete McGarvey, Old Brewery Bay (*Toronto: Dundurn, 1994*)

In his summer home on Brewery Bay, Leacock wrote, entertained friends and family, and horrified the pious of Orillia with his love of the spirits and eccentricity. He loved Brewery Bay and, after his wife died in 1925, built a beautiful home there. On his death in 1944, the home passed into the hands of Leacock's strange son, Stephen Leacock Jr. and the beginning of decay.

THE CENTRE A COMMUNITY BUILT

The Community Centre in Orillia means more to the city than a place to play hockey. The community built the centre, not only with the usual fundraising dinners and canvasses. Volunteers hammered nails and cut wood, served workers coffee and painted walls each weeknight for months to save time and money. Much maligned over the past ten years, the centre remains one of the best examples of community spirit in Orillia.

Until the late 1940s, a natural ice rink inside a corrugated medal shed on West Street at Coldwater served as Orillia's arena. After the war, a few communities in Ontario built artificial rinks as memorials. In 1947, just about the time the Orillia, Water, Light and Power Commission (OWLP) bought the site of the natural rink for a new building, a small group of service club representatives led by lawyer and Y's Men Club member Mac Carter started talking about building a modern arena. That small group turned into the Community Centre Association, headed at first by Carter, and went through the usual discussions about when and how and where to build an arena. What was different about this project was the funding. The town had little money to spare, as it was paying for two school projects and a new sewage plant. So it was left up to the service clubs in town to initiate and pay for the $150,000 project.

But interest in the centre appeared flat after the first four months of campaigning. Looking for a way to heighten interest in a new arena, Carter came up with an unusual solution - shut the old one down. Without a rink in the winter of 1948, town residents might better appreciate the need for a new one, said Carter when he first brought up the idea with town council. The media, some sportsmen, and city leaders, including the president of his own club, the Y's men, cried foul. Carter's enthusiasm was clouding his judgment and it was time for older heads to prevail, said the editorial writer for the Newsletter. Later a prominent judge, Carter battled back in a lengthy, articulate letter to the editor. The OWLP had promised the $15,000 from the sale of the old, corrugated-sided rink to the new arena committee, said Carter. If the OWLP delayed, the price of the old rink would likely drop. If no buyers were found soon, the OWLP would have to move the rink

to build its new headquarters, and subtract the costs of that move out of the money handed over to the new arena committee, argued Carter. It was best to shut the old rink down, let it be sold as soon as possible and be out of the OWLP's way. His arguments won the day, and the town shut down the old rink for the duration of the campaign. Skaters and hockey players had to settle for outdoor rinks.

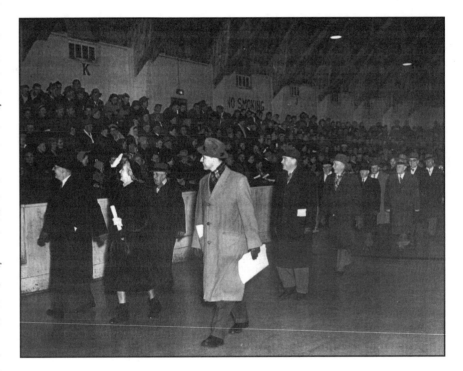

A young Mac Carter, centre, led the dignitaries on a tour of the new Community Centre on January 28, 1952. Following Carter is Maple Leaf goalie Turk Broda. Carter shocked his older colleagues on the arena committee by persuading town council to shut down the old arena before the new one was built. Carter figured hockey-hungry Orillians needed a little push to put more money into the new arena campaign. Volunteer labour cut about $85,000 off the cost of the arena. Carter later became a respected judge.

Courtesy of Mac Carter

It took several fundraising drives in 1948 and 1949 before enough money was raised to begin building. Interest in the project, like any other, waned several times. The community centre group had to re-organize and scale down plans in 1949. But once the sod was turned in 1950, the arena became a community centre even before it was built. Local contractors and manufacturers donated material and services valued at about $48,000. About 3,000 volunteers hammered, nailed, sawed and helped lay bricks over the two-year construction. Service clubs provided teams of twenty or more one night a week, with as many as 100 volunteers working at a time. Town residents did most of the work in every phase of construction except laying the floor and artificial ice. Government inspectors and contractors praised the work. Volunteers contributed more than 100,000 hours of labour, worth about $85,000 and cutting the labour costs in half. Fundraising brought in another $110,000, and the province gave $10,000, leaving the city with only $25,000 to borrow, one of the lowest loans for a municipal arena in the province at the time.

The opening-night gala on January 28, 1952 featured Toronto Maple Leaf goalie Turk Broda and champion figure skaters from Toronto. About 2,400 people watched Premier Leslie Frost, a native Orillian, cut the ribbon. The OHA Junior A Barrie Flyers and Galt Black Hawks put on an exhibition game, with Barrie winning 5-1. Touring the new arena that night, George Dudley, secretary manager of the Canadian Amateur Hockey Association, told reporters, "If more beautiful arenas like this one are built, hockey would be brought up to an even higher standard than it already enjoys in Canada."

SOME DREAMS JUST WON'T DIE

lat on her back with the flu in 1961, Orillia housewife and mother of four Ruth Jones had nothing else to do but think — about Orillia, her home of the past five years; about the notion espoused recently by a tourism expert that each community should have something unique to draw people; about how she loved to get away now and then to Toronto and listen to the rising young folk musicians. By the time the flu bug had worked its way through Ruth Jones that winter, she had worked through an idea that would marry her love of folk music and her love of Orillia — the first-ever Canadian folk festival, held, of course, in Orillia. Six months later, hundreds of teenagers from across the country and hundreds of bewildered Orillians heard the opening songs of the first Mariposa Folk Festival. On that peaceful night, when Jones' dream had come true, no one could predict the rocky ride Mariposa and the 1960s would take, with Orillia just barely hanging on.

The Mariposa Folk Festival began like many of Orillia's dreams that decade, with naivete and energy. Ruth Jones sent letters to major folk stars such as Pete Seeger to invite them to an as yet non-existent event. Few replied, but it did not matter to Jones. Within weeks she had a committee working for her. Alderman Pete McGarvey, fresh from his Leacock Home victory, liked the idea and dubbed it the Mariposa Folk Festival. Jones and her volunteers roamed the province, trying to gain support and publicity. The festival committee found strong acceptance in Orillia. A folk festival was a nice, clean way to promote Orillia and bring thousands of tourists into town. In 1961, folk music was riding a crest of popularity, attracting both clean-cut college students still many years away from Woodstock and the hippest of their middle-aged, middle-class parents. The organizers' aims were simple and noble. The Mariposa Folk Festival would teach Canadians about their own national folk songs, give rising musicians the publicity they needed to attract record contracts, allow Canadian singers a chance to earn a successful living at home, and promote the world's folk music to the world.

The first festival accomplished all that. On a warm August night at the Lions Oval in 1961, about 2,000 people sat before a stage that looked like a medieval jousting tent and listened to rising stars Ian Tyson and partner Sylvia Fricker, later known as Ian and Sylvia Tyson. So good was the music, some Orillians even moved out of their chairs to sit on the grass near the stage, reported The Packet & Times. That was as wild as things got. After the Friday night performance, hundreds enjoyed a square dance on Mississaga Street and throughout the festival, watched films about folk music. In true folk festival fashion, it rained the Saturday evening. About 4,000 people crowded into the community centre to watch newcomers such as Bonny Dobson and seasoned folk-singers The Travellers. Afterward Traveller Jerry Goodis proclaimed, "This could be another Stratford." The Packet & Times agreed. It called on any suspicious Orillians to accept the eccentric folk musicians and their fans, just as Stratford residents finally accepted the strange theatre people who descended on their town each year. Mariposa was just the thing to give Orillia an extra edge in the tourism industry.

The second year proved just as successful, with a bit of hometown pride thrown in too. Orillia native Gordon Lightfoot, starting to make a name as a folk-singer in Toronto, brought fellow Orillian Terry Whelan to the festival and they performed as the Tu-tones. The second festival featured workshops on folk music, including a serious look at the art form with critics from the New York Times and the Folklore Center of New York.

The 1963 lineup was even more impressive, with a midnight jamboree and hootenany, tempered by lectures from Edith Fowke, an acknowledged expert on folk music and host of many CBC folk music programs. Festival organizers expected 25,000 people to congregate in the town of 15,000 and pleaded with homeowners to rent out their rooms. People from across the United States and Canada were phoning for accommodations and the motels were full. A businessman in Severn Bridge cleared some land and created the Silver Sleeve campground to handle the overflow. Homeowners responded by opening their doors and the police, worried about traffic, asked the OPP for extra officers. About 5,500 people watched the Friday night performance on August 10. That was twice as high as the year before and convinced the show's producer, Jack Wall, earlier worried about Orillia's interest in the event, to keep the festival in the town. Wall had taken over organizing the festival from Jones. The third festival gained Orillia international recognition, with crews from CBC television, NBC and CHUM Radio recording the event. The crowd that first night listened quietly to the songs of Ian Tyson and Sylvia Fricker and veteran folk-singer Alan Mills. The only trouble for the fifteen town police and ten OPP officers were the traffic jams downtown and up the highway to Severn Bridge. The party that night centred on Silver Sleeve, where a jamboree and impromptu, bonfire singalongs kept teenagers up most of the night.

Saturday turned rowdy in Orillia itself. According to press reports, more than 23,000 people, including members of the Black Lancers motorcycle gang, streamed into Orillia. About 11,500 of them turned up at the Oval for the concert. Men armed with baseball bats tried to keep out gate crashers. The field was so jammed with people, organizers warned concert-goers if they left at intermission, they would not be allowed back in. That sparked trouble and hundreds tried to get back in by climbing over the fence. One girl fell from the fence and landed on a beer bottle, breaking her arm. The crowd settled down when The Travellers took to the stage, but people were still restless and a post-concert singalong drew little interest. The teenagers in the crowd poured downtown, where they joined thousands of others who had come into Orillia just for a party. They took over the main street. Silver Sleeve had closed its gates to the crowd at 8 p.m. because it was full. Police on duty there reported seeing thirteen and fourteen-year-olds drunk, and campers using neighbouring lawns for toilets because there weren't enough washrooms in the park.

"The morals at Silver Sleeve were deplorable. It was disgusting," OPP Sgt. Ken Chalmers later told the press.

Things were worse, or at least closer to home, in Orillia. Gangs of youths drank and fought in the streets, said newspaper reports. Doorways

Kids, there were kids everywhere! Orillia had seen nothing like the Mariposa Festival weekend in August 1963, when an estimated 23,000 people, mainly teenagers, descended on the town. They drove up and down the streets, crowded into the Lions Oval to listen to music and started bonfires at a nearby campground. A raucous street party on the Saturday night convinced council to put an end to the festival in Orillia.

The Packet & Times

became toilets. Teenagers swarmed around a police officer as he tried to arrest a youth, and the youth escaped into the crowd. One officer checked a man in a sleeping bag on the street and came face to face with a gun. Teenagers rolled pints of beer down the Mississaga Street hill to friends at the bottom. They showered and bathed each other, and the Champlain monument, dubbed Sam's Place, with beer. According to police and newspaper accounts, one mob of teenagers broke into a University of Toronto bus, and smashed all the camera equipment and scattered clothes on to the street. A hundred youths held up a police cruiser on the main street, refusing to let it pass for several minutes. Parked cars were ransacked and thieves stole anything inside. Police arrested hundreds, but a thousand officers could not have handled the crowd, they said. "Bloody noses and black eyes" greeted police officers everywhere, said Chief E. W. McIntyre. The forty town, OPP, and RCMP officers could not handle the mobs. Not even the worst brawls of the lumber days sparked such outrage in the town.

"It is obvious there cannot be another festival here," Alderman McGarvey, one of the festival's founders and biggest supporters, said the next day. There was no doubt the festival made money — restaurants reported triple the business.

"We need the money, but not at the expense of the town's good name," said Alderman Murray Robinson.

Not everyone found the Mariposa Folk Festival the nightmare reported in the press. The Orillia establishment over-reacted to a few small problems and the sight of so many young people in the streets, maintains Frank Gold, who owned a clothing store in the middle of the fracas downtown.

"The oldtimers couldn't believe the young people," he recalled in an interview for this book. "It was the Woodstock generation, and this town wasn't ready for it. The stories were exaggerated." Ruth Jones agrees. The Globe and Mail sent a reporter just to do a story on the riots before the festival even started, she said in an interview. Festival organizers conspired to get the reporter drunk, and he missed his deadline. But the image of the town had been tarnished, and city leaders felt any threat to Orillia's good name, and year-round family tourism, had to be quashed.

Council and organizers told the producers to go somewhere else, preventing the festival from being held near the town in 1964. The festival moved on, looking for permanent home on the Toronto Islands, Barrie's Molson Park and a few other places in between. For awhile in the 1970s, the Mariposa Folk Festival became the hippest musical event in the country, attracting visitors like Bob Dylan, Neil Young, Jackson Browne, Joni Mitchell and Gordon Lightfoot. The name Mariposa remains synonymous with folk music. And Orillia seemed ready in 1996 to bring Mariposa home. The Orillia Folk Society asked the Mariposa Folk Foundation to consider putting on the financially-troubled festival in Orillia. Two other communities, Bracebridge and Cobourg, heard about the move and joined

the competition. The Foundation decided to split the festival in three places, but Orillia's organizers rejected the idea. Either Mariposa would come home intact, or not at all. The folk society was considering setting up its own festival and looking into the legal rights of the name Mariposa.

The Orillia Curling Club's Harry Barons, far left, and Mayor George McLean, far right, congratulated the "Sputniks", from left to right, Ross Coward, Frank Milligan, Tom Caldwall and Tre Behan after winning the provincial curling championship in 1961.

Company manager or factory worker, when you walked through the doors of the Orillia Curling Club you became an equal. The beer was in the cooler. The chairs were set around the legendary Black Table. The best curling won on the ice. The best tall tales won at the table. Like the other clubs and organizations that swelled with memberships after the Second World War, the curling club offered comraderie, democracy and entertainment. Estimates of the membership in the glory days from 1945 to 1975 range from 700 to 900 people. Clubs from across Ontario, including the prestigious Granite Club of Toronto, made sure they attended Orillia tournaments because the club had a such a good reputation for hospitality. Since its beginning in 1873, the Orillia Curling Club has seen its various buildings burn in fires, collapse under the weight of snow, and get shut down by government safety regulations. The 1964 club on West Street was shut down by the ministry of labor in 1989, and club members played in Gravenhurst for several years. In 1996, the club began a campaign to build an Orillia facility.

The Packet & Times, Courtesy of Harry Barons.

A similar dream of the 1960s met a similar fate, and refused to die into the 1990s. Just as the Mariposa Folk Festival packed up its tent stakes, Orillia embarked on an even more ambitious plan to please its youth, while making money and boosting the town's image at the same time. The way to do that seemed simple — build a university. Universities do more than keep young people at home and bring in students and their money. They give a community an intellectual centre, and a focus for arts and entertainment, from varsity sports teams to better pubs. And Orillia came agonizingly close to achieving the cachet of a university town a half dozen times during the stormy rise and fall of Simcoe College. For the first few heady years in the 1960s, it appeared certain the town would get its university. Enrolment at existing universities was rising and the Orillia area was growing. A group of educators and residents formed a university committee in 1964. In a report of that year, the committee proposed building a university called Simcoe College that would cost $1.25 million, to be built in three stages. Besides a 35,000-square-foot teaching centre, Simcoe College would have a library, residence, and gymnasium/auditorium. Waterloo Lutheran University was interested in operating the satellite campus until someday, perhaps, the university would achieve independence. The first stage would enrol 600 students, with another 600 enrolled when completed.

The campaign to raise the construction money started with the largest banquet held in Orillia. About 700 people sat down to a fundraising dinner in the community centre June 4, 1966. Excitement gripped Orillia, the county, and Muskoka, for the university was to serve a large area. The eighteen campaign leaders themselves pledged $41,400. The Simcoe College Foundation hoped to raise the $1.25 million by September, so the buildings would be complete the year after, 1967. In the fall of 1966, the Simcoe College Foundation paid $115,300 for 228 acres of wooded land on the west side of Highway 11. So optimistic was the foundation, it bought more land than originally planned, in order to allow for college expansion. The site seemed ideal for a university, with a stream, pond, and rolling hills that gave a view of Lakes Couchiching and Simcoe, and frontage on Highway 11. Stephen Leacock himself had used the pond as a secret fishing retreat and wrote about it. But fundraising slowed after the initial kick start, and the September 1967 opening was delayed. Meanwhile, the foundation had to bump its goal up to $1.8 million to cover the extra land bought.

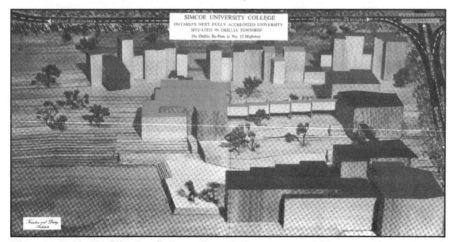

The plans of the Simcoe College Foundation were ambitious - a three-staged construction of a lecture hall, classrooms, library, and laboratories (foreground); student lounges, a cafeteria, and gymnasium (middle); and behind those buildings, residences. The original proposal had the university being erected at the intersection of the Highway 11 and Highway 12.

The swing bridge at The Narrows, built in 1925, was replaced by a new bridge in 1964. The girders for the new, $600,000 bridge dwarfed the swing bridge.
The Packet & Times

106

Foundation chairman Sue Mulcahy appealed for the public's help. A sod-turning ceremony a year after the dinner may have been a sign of the public's waning interest. Thirty-five people working in shifts called 9,796 residents by phone to personally invite them to the June 17, 1967, sod turning. About 200 turned up to stand in the rain that day for the dedication ceremony by the Hon. Earl Rowe, then the Lieutenant-Governor of Ontario and Honorary Patron of Simcoe College. That same year, the federal government announced a shift in funding that saw Waterloo Lutheran lose some grants. The university pulled back on its commitment to Orillia. At the same time, the province announced it would offer grants only to universities in existence in 1967. Although the Simcoe College Foundation had been incorporated in 1965, the province refused to offer it any grants.

For the next thirty years, the foundation and its supporters rode a rollercoaster of hopes risen and dashed. Each time the province announced a new direction in post-secondary education, the foundation grew hopeful money would finally come. The Conservative provincial government alternatively warned there would be no money for universities and promised Orillia it would be the first to get one when money was available. In 1974, Premier William Davis fanned the dying embers of the dream by suggesting university enrolment was rising again and Simcoe College would get permission to build. No free-standing universities would be approved, said Davis at an Orillia fundraising dinner, but Simcoe College was affiliated with Wilfrid Laurier University (formerly Waterloo Lutheran University), and that meant it could go ahead.

That promise was broken, and as the years went by with no construction in sight, the pledges of service clubs and businesses died a natural death. Georgian College's construction of a new facility in 1980 likely ended for good Orillia's chance of getting a university.

Meanwhile, the foundation had to endure charges about the mishandling of funds and wasting everyone's times. In 1981, Orillia council took back about $284,000 raised in taxes for the university. That money was for bricks and mortar, and nothing else, council members said. For much of the eighties, the remaining foundation members held on to the slimmest of hopes for a university in the face of demands it put the land and assets to another use, whether for a recreation centre or a new hospital. Volunteers cleaned up the property from time to time, as hikers, mountain bikers, and cross-country skiers became the only visitors to the site. The foundation continued to help students taking York University courses at Georgian College and gave $10,000 for a college library. The pressure to sell grew heavier when Richmond Hill, Ontario developer Lou Orsi started buying land around Orillia in the late 1980s. He offered the foundation from $1 million to $1.5 million for the land. Longtime college backer Sue Mulcahy and other board members refused. Meanwhile, the province told the foundation to forget any idea of a new university for a long time.

By 1989, the foundation had had enough of the pressures and asked the province for help in dissolving the foundation and dividing up its assets. Under its charter, the foundation's assets had to go to charities, but there was little charitable about the scrabble for the 228 acres of land and $77,000 in the bank. The Public Trustee of Ontario announced it would hear from groups interested in the assets, sparking a bizarre battle between a range of non-profit groups. Local service clubs, the hospital, the Orillia Naturalists Club, Georgian College, the St. James Court Non-Profit Housing Corporation, the Orillia Heritage Centre, city council itself, and a new-age church called the Fellowship of White Light all claimed to have the best plan for the land and $77,000 in assets. The proposals ranged from the prosaic to the poetic.

The Orillia Lions, Rotary, Kinsmen, and Quota Clubs joined forces to push for a nature and recreation park that would attract tourists and help residents. The Naturalists Club had a similar idea, but favoured a wilderness area. Hospital officials would not say why they wanted the park, but it was likely for a new facility or to resell and pay for a new facility. The Orillia Heritage Centre wanted some money to help build a museum in Tudhope Park. Georgian College wanted some money to pay for scholarships and capital works projects. The non-profit housing group wanted to build non-profit housing.

The new-age Fellowship of White Light wanted to build a "mystery school." That's how leader Stephen Ginsberg described his proposal. The group had 1,500 members devoted to health, peace, and "focusing on the white light". The Fellowship's conference centre, restaurant, dormitories and nature trails would offer adults a place to learn how to eat better, relax, and re-gain their spirituality, said Ginsberg. "We believe we can change the world," he said. Just to make things even more confusing, some of the previous owners of the land claimed they should get the land back. The owners said they had been forced into selling their land by the threat of expropriation for a university. If there was going to be no university, the land should return to them, they argued. Each group lobbied council and the public before a Supreme Court hearing into the assets. The fighting grew so intense Mayor John Palmer, usually the spark of such controversies, pleaded for calm.

"We're looking like a bunch of little pigs," he told The Packet & Times. "It seems a little unseemingly, like someone threw a loaf of bread into a crowd of starving people."

In the midst of the interesting little battle, council, the service clubs, and the Naturalists Club got together to propose —what else — a university. The rollercoaster headed up the track again. Former education minister Bette Stephenson, heading a group trying to build a private university, gave initial support. The Ontario Public Trustee's Office, which supervised charities in Ontario, thought that was a great idea.

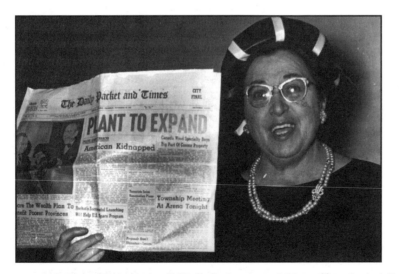

It was a good time to be mayor. Orillia's first woman in the office, Isabel Post, celebrated several plant expansions in the 1960s. One of the town's largest industries, Fahralloy Canada Ltd., built a $2.5 million plant on fifty-two acres on Highway 11. In this photograph, Post celebrated the expansion of Canada Wood Specialties. Post served as mayor six times in the decade, during which time the economy continued to grow.

The Packet & Times

The "twelve-foot Indian" finally got a break in 1964. The original 1912 design, top, was drawn by Mayor William Frost. The rather large Indian figure became the butt of many jokes. A local artist, Don Tunstall, revised the Coat of Arms to make the Indian smaller and the canoe longer. The deer, called greyhounds with antlers by some critics, were also changed.

The Packet & Times

A district judge delayed the hearing on the assets to give the university backers time to prepare a proposal. Most of the other city groups fell in behind the idea, although the property owners and the non-profit housing corporation continued to make a plea for some of the assets. Meanwhile, yet another government study came out, giving Orillia new hope. The Institutional Policy Committee of the Ontario Council on University Affairs suggested the province consider ways to help fund proposals such as Simcoe College. In February 1990, the dream of a university received official rekindling. A county court decided the Simcoe College Foundation should expand its board of directors and work toward getting a university in Orillia. Mulcahy and other foundation members could hardly believe that in less than a year they had bounced from a bitter dissolution to an optimistic expansion. Ironically, the legal battle over the foundation drained all but $13,000 of the assets which had tempted so many groups.

For most of the next five years, the new Simcoe College Foundation tried to establish a centre for environmental studies, offering graduate students and professors a place to conduct research. The centre would not have to gain any university accreditation, but would get the status of university research in exchange for supplying a facility, technical equipment, and support staff. Orillia's unique location between the urban and agricultural south and wilderness north provided an ideal setting for studying a range of environmental issues, said supporters. With $3 billion available in the federal government's Green Plan, Conservative MP Doug Lewis in cabinet, and a local Conservative leader, Jack Stewart, heading the foundation, it appeared finally that Orillia would get something. The federal government financed two of three studies into the centre's development, which outlined not only what the centre would do, but in what buildings and how. The foundation pressed the federal government for $500,000 to prepare site plans and architectural drawings. But in May 1993, the government balked, perhaps because any more help would put it on the line for the rest of the $15 million needed for the centre. A $50-million government cut had turned the vibrant Green Plan pale. A few months after the federal government's rejection, foundation president Jack Stewart died. The Tories themselves lost the election a year later.

With the February, 1995 deadline approaching, the foundation disappeared from public view. Behind the scenes, foundation members lobbied the Ontario Public Trustee and anyone who might object to a further extension. A county court order issued on February 2, 1995 gave the foundation three more years to make substantial progress in setting up an environmental research centre. The foundation also made an agreement with Georgian College, the occasional burr in its side, to let college students use the 228 acres in Scout Valley for environmental studies. In exchange, the affiliation with the college may give the foundation a break from the taxes that continue to eat up assets. In three years' time, the foundation must get another $50,000 for its final report and hire someone to get a commitment to the plan from Ontario universities. Meanwhile, the foundation has a few other ideas to consider, including affiliation with the Canadian Memorial Chiropractic College or building a centre for construction excellence with the city's construction association.

After thirty years of false starts, sudden stops, skirmishes with money-hungry politicians, land-hungry citizens, sceptical media and bitter donors, and court battles and public relations nightmares, Simcoe College remains the hardest-to-kill dream in Orillia.

With its beautiful shoreline, clean water and Indian motif, Camp Summerland was the classic camp of the 1960s, when this photograph was taken. Thousands of Orillians and others across Canada spent childhood summers at the camp on the east side of Lake Couchiching. It was closed in 1989.

In spite of the failure of the college and the Mariposa Festival, the 1960s ended with optimism in the city. For one reason, Orillia could finally be called a city by the end of the decade. There had been several attempts to turn the town into a city, usually tied to annexing some land. So optimistic were city fathers in 1917, they named the Opera House the Orillia City Hall. Progress never seemed so certain after those years. Mayor Ben Johnston tried in the 1930s to expand the town's borders to include 10,000 people, enough for a city, but failed. Other attempts in the 1940s and 1950s failed for the same reasons, fear over costs and fear over a loss of small-town identity. From 1915 to 1952, the town did not expand at all. The 1950s saw a series of annexations. In 1952, about 109 acres north of Brant Street and west of West Street was annexed. Much of that land had been a farm owned by Reeve James Quinn of Orillia. He had used his influence for years to keep the farm safe from annexation so he could pay the township's lower tax rate. The town annexed two more parcels in 1956, including the land where Park Street Collegiate sits today, and a small parcel in 1959.

By 1965, Orillia Township (now Severn Township) had had enough. But more people were moving into Orillia Township on the town's borders, taxing the town's facilities, without giving the town taxes. The western edge of the town was Westmount Drive and West Street, its northern border a zig-zag of streets well below Highway 11. Across Westmount especially, hundreds of new homes were springing up. They weren't tied to city services and there was fear the septic tanks couldn't handle all the sewage. Council commissioned a study of the problem and the consultants recommended the town annex 3,000 acres of Orillia Township. With the typical optimism of consultants, the report predicted the town would grow to 30,500 people by 1985 and needed the room. Growth had been stalled since 1951 by lack of space, while the township had been booming. But all those people used city facilities, and the city needed to get something in return, concluded the report.

At first the town and township played down any potential animosity over the recommendations. Mayor Isabel Post suggested the township hand over the land quietly, without a fight. Township Reeve Tom Joslin said his taxpayers would not approve of that, and suggested the township and town consider uniting. That and other compromises failed, so the town took its annexation plans to the Ontario Municipal Board in 1966. Orillia Township opposed the move.

Town lawyers argued that by 1985, without annexation, Orillia would have only seventy-five acres left for residential development. There were only twenty-five acres of industrial land left in town, and two industries, Dominion Rubber of Kitchener and CCM Bicycles, had rejected Orillia because there were no suitable industrial sites, argued town lawyers.

Orillia celebrated the Centennial of the town's birth in May 1967 and the country's birth in July. Parades, fireworks and costume contests, where the old mixed with the new, marked the celebrations.

The Packet & Times

The spectre of the town's leading industrialists opposing new industry rose again during the hearings. S.F. Saunders, the president of Dorr-Oliver-Long, the town's biggest industry and chairman of the Orillia Industrial Associates, told reporters he was against annexation because it would increase taxes. His point was well-taken. Orillia's taxes were already higher than average for towns its size, and higher than Barrie's. The town's debt per capita was the fourth highest for municipalities that size.

The township lawyer argued that the annexation was piece-meal and would destroy the township's tax base, pointing out a previous annexation attempt in 1957 was turned down by the OMB.

The hearings turned nasty several times, such as when the township officials suggested Orillia clean up its "slums" in the south ward before worrying about getting more land.

Time, ice and fires took their toll on the boathouses along the waterfront. The Ross boatworks burned down in 1964, damaging the neighbouring Rolland boat livery. In 1966, the town had the remains of the Rolland boat livery knocked down and started its Centennial project, a new waterfront park. Workers added four and a half acres of land to the waterfront to create Centennial Park, which stretches from Couchiching Beach Park to the town dock at the foot of Mississaga Street. The shoreline was extended up to 200 feet from the Canadian Pacific Railway tracks. The park and Centennial Drive were officially opened July 1, 1967. There was no boardwalk and few trees, but it was a start.

Orillia's main street in 1966. There wasn't a tree or bit of cobblestone to be seen.
The Packet & Times

"You'd think you were a criminal on the stand," Mayor Isabel Post recalled years later. "...You had to stand through all this, through all this cross questioning. I remember someone saying, that the lady ought to be offered a chair. And I remember retorting quite caustically," She's quite able to stand." It was a sort of bitter business."

The Ontario Municipal Board ruled in September 1966 that Orillia could annex about 3,000 acres of township land, because the built-up areas around Orillia should come under an urban administration. The annexation doubled the size of Orillia and raised the population from about 15,000 to 20,000. That was enough for a city, but no one was rushing into becoming a city, at least officially.

"I don't see any city status for Orillia in the near future," said Mayor Isabel Post shortly after the annexation victory.

The next year, 1967, Orillia celebrated its own and Canada's 100th birthday and did a study on the costs of leaving the county and becoming a city. The relationship between the town and the county was beginning to sour. The county refused to give large municipalities such as Orillia more voting power, prompting Mayor Post to do a preliminary study of becoming a city in the fall of 1967. Her figures showed that Orillia was paying more for county services than Barrie, which had loosened its relationship with the county when it became a city in 1958.

Post wanted to delay doing anything for a year because there was no money budgeted for an official study, but council pushed ahead. Council members said they were tired of fighting the county over money, and feared the province would force regional government on them. Next spring, 1968, a chartered accounting firm from Toronto decided leaving the county would cut taxes in Orillia. No one objected to the proposal when the city applied to the Ontario Municipal Board. The board took about two minutes on May 6, 1968 to decide Orillia could finally become a city.

Residents expected becoming a city would bring more industry, Simcoe College, jobs and status to Orillia.

"We'll start acting big," predicted resident Reg Irwin, interviewed by reporters after the announcement.

"I wouldn't like to see Orillia get too big though," said Violet Mintz.

When fireworks, speeches and the ringing of church bells proclaimed the birth of the city January 1, 1969, civic leaders offered the same optimism, and caution.

"Our day is tomorrow," proclaimed Mayor Burt McIsaac. "Look, We Are a City! But We're Still Orillia," proclaimed The Packet & Times. How true that was. For the next 20 years, residents struggled to reconcile Orillia the City with Orillia the Sunshine Town. The Orillia Spirit was splintered by internal division and bashed about by external forces, leaving an entire city with a splitting headache.

In the 1960s, progress often meant tearing down or hiding Orillia's older buildings. The first town hall, built in 1874, was torn down in 1962. The public library had its facade covered by angular additions in 1968, shown above, and in 1982.

The Packet & Times

THE LONG WAIT FOR A DRINK

It took almost a hundred years, but Orillia finally got a drink.

The city's status as a dry town, always more official than real, began back in 1874 when taxpayers voted 144 to 3 to prohibit stores from selling liquor. The issuing of "shop licences" continued until the early 1900s, partly because the bylaw had not been signed and the courts refused to recognize it. Orillia voted again in 1906 to prohibit the shop licences and in 1908 to shut down the town's bars. Alcohol merchants and thirsty drinkers made several futile attempts in the 1930s to change the laws. The colourful Wilbur Cramp and a group of merchants led the vote in 1950 to allow a beer and liquor store in Orillia, but residents still had to drive across The Narrows to Atherley for a drink in a tavern. The first bar across the bridge is still named The First, although The Second, which was of course next in line, has disappeared. Between trips to Atherley and dipping into the cooler at the curling club, Orillians had enough places to get a drink. But it still galled many that residents or tourists could not buy a drink with a meal in as modern a time as the 1960s. Focusing on the benefits to the tourist trade, a group of seventy-two residents signed a petition in early 1967 asking council for a plebiscite on the issue. Council agreed to the vote, and the last great liquor fight began. The Orillia Yes Committee included doctors and developers and hired a professional manager to help bring bars and lounges to town. The committee stressed that opening lounges and beverage rooms would please tourists, but have no effect on Orillians' drinking habits. Opposing the committee were the Concerned Parents Movement and some local churches. The churches became the rallying point for the No side, when radio station CFOR cut short the weekly broadcast of a Sunday service. Station management had asked the churches not to bring up the liquor vote in the weekly shows. One minister told his audience about the restriction, then joked that he planned a long dissertation on the demon rum. The radio station cut him off the air, playing a few records and returning only when the minister began his sermon. The churches and Temperance supporters cried censorship. The Concerned Parents stepped up their advertising, which claimed lounges and taverns increase alcoholism. The Packet & Times reversed a century of editorial policy and endorsed the vote for lounges, concluding Orillia needed lounges and licensed dining rooms to attract tourists. Temperance officially ended on April 24, 1967, when slightly more than the required 60 per cent of voters approved licensed lounges. A few months later, the first tavern sign went up on Jin Seto's Shangri-La Gardens. The licensed Terrace Room attracted a steady stream of businessmen enjoying the first public drink in Orillia since 1908, and the end of a long, dry season.

FISHING FOR A COUNTRY'S MYTHOLOGY

He has given Canada a sense of its own mythology — the drama of building a railway across the country, the tragedy men reach on the Great Lakes. He has survived struggles in his own life with a sense of humour, and he has become one of the country's most successful songwriters and performers. In all these efforts and achievements, one can see Orillia in Gordon Lightfoot. Ask him what he thinks about when he remembers Orillia and the answer is quick — fishing.

"I think about the North River. I was drawn to the countryside," said Lightfoot, fifty-seven, in an interview in the summer of 1995.

The Two-Timers: Orillians Terry Whelan and Gordon Lightfoot, in the early 1960s.

Photo by James Pauk

Born in 1938 and raised in a modest house, his boyhood in Orillia wasn't much different from many others. He fished; he hiked; he sang in the junior church choir at St. Paul's United Church. He performed in barbershop quartets, plays, and music festivals at the Opera House, and he formed bands with his friends.

"It was just a great place to grow up," he recalled.

The small-town life did not restrain him. It fed him. Good music teachers and plenty of opportunity to perform taught Lightfoot discipline and professionalism. He left in the 1960s, not to throw away the shackles of a small town, but to learn more about composing and writing.

He remembers Orillia now as a typical small town, with a heightened sense of humour because of the influence of Stephen Leacock. Lightfoot refuses to either worship or patronize the city. When he names the overwhelming trait of ordinary Orillians as kindness, it is a compliment. The kindness of others helped him through rough times, and he values it highly.

Lightfoot's relationship with the city has occasionally been strained, especially when a fundraiser has expected Lightfoot to perform simply because his hometown asks. He does perform for charities, for free, once or twice a decade to enthusiastic and sold-out audiences.

Some of his music comes from specific places around Orillia. There would not be the song "Pussywillows, Cattails" without Orillia and the North River, Lightfoot has said. And his music has a feel for home, which will always be partly in Orillia.

"When I go out and see The Narrows," said Lightfoot, "and look north up to Lake Couchiching, it feels like home."

Skid Watson, head of Orillia's YMCA and Camp Summerland, touched the lives of thousands of Canadian children. The eulogy at his funeral in 1984 was given by his nephew, Patrick Watson, a Canadian author and broadcaster. Watson went to Camp Summerland and recalled how Watson taught by example. "...the only instruction that I can remember receiving from his lips was "Wakee, wakee" early in the morning; and in the evening, quietly, "Don't forget your devotions boys.'".

BIG CITY DREAMS, SMALL TOWN REALITY

f everything had gone according to plan, by 1990 Orillia would have had a new community centre, a new hospital, one of several waterfront plazas, a huge downtown mall, a huge Highway 11 mall, a lot more jobs, and a lot more people.

So much for plans. Instead, throughout the 1970s and 1980s, Orillia suffered through bitter arguments, failed or derailed projects, fewer industrial jobs, stagnant population growth, and an undeveloped waterfront where the only thing expanding was a scrap yard. That being said, things weren't all that bad. The city gained a new college facility, some new companies, and a much improved downtown that has become a key to tourism. The local hockey club brought the city to its feet with two championships. But all the failed plans, hollow hoopla, and missed projections of greatness left Orillia with a hangover of cynicism about new ideas and projects, which lingered into the 1990s. The only constant in the years from 1970 to 1990 was the desire to grow out of being a small town, yet avoid growing into a city. That mixed-up wish left the city...mixed up.

The first sign of trouble came at the start of the decade in a provincial plan for the growth of Southern Ontario. The Toronto Centred Plan, released June 5, 1970, after months of discussion, focused on the roles of Toronto and the communities around it. The plan suggested communities such as Barrie and Midland grow as industrial centres. Orillia? It was best suited for recreation and parkland, as one government spokesmen said, a place for horseback riding and snowmobiling. "For Orillia, it's a blueprint of doom," The Packet & Times declared. "The plan sentences Orillia to a lifetime as the centre of a playground for the idle rich from Metro..." An infuriated Mayor David Brown vowed, "We will fight like hell." In public meetings, local politicians reminded provincial bureaucrats and cabinet ministers Orillia had already proven itself a successful industrial city. The city sent off an official response to the Toronto Centred Plan, calling its conclusions false and its implications for Orillia dangerous. Orillia had proved through hard work, imagination, and determination industry could and would locate here, said the city report. Angry city officials said retailers and professionals in the city were suddenly reluctant to expand because of the stigma the report gave Orillia. Reports come and go, and in the 1970s and 1980s especially, one report was hardly printed before another put it out of date. Yet in Orillia there is a suspicion the Toronto Centred Plan did hurt the city, at least for a while. Developers and company owners looking to expand likely did consult the plan, an important one in Queen's Park. And that plan certainly discouraged them from moving to Orillia. The plan proved so controversial, its recommendations were dropped. But Orillians suddenly had a bad feeling about their standing in the rest of the province.

It would get worse. In 1975, a CBC television crew filmed a documentary called "Orillia, Our Town." The CBC focused on fifteen people in Orillia, basing their look at small-town life on the Thorton Wilder play, Our Town. The ninety-minute documentary accented Orillia's quaintness and manufactured some of its own. The soundtrack ambled along on barbershop quartets, Movietone music, and ragtime, and the camera focused mainly on old salts and the salt of the earth. Old home movies were cut into shots of empty streets. Old cars, old factories, old people, and the old theme of a nervous bride and groom approaching their wedding day. As a look at ordinary people's hopes and dreams, "Orillia, Our Town" worked fine. As a mirror held to a nervous, young city hoping to attract suitors, it was a distorted disaster.

The show was first aired to a crowd at the Opera House, which gave it fair reviews. But when "Orillia, Our Town" was shown on television coast to coast March 19, other Orillians getting a first look at it were horrified. Hundreds called the mayor's office, the Packet & Times, radio station CFOR and Conservative MP Dr. P.B. Rynard's office. None were too happy, and many echoed the comments of CFOR announcer Rusty Draper: "We've been made fools of in the eyes of Canadians." Letters to the editor in The Packet & Times carried Orillians' complaints: The documentary showed nothing of Orillia's growth or energy. Orillia was depicted as Dullsville with a capital D. Where were the new buildings, the prominent people, the heroes, people under forty-five? How could anyone think Orillia was still Mariposa?

Actually, all anyone had to do was look around. At the same time some Orillians were complaining that outsiders were making the city look like Mariposa, others were invoking the myth of Mariposa to make sure Orillia didn't look too much like a city. Their fears focused on high-rises and they made the choice clear to Orillia: the city could have Homes or High Rise. The group by that name forced the city into a rollicking and mud-slinging debate on the future of Orillia. Members of the group take credit for the preservation of the city's church spire and municipal tower skyline, and with good reason.

Development-hungry city politicians in the early 1970s had opened the door to builders. The planning board and council had approved a few eight- and seven-storey apartment buildings without much opposition. But in 1973, a handful of influential and wary north ward residents heard rumours an apartment complex proposed for their neighbourhood, on the southwest corner of Laclie Street and Fitton's Road, was going to be eight and twelve storeys high.

After a bit of a tangle with the city's planning department, which appeared reluctant to give out too much information, the residents learned that the buildings were indeed going to reach the 120-foot mark. The residents happened to be leading members of the Orillia Historical Society and the Orillia Chapter of the Ontario Architectural Conservancy. Jay Cody, president of the Historical Society, made a short but controversial presentation to council January 15, 1973. He suggested the planning department did not want residents to know about the height of the new buildings and that council members should declare any interests they had in building developments. Cody raised several questions about the effects of high-rises on sewage, traffic and the health of residents. Several Toronto

urban planners were claiming that high-rises led to crime, a breakdown of community, and did not make much money for landlords. Supporters of high-rise development argued that the city needed more housing. After all, the population was expected to reach 40,000 people by 1985.

But the high-rise debate really centred on one issue: Orillia's image.

"I'm here on a bigger mission...to keep this place like Mariposa," stated Doug Sneyd, leader of Homes or High Rise.

The North Warders took their worries to the streets, and in no time had 2,500 names on a petition against the high rise. The city had a bylaw restricting buildings to thirty-five feet in height, passed many years earlier when fire fighting equipment could reach only that high. But that bylaw did not cover the area annexed by the city in 1967.

Supporters of the high-rises argued Orillia needed more rental units, and that the well-off Homes or High Rise members living in the north ward were simply worried about their property values declining if apartment buildings were erected in the neighbourhood. Sitting before council were five plans for apartment buildings, and aldermen were not keen on turning down developers or their tax dollars. Even doctors for the Simcoe County Health Unit joined the fray, telling the city's planning board that high-density apartment buildings caused an increase in mental problems and offered little space or imagination for children.

The two-year fight over the high-rises raised all the questions and prejudices that surfaced, not always at the same time, when Orillians tangled over their future. Who had the right to speak for Orillians? The longer one's family had lived in Orillia, the more credence one's arguments received. Many of the opponents to high-rises had moved here from Toronto to escape city life. A lot of them had settled in the peaceful north ward. That gave high-rise supporters a couple of weapons. How dare outsiders, rich outsiders, tell us how to run our city? "It amazes me all the people who move here from the big city and retired ones who move here don't think we should think like a city but like Stephen Leacock's so-called little sunshine town," wrote one resident to the editor of The Packet & Times. Then Stephen Lewis, leader of the Ontario New Democratic Party, publicly stated his opposition to high rise development in Orillia. That put high rise supporters into a frenzy. Not only was Lewis from Toronto, but he was a politician. And not only was he a politician, but he was with the New Democrats. "Who does Stephen Lewis think he is trying to tell us how to live in Orillia?" asked one letter to the editor. Homes or High Rise, though, had gained support throughout the city.

The petition of 2,500 names had several hundred from the south and west wards. "It just happens that I live in an $8,000 home in the south ward and I am sure that it is as dear to me as those lodgings are to the folks over on the lakeshore. I don't want a high rise next to my home!" read one letter to the editor, signed by an "Old Low-Downer."

As the debate continued throughout 1973, the two sides became more determined. Homes or High Rise spelled out its fears in a letter to Ontario treasurer John White. Because there was no official plan for the annexed land, residents had no right to appeal a development to the Ontario Municipal Board, said Homes or High Rise. A few days later, White's ministry sent a letter to the city planning board suggesting the city put some kind of interim planning controls on the annexed land, or the province might. Homes or High Rise threatened to take the issue to the Ontario Municipal Board if council did not act quickly. In March, council agreed to make developers wishing to build over the thirty-five foot limit in the annexed area apply for a site zoning bylaw. That meant residents had the right to appeal any development to the Ontario Municipal Board.

Homes or High Rise did not stop there, and throughout 1973 won and lost several battles. Council refused to limit development in the annexed area to single-family dwellings under thirty-five feet, but turned down one application for an eight-storey apartment. As opposition grew, few high-rises were built.

Council finally got its official plan back from the province, and began considering an overall zoning bylaw for the annexed land. Opposition to high-rises mounted, and five other ratepayer groups joined Homes or High Rise in calling for height restrictions. But council voted 6-2 on May 18, 1974 against putting a limit on building height in its zoning bylaw. Homes or High Rise had one chance left. The final vote on the zoning bylaw would not take place until June. By then, eight ratepayer groups, including Homes or High Rise, had joined in one association to fight the high-rises. The groups warned aldermen to change their votes or face defeat in the next election. A poll conducted by The Packet & Times showed 60.4 per cent in favor of height restrictions. "Orillia's a sunshine town, keep it that way," said one resident polled by the newspaper. The pressure worked. In July, the planning board recommended the thirty-five

foot height restriction be placed on development throughout the city. Council agreed, and put the restriction in its new zoning bylaw. But the zoning bylaw still gave council the flexibility to ignore the height restriction if it pleased.

That flexibility in the bylaw encouraged developers to continue planning taller buildings. That forced Homes or High Rise into Ontario Municipal Board battles on individual developments. Although they won only a partial battle politically, the leaders of Homes or High Rise point out today that there are few high-rises in the city, and none in areas that might block views of the lake. Few high-rises actually went up over the next few years.

But the issue did not go away. In August, 1978, council lifted the restriction in the downtown core to approve plans for a ten-storey, ninety-four-unit apartment building behind City Hall on the site of a former creamery. The proposal was backed by influential Toronto developers Mike Huang and Bela Danczky. But in Orillia, visions of glass and steel boxes competing for space with the city's spires, treetops, and church steeples arose. So did another opposition group, this time called Save Our City. At eighty-nine feet high, the ten-storey apartment building would be a foot higher than the Opera House spires, said opponents. They marched in front of the Opera House on Saturdays, hanging a balloon in the sky above the heritage building to show high how the apartment building would be. That debate landed in front of the Ontario Municipal Board. The board ruled in 1979 that council had the right to develop the downtown as it saw saw fit, in spite of the thirty-five-foot height restriction. Rising interest rates and vacancy rates did what the protesters could not, forcing the developer to limit the apartment to seven storeys.

The high-rise battle and the furore over the CBC show highlighted the city's split personality: half the time looking to shed its Mariposa image and move on, half the time running back to it. Ironically, the city's biggest success in the 1970s came when Orillians returned to the past, in order to get ahead.

By the 1970s, Orillia's downtown was suffering a little from age and the attraction of suburban malls in neighbouring centres such as Barrie. Downtown was hardly dying, and you could still buy everything from hardware to women's clothing within a few blocks. But downtown merchants and professionals figured they had better do something before a

Downtown merchants turned Mississaga Street from West to Peter streets into a pedestrian mall for a couple of summers in the 1970s. Temporary planters and even a small fountain were put up to give pedestrians a little scenery. The Mariposa Mall only lasted two years, but it inspired merchants to think about revitalizing the core.

The Packet & Times

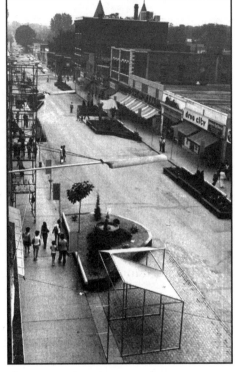

boxes and, of course, storefronts. It was called the Mariposa Mall and was all very pleasant for two years, 1974 and 1975. But merchants soon learned shoppers wanted parking more than flower boxes. A shopper heading to a mall will park a kilometre away from the entrance without a thought. However, a shopper heading downtown wants to park in front of his or her chosen store, or at least within sight of it. Operation Pride ended when too many people complained about merchants messing with their main street and too many merchants complained about losing their customers.

Downtown merchants and other businessmen agreed in 1975 to start a $3.5 million, five-year improvement of the city core. The work turned Orillia's downtown into a more pleasant place to shop. A plan to build an civic centre and amphitheatre beside the Opera House was abandoned.

The Packet & Times

mall moved into the city. Former Conservative cabinet minister Doug Lewis, then a lawyer looking for ways to make his mark, started promoting the Norwich Plan, based on the Norwich Insurance Company of England. That plan called for the painting of brick buildings in a variety of colours to brighten up a city's downtown. With the help of some downtown merchants and professionals, Lewis convinced landlords and tenants to go along with the idea. In retrospect, even supporters of the plan wonder if painting buildings from the 1800s was such a good idea. But the colouring of the downtown did bring downtown merchants, landlords, and professionals, such as lawyers and bankers, together.

The Norwich Plan gave birth to another proposal, with the typically 1970s boosterish name, Operation Pride. So proud were downtowners, they closed off the main street, Mississaga, from Peter to West for two months in the summer to give shoppers time to stroll under canopies and by flower

But the downtown boosters weren't through yet. A few of them discovered a little used part of Ontario's Municipal Act that allowed municipal councils to appoint a board to manage downtowns and provided provincial money for capital projects. Toronto's Bloor Street West had already received money, and Orillia decided to follow that lead. The downtowners set up a management board in 1975, created a business improvement area, and hired a consultant to draw up plans. About thirty members of the Downtown Management Board gave unanimous approval for a $3.8-million, five-year revitalization. The money came from downtown landlords and the province. Over the next two decades, Orillia's downtown changed from the typical cement and concrete, straight and square fashion of the 1950s to a more comfortable-looking blend of cobblestones, benches, flowers, planters, and decorative lighting. Left behind because of dwindling finances was a proposed civic centre stretching from city hall to the Opera House, which would have included an amphitheatre and public plaza.

The redevelopment occurred just in time. The Orillia Square Mall opened up in November 1975, and the economy of the downtown began to hurt soon after. From 1977 to 1978, retail sales in the downtown dropped $20 million as several stores closed. Even some of the oldtime stores began to close. Yet throughout the recession of the early 1980s, downtown redevelopment continued. And it was about the only major development in the 1970s that worked.

For a brief heady period in the middle of the decade, Orillia had two suitors romancing it at the same time with promises of giant commercial developments. By playing its cards right, the city lost both of them. The first proposal came from a Toronto development group called Willmore-Trizec in May 1974. Trizec had built the Yorkdale shopping mall and had plans to put up a 300,000-square-foot shopping centre and 558-unit housing subdivision on a site southwest of Highway 11 and the Coldwater Road. The developers promised the mall would create 400 to 500 new jobs. At the first council meeting on the proposal, spectators crowded into the packed council chambers cheered for the development and booed anyone speaking against it. Twenty years later, city council did backflips in an effort to get a developer to build a mall on the same site, but in the 1970s, council held a little more tightly to the dream that industry would someday come to its senses and move to Orillia. The land Willmore-Trizec owned was zoned industrial. And some council members thought it should stay industrial to entice new firms to the city.

A few days after the Trizec proposal, the real estate arm of Canadian Pacific, Marathon Realty, unveiled its plan to build an enclosed mall, hotel, marina, and community civic centre on twelve acres of downtown waterfront. That project would create a minimum of 300 jobs, the developers promised. At the first council meeting on the proposal, spectators crowded into the packed council chambers cheered for this development too, and booed anyone speaking against it.

Each proposal promised a major department store. It appeared Orillia was finally going to boom. The trouble was, with the Orillia Square Mall going up, there was room in town for only one more big player. Marathon immediately asked council to oppose any other large retail projects — in other words, Trizec. As a new council began to consider the two proposals in January 1975, The Packet & Times released a poll showing most Orillians favoured the Marathon development on the waterfront. The Trizec plan would pull shoppers away from the downtown, while the Marathon plan would draw them into the core. In spring, the Chamber of Commerce voted 31-5 in favor of Marathon, partly to keep the Trizec land industrial. Yet another newly formed citizens' group, Heart of Orillia, also backed the Marathon proposal.

But Mayor Frank Dolcort suggested Marathon wanted a monopoly and, in what some aldermen called a last-minute surprise vote, council approved an amendment to its official plan to allow the Trizec proposal to go ahead. Marathon asked for at least a hold on development until it completed a feasibility study on the proposal. At the same June, 1975 meeting, council turned down the Marathon request and hired a consultant to prepare its official plan amendment for the Trizec development. A month later, Marathon said so long to Orillia. Council continued with the plan to develop the land across Highway 11 with Trizec. But after a year of study, the consultant concluded Orillia could not support another commercial mall such as Trizec's, and the city should concentrate on developing, what else?, the downtown core. The city kept that study secret for a month or two, but it could not stop the inevitable. After the study became public, Trizec said so long, too.

That was the way it went in the 1970s and 1980s in Orillia. Huge development plans drew huge headlines, and after a few years of excitement nothing happened. In 1972 and again in 1980, two different developers announced plans to put up commercial complexes on the Tudhope Block. Primesite Developments' 1980 plan was stunning in its immensity. Wiping out twenty-six businesses, including three major industrial employers, five residential units, a church, a bus terminal, and three vacant offices, the commercial plaza would have taken in two blocks bounded by Mississaga Street West, Barrie Road, Andrew Street, and West Street. Only the new Canadian Imperial Bank of Commerce at the corner of Mississaga and West streets would have survived. Such was the optimism only months before the

The sun, the lake, the Opera House, and, of course, Samuel de Champlain in a plume-feathered cap playing a bagpipe shaped like a perch. The 133 entries for the design of Orillia's flag in a 1984 contest covered all of the city's symbols and landmarks. The entry that combined the French explorer, the Scottish heritage and the annual Perch Festival did not win. Orillia resident Don Tunstall won the contest with his design, which represents summer and winter in the city. The flag that flies over city hall is centred by a two-sided sun - the sharp points on its right symbolizing winter and the wavy ones on its left symbolizing summer. The blue waves and green top and bottom sections suggest summer and the white waves suggest winter. The meeting of the waves at the sun symbolize Orillia's location on lakes Couchiching and Simcoe.

Courtesy of Phyllis Roberts

peaked in workforce strength in the late 1970s. But the mining industry, which gave business to Orillia foundries, went flat, and the jobs began to disappear. The recessions of the 1980s and 1990s did even worse damage. By 1995, membership in the United Steelworkers Union had dropped so far, the union sold its hall on Gill Street. The population growth of the city also slowed to a crawl, moving up only 2.16 per cent from 1971 to 1976.

But in Orillia, you can't keep a good scheme down for long. Once the recession of the early 1980s was over, a flotilla of proposals to make Orillia unique and wonderful again jostled for the public and politicians' favour. With the downtown being re-developed, and malls out of the question for years, attention turned again to the waterfront. Many residents were angry the city had let Marathon slip away and wanted the mess of old boathouses and a scrapyard owned by the intractable Max Schachter cleaned up. A team made up of the province, the city, and local businessmen seemed eager to comply in 1981. Conservative MPP Al McLean announced the province would hand over $3 million to Orillia for a waterfront marina, on the condition the city assemble the land and the private sector build a hotel. City businessman Ralph Cipolla and his partners in a company called Oldco owned some of the land, and the city encouraged them to work on a proposed convention centre/hotel. The city and the company signed a deal in 1984 to sell their separate parcels of property to a parent company called Newco. That company was made up of Oldco partners, city officials, the city's Economic Development Commission, and immigrant investors grouped together in the Orillia Development Corporation. The Orillia Development Corporation, working with the federal government, had attracted seventeen foreign investors to Canada, offering each one landed immigrant status for a $100,000 investment. "In 40 years in business I don't think I've ever seen a project so complicated and complex," said Orillia alderman Jack Andre. "It's a consultant's, lawyers' and accountants' paradise."

The province handed over half the money, which the city used for a 130-slip marina. The other half was to come with the construction of the hotel. The federal government jumped in with its $800,000 worth in 1984, building a breakwater to protect the slips and the proposed hotel. That was as straightforward as things got. The deal between the city and the developers began to fall apart. Newco, the parent company, hired a consulting firm to look at waterfront development and concluded the costs

recession hit. Two years later, that proposal too was dead. Primesite could not find a major department store for a tenant and scaled down the plan to a $7.7 million mall. Council refused to allow a small commercial plaza that would compete with, rather than enhance, existing stores downtown.

The failure of the huge commercial ventures grabbed the headlines, but none of the proposals were solid or realistic. And there was worse news, that didn't get the same attention. The city's industrial base was shrinking, especially in relation to the population. In 1966, there were seven Orillia companies with more than 100 employees. By 1982, there were five companies with more than 100 employees, showing a decline in the best-paying, unionized factory jobs. Some of the companies, such as Dorr-Oliver-Long (once the E. Long Ltd) and Fahramet (formerly Fahralloy)

Orillia's waterfront underwent further changes in the 1980s. In 1985, the municipal, provincial and federal governments joined to build a marina and breakwater at Centennial Park. Workers drove steel piling along the park to widen the shoreline by about three feet and allow the construction of a boardwalk.

Courtesy of Don Hunter

of developing the land were too high to make any project feasible. City officials and the immigrant investors balked at giving Cipolla and his partners $800,000 in cash and twenty-eight shares in Newco, worth another $700,000, for their property. The remaining members of Newco tried to buy the city's land but that deal fell apart too.

Nothing seemed easy in Orillia in the 1980s. Even championships in sports seemed to draw trouble. The Orillia Terriers won the Senior A Allan Cup in 1972, and the Orillia Travelways won the Centennial Cup in 1985. The sudden closure of the city's community centre in 1986 disrupted the season of the defending champions, and sparked a fight that left a bitter taste in opponents' mouths ten years later. And it became a defining round between those in Orillia who resist spending tax dollars and those who encourage it.

Concern surfaced in the mid-1980s that the community centre, the pride of volunteers and symbol of community, was falling apart. Building and fire codes had changed since the 1950s and since renovations to the building in 1970. A study in the late 1970s gave the arena another five years.

Some Orillia residents tried to persuade city council to abandon plans to build eight-foot high berms between Centennial Drive and Lake Couchiching in 1985. Seniors argued that they could not see the lake while driving by. Alderman Myrtle Bowlen, a long-time opponent of high buildings, found nothing wrong with the berms. People should get out of their cars and walk if they want to enjoy the park's beauty, she suggested. Council stuck to its original plans, which called for berms to hide the road from the waterfront. The tempest in a teapot prompted cartoonist Don Evans to name the berms "Mariposa's Mountain High"

Courtesy of Don Evans and the Simcoe County Archives

Two Orillia hockey teams won national championships in the 1970s and 1980s. The Orillia Terriers won the Allan Cup, the senior championship, in 1973. The Orillia Travelways won the Junior A Centennial Cup in 1985. More than 2,000 fans crowded into the Community Centre watched the Travelways skate a victory lap. In the middle of playoffs a year later, the defending champions were suddenly left without an arena to play in.

Courtesy of Mike Dodd

It seemed likely in 1985 the arena needed work. The city hired consulting firm Proctor & Redfern to examine the arena in the fall of 1985. By March the next year, Mayor Ted Emond began warning the public that the arena might have to be shut down and worried aloud that Orillia might have to build a new one.

Emond had already been meeting privately with investors about building a new arena, and his warnings may have been testing the public for support of a new building. Yet no one expected the dramatic announcement that came March 12, 1986. Travelways coach Gary Marsh arrived at the arena at 4:30 p.m. to prepare for a playoff game only to find the doors locked. The first look at the consultant's report the night before had prompted council to close the centre immediately. The report concluded the arena was safer than it ever was, but it still failed to meet building and fire codes. Nervous about the building's safety and fearing potential lawsuits, council locked the doors. It was not a popular decision among council members, and Orillia's sports fans couldn't believe it. The closure forced the Travelways to play home games in Gravenhurst and put hundreds of minor hockey players on the bench. Summer lacrosse and ball hockey leagues had nowhere to go. Community groups that used the centre for fundraisers had to look elsewhere. Angriest of all were the volunteers who built the centre. How could an arena last thirty-five years without any problems then be shut down in a day? they wondered. If it was so unsafe, why did city staff let the report sit on the shelf for a week before council saw it, a week in which 600 people attended a Travelways game?

Council began considering building a new arena. But Alderman Clayt French, who had voted against the closure, insisted a committee be set up to look into the arena issue. French told council in May his own survey showed Orillians favoured rebuilding the old arena by nine to one. He persuaded council to shelve fledgling plans for a new community centre and rebuild the old one for $500,000, with an opening expected in October.

Mayor Ted Emond and Alderman Jerry Wink argued council should build a new centre instead, calling the $500,000 estimate ridiculously low. They were right. The only company that bid for the repairs would have charged $970,000. The city approached three firms to see if they could at least repair the arena's trusses for about $500,000. As fall approached, angry residents pressured council members for a solution. A slight majority of arena users favoured a quick fix instead of a new building, but they all criticized council's lack of direction. The big players, the Junior A club and

Doug Leigh's Mariposa School of Skating, called for a new arena. But minor hockey and lacrosse officials wanted the old one repaired. A group of residents calling themselves the Friends of the Community Centre volunteered their time to rebuild the old arena.

The new estimates for the repair work, about $700,000, solved nothing. A report from a second council arena committee said it would cost $1.3 million to fix the old arena properly and about $3.5 million to build a new one on the same site, with government grants available for either project. A third proposal would tear down the walls and roof of the centre and put up a temporary bubble for about $160,000.

The high costs of fixing the old building persuaded council to reverse its earlier decision and build a new centre. Meanwhile the roof of the old one would be torn off and a temporary bubble roof installed. The decision was hardly unanimous. Barely a week after the vote, supporters of the new arena and supporters of the old were caught by the press swearing at each other just after a council meeting ended. The normally civil Emond and French had a profanity-filled shouting match that prompted an alderman to suggest they carry on in a more appropriate setting, such as the washroom. Council was hardly a year into its term and already bitterly divided.

Things would get worse before they got better. Although council had approved the bubble plan in September, supporters of the old arena continued to lobby aldermen. The $160,000 price tag of the bubble turned out to be unrealistic and now stood at $300,000. Council reversed itself again — residents needed a scorecard by now to keep track of the game — and voted to repair the old arena with $800,000 of city money and $200,000 from the province. French led the fight again for the repairs, promising the arena would need no major renovations for many more years.

The Mariposa School of Skating and the Travelways Junior A team immediately announced they would look elsewhere to set up shop. The news rocked sports-hungry and image-sensitive Orillia. To small communities, Junior A hockey is the pinnacle of big-time sports. The Mariposa School of Skating, eighteen years in Orillia, and its star student Brian Orser were making Orillia famous. Coach Doug Leigh complained that the city's second ice surface, the Brian Orser arena, was too small for his expanding school. He needed an Olympic-sized ice surface. With a new arena now ten to fifteen years away, it was time to move. He opened negotiations with Barrie, the worst possible news for Orillians.

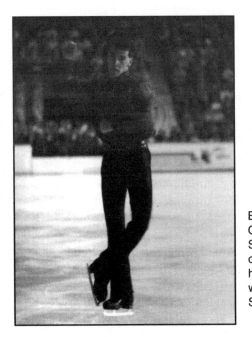

Brian Orser set off a celebration in Orillia when he won the World Figure Skating Championships in Cincinnati on March 16, 1987. Two months later, his coach, Doug Leigh, announced he was moving the Mariposa School of Skating to Barrie.

Courtesy of Mike Dodd, The Packet & Times

Travelways president Bob McFadden said he was counting on a new arena to attract more fans and pay off the team's operating deficit. The Travelways played in the lower tier of Junior A, but their success inspired hopes of a major Junior A club in the city. Those hints were enough to get council to set up yet another arena committee, this one to examine building a new arena even while the old one was being repaired. Time was running out. Soldiers' Memorial Hospital was about to launch a major fundraising campaign and no one believed the city would support both at the same time. Alderman French opposed spending $20,000 on the new arena study, saying the city could not afford a new arena, given its high debt. But by the time the old arena opened in February 1987, the momentum for a new arena had risen again. The Chamber of Commerce and Downtown Management Board backed the efforts to build a new arena. Businessmen said Leigh and his skating school brought about $1 million a year into the community, the same amount a new arena would likely cost taxpayers.

Several businessmen offered to renew pledges made a year ago for a new centre. Faced with that kind of pressure, council backed a new,

$5-million centre, which would have an Olympic-sized ice rink, 3,000 seats, and meeting and training rooms. The city would have to put up $1-million, a public fundraising campaign another $1.6-million to $2.6-million, and the provincial and federal governments the rest. So unified was council, Alderman French introduced the motion for the new arena. The enemy now was Barrie. The federal and provincial governments suggested only one of the two cities would get substantial funding for an arena that year. Federal sports minister Otto Jelinek sweetened the pot, saying his government wanted to establish a national skating school in the Simcoe County city that offered the best proposal. Barrie had the early edge. While Orillia council waffled about a new arena, Barrie's parks and recreation department wooed Doug Leigh and his skating school. Orillia's parks and recreation department took its direction from council, whereas Barrie's more aggressive city hall staff had been working behind the scenes for four months with Leigh.

Still, Orillia's eleventh hour fundraising campaign got off to a grand start, with business leaders committing their resources to the effort. Longtime hockey backer Bill Smith began negotiations with the Ontario Hockey League to bring a Major Junior A team to Orillia. Leigh continued to negotiate with Barrie, or as some angry Orillia residents claimed, continued to play the two cities against each other for the best deal. Through 1987, the competing arena campaigns, especially Leigh's role, riveted the city. In May, Leigh delivered the bad news — he was taking his school to Barrie. Orillia moaned. Barrie celebrated. It seemed to Orillians once again that Barrie got everything. In the gnashing of teeth and pointing of fingers, a few people suggested that Leigh had no real intention of staying in Orillia. Shortly after sparking the campaign for a new arena in Orillia, Leigh had privately signed a letter of intent with Barrie. The Orillia arena would have been larger than Barrie's, but the bigger city to the south offered Leigh a better financial incentive and proximity to Toronto and national media.

Leigh's decision damaged Orillia's pride. Residents believed they had done what Leigh wanted — agree to build a new arena — yet he still spurned his family of the past eighteen years. Mayor Emond criticized Barrie for spending $1-million in taxpayers' money to lure an industry from a neighbour. Watching Leigh build the most successful figure skating school in the country, with Elvis Stoyko following Orser's success, was difficult for Orillia sports fans and businessmen. His departure and official signing with

Barrie in July 1987 threw the new Orillia arena into question again. The province contributed about $900,000 to the arena in July, but opposition to a new centre, led again by French, resurfaced.

The bad news for arena supporters came in March 1988, almost two years to the day the old arena was closed. A consultant's study determined Orillia could not raise the $3.5 million for an arena in a fundraising drive, mainly because the hospital campaign had begun. The good news was the city might be able to raise $2-million, and get the rest from the federal government, the report concluded. That was good enough for deputy mayor Jerry Wink, the biggest supporter of a new arena. But the consultant's recommendations sparked a whole new debate. The report concluded the arena had a lot of support, but French argued an influential minority had biased the consultants. A 5-4 council vote kept the arena project on track. Alderman Geoff Hewett, French's ally up to now, voted for the arena. Mayor Emond cast the deciding vote, but made it clear any new arena depended on getting $1.5-million from the federal government. The city applied for the money through the local community futures board, which determined which city projects should get federal money. Two other groups were looking for money, the Orillia Heritage Centre, which hoped to build a huge museum on the waterfront, and the CN Station committee, looking to renovate the old station on Front Street. The board turned the arena down. After three years of nasty arguments and several reversals, the entire term of council, a new arena was dead. For his efforts in defeating the new arena proposals, Alderman French had the old community centre unofficially named after him. Residents who shiver in the cold seats call the arena French's folly.

The arena debate set up a battle for the next election between those who wanted to cut spending and those who wanted to spend to spur development. In 1988, Ontario's economy was still booming and Orillia seemed ready to bust out of its long economic hibernation. The city was moving to annex about 3,000 acres of land from Orillia Township, much of it for industrial expansion. Richmond Hill developer Lou Orsi was buying up thousands of acres around the city, obviously optimistic that Orillia would grow. A pro-development faction remained strong on city council. It was led by Mayor Ted Emond, architect behind many of the deals over the past few years. When Emond announced in 1988 he would not run for re-election, his hand-picked successor, Jerry Wink, appeared ready to walk into

the mayor's office. Instead, Wink found the doorway blocked by a six-foot, eleven-inch giant with a gravelly voice and his own large hands on the doorknob.

Born on the Chippewas of Rama reserve near Orillia, Arthur Shilling (1941-1986), lived a short but passionate life. The vivid colors, inward glances and broad yet complex strokes that became the trademarks of his work could as easily paint his life. Success came early, but so did trouble. At 29, he underwent heart surgery and he fought alcoholism for years. But he continued to work and build a native art gallery. His works hang in major galleries across Canada, including the Royal Ontario Museum and the McMichael Canadian Collection, celebrated for the native pride they rekindled and their unique beauty. Shilling was inducted posthumously into the Orillia Hall of Fame in 1989.

Courtesy of Kate Grigg

A SMALLER DREAM

Sometimes the smaller dreams have a better chance of coming true.

While the campaign for an Orillia university sputtered throughout the 1970s, a small adult training centre grew into Georgian College's Orillia campus. Under Mayor Isabel Post, the town and school board began adult training in 1963 to help the unemployed and those without proper business and industrial skills. Classes were held in the evenings at Orillia District Collegiate and Vocational Institute. The program grew, and in 1968 was moved to the town's Armoury on West Street, which was renamed the Adult Education Centre. A year later Georgian College of Applied Arts and Technology in Barrie took over the 22 courses and 400 students. As the program grew even more, the health classes had to be held in a storefront on Mississaga Street. By the 1970s, courses were taught at five locations in Orillia. The college's quest for a larger, permanent site ran into several barriers, including a city council reluctant to support the college at the expense of the proposed university. But in 1977, the province declared two parcels of land at the Huronia Regional Centre surplus. That cleared the way for Georgian to buy the land, and with a $3.6 million grant from the province, build a $2.6-million facility on Memorial Avenue. Mayor Frank Dolcourt turned the first sod at a November 3, 1978 ceremony, and Premier William Davis opened the campus April 18, 1980.

THE HOUSE THAT LOVE BUILT

Each time someone told the story about the kid in the house fire, his heroics grew. In no time at all, Joe Philion was a national hero and just as quickly destined for a fall.

Before the house fire on March 10, 1988, Philion was just another boy living in the small community of Cumberland Beach north of Orillia. That morning about 7 o'clock, Philion, fourteen, crashed through a rear window of his single-storey wood house, on fire from head to toe. Neighbours rolled him in the snow to put out the flames licking his body. He was the only one hurt. His mother, Linda Hawkins, had left earlier to drive husband Mike to work. His brother Danny escaped without burns. Philion was rushed to Soldiers' Memorial Hospital, where doctors took the first

When Joe Philion jumped out of his burning Cumberland Beach house in 1988, he became an instant media star. As he slowly overcame the complications of a serious burn, he faced more time in the public spotlight. The family split apart under the pressure, and Philion got a court order to keep his mother Linda, at his side in this photograph, out of his life.
The Packet & Times

steps toward an unlikely goal, saving his life. From there he was transferred to the Hospital for Sick Children in Toronto, where doctors gave him a 10 per cent chance of survival. A few days later, when Philion was transferred again, this time to the Shriners' Burn Centre in Boston, Massachusetts, his chances had risen to 25 per cent. For the next seven months, the frail boy underwent more than forty painful skin grafts, fought several bouts of pneumonia and blood infections, and returned time after time from the brink of death. Through the media hype and mistakes, the family disintegration, and the pain in Orillia that followed, one fact remained — it took Philion incredible courage and strength to survive.

His struggle seized the attention of people throughout Canada and the United States. Retired National Hockey League star Bobby Orr visited him in the hospital, and the truckers of Country Bob's Roadhouse in Binghampton, New York raised money for the family. Somehow the story grew in the Toronto media. Reports had Philion running through the flames to carry his brother to safety, then returning to the house, back through the flames, to look for his mother, before finally collapsing in the yard.

If the media hype bothered people in Cumberland Beach and Orillia, they did not show it at first. They raised money for a family trust fund in the hundred different ways all communities do — benefit dances, auctions, car washes, high school rallies, service club donations, companies and unions challenging other companies and unions. Canadian Music Express magazine donated the proceeds from its annual awards show, about $40,000, to the fund. Rock stars Phil Collins, Robert Plant, and Rod Stewart taped a get-well video. Toronto schoolteachers recorded a song, "Soaring Free," to raise money. By the time Philion returned to the Hospital for Sick Children in October 1988, his trust fund stood at $95,000.

It wasn't clear if the money could go to a new home for the family or would have to be used for rehabilitation. That got local contractor Ken McCann talking to his wife one day over lunch about Philion. They had healthy children and a nice house. Local contractors were doing well and should give something back to the community. Why couldn't Orillians simply build Philion a new house, McCann wondered. He appeared to be an unlikely leader for the project. The unassuming forty-four-year-old contractor had stuttered since birth and was uneasy speaking in large crowds. But two hours after lunch that day, he dropped a letter off at The Packet & Times, challenging everyone in the building trade to help build Philion a home.

The letter and an interview in The Packet sparked an immediate and overwhelming response. Within days, eighty carpenters, plumbers, painters, and companies had signed up. Over the winter, more than 500 skilled volunteers, with donations from more than 200 companies, built Philion and his family a two-storey, aluminum-sided house with a fire sprinkler system, smoke and fire alarms, air filtering, a new well, a handicapped elevator, and a whirlpool bath. People named it the House that Love Built. When Philion finally returned home on April 17, 1989, after 404 days in hospital and rehabilitation, Cumberland Beach and Orillia residents gave him a rousing welcome. The story should have ended there, with a little epilogue of how Philion continued his brave struggle to win back acceptance in school.

But the House that Love Built wasn't a home, and it began to crumble from the inside. Five months after the triumphant return, reporters discovered that Hawkins and Philion had slipped out of Cumberland Beach to a new home in British Columbia. Surprised Orillia residents wondered why they would leave the beautiful new home. Philion told the media he just wanted to be left alone. Living in Cumberland Beach, he had no peace. McCann and other residents tried to block the Hawkins from getting Philion's $100,000 trust fund, although Philion himself was going to take it over in nine months.

Two years later, in 1992, Philion was back in Cumberland Beach with his mother and natural father, Wally Herdman, a self-described born again Christian. The stories in the media, once about his courage and the family's love, turned instead to the soap opera being played out in Cumberland Beach. The next spring, Philion, now nineteen, went to court to get his mother out of his life. He told police she and Mike Hawkins had drained his trust fund. The happy family life portrayed in the media was a sham, Philion said. With little government money coming in, the House that Love Built had no phone or batteries for the smoke detectors, and the custom-built elevator had failed a safety inspection. Linda Hawkins agreed to sign a peace bond forbidding her from seeing or talking to Philion for a year. Two weeks later, Linda was back with her son. A month after that, April, 1993, both she and Herdman were out of the house, living in a local hotel.

After an OPP investigation concluded there was not enough evidence to lay charges against the Hawkinses, interest in the rollercoaster family life of Philion faded quickly. Philion married with little fanfare, and the wedding received little press. As the media decided this story was finished, Joe Philion finally began his new life.

THE OPERA HOUSE SCANDAL

It will forever be remembered as the Opera House scandal. But as time passes, the scent of scandal drifts away from the men charged with homosexual acts to the people in Orillia who so eager to condemn them.

City police stunned Orillia in September 1983 by charging thirty-two men with fifty-five acts of gross indecency, including homosexual activity, at a public washroom in the Orillia Opera House. In the summer some youths had complained of being harassed in the men's washroom, just off Mississaga Street. So city police set up hidden cameras in the washroom ceiling. At least one looked down directly into a cubicle, while another filmed the cubicle doors. Police said their films showed incidences of buggery, masturbation, and fellatio. Fifteen of the thirty-two charged were from Orillia, including three school teachers, but police refused to release their names because of the sensitive nature of the charges and because the investigation was continuing.

Richard Clarke, a lawyer representing seven of the charged, announced he would seek a permanent ban on publication. Clarke, later a respected judge, argued that publishing the names of the accused would hand them a far greater punishment than any court penalty could. Many Orillians and the media reacted to his plans with indignation. Most letter writers told The Packet & Times the names should be released. Some argued that everyone charged with a criminal act has his or her name published. High school law students pointed out the publishing of names protects both the accused and the victims. One man insisted that all males in Orillia would be suspected of being gay until the names were published. In all the arguments ran a strain of simple curiosity. Who was it? Who among us was homosexual?

At the September 16 Ontario Supreme Court hearing, Clarke argued the release of the accuseds' names would be a humiliating experience that could lead to marital stress, the loss of jobs, anguish, and even suicide. Affidavits from the accused, their wives, doctors, a social worker and a city alderman supported the ban on publication. Clarke and another defence lawyer, Bill Holdsworth, based their arguments on the new Charter of Rights and Freedoms. The rights of security to persons included the rights to protection of health and reputation, Clarke argued. Publishing the names would infringe on those rights. Lawyers for The Packet & Times, The Toronto Star, and the Toronto Sun argued a ban would infringe on the principles of equality in the Charter and the rights of the public to be informed.

Justice Joseph O'Brien agreed that the rights of the public were greater than those of the accused, and neither the standing of the accused nor the nature of the crime should ever protect the accused from the public.

"If there is no publicity, there is no justice," said Justice O'Brien.

The day after the ruling, The Packet & Times published the names of the accused on the front page below the story about the hearing. The nature of the police investigation, the charges, and the release of the names put Orillia in the crosshairs of civil liberties' spokesmen from Toronto. Michele Landsberg, a well-known Toronto Star columnist, publicly condemned the police, saying warnings would have been more appropriate than a full-scale investigation involving hidden cameras. Alan Borovoy, counsel for the Canadian Civil Liberties Association, appeared before city council and asked it to condemn the police force's action. How could the habits of gay men warrant police surveillance and the torment that accompanied the charges? he asked council. The investigation would not prevent such acts, only punish them, Borovoy argued. Council refused to discuss the issue at length because the matter was before the courts.

The scandal tested the city's character, and for some, that character was found wanting. The first of the accused to appear in court ran a gauntlet of twenty-five spectators lined on the street outside the Orillia courthouse. The crowd shouted insults at the accused men and identified those they knew for newspaper photographers. When the cameras were turned on them, they threatened the photographers. It was a carnival. One man followed two of the accused up the street and taunted them with insults. Several of the accused received threatening phone calls.

The fines the men received were hardly as severe as the punishment handed out by the community. Yet they had their defenders. Editorial writers and columnists urged that the men not be judged harshly. And the managing editor of The Packet & Times quit, partly because of the paper's position on the names. The investigation was the first of several similar ones across Ontario. It was an "Orillia first" many would just as soon forget.

THE END OF EXPANSION

It was a gamble that lost. Soldiers Memorial Hospital expanded several times since it was first built, its early, graceful facade overtaken by steel and concrete additions. When the province announced in 1987 that the hospital would receive a $30-million grant, further expansion seemed inevitable. But hospital officials did not celebrate. Instead, they turned down the money, saying it wasn't enough. Orillia needed more provincial money, about $45 million, to renovate the existing hospital and build a second facility, said the hospital board and management. What Orillia needed was a chronic care facility, to be built in the existing hospital, and a new building for acute care. Get back to us, hospital officials told the province and confidently began a fundraising campaign for a new hospital.

The new hospital campaign sought $15-million to go with the expected $45-million from the province. It derailed two other fundraising efforts in the city, one for a new arena and one for the Heritage Centre, a museum for antique cars and boats. Neither group wanted to go head-to-head with the hospital's drive for a new building.

The hospital raised about $5.8 million without any word from the province about the new building. Several times in 1988 and 1989, the province promised publicly that word about the funding would be coming within days. Meanwhile, ministry of health officials began giving hints the project was in trouble. They started promoting the idea that care in the home, not in the hospital, was the new direction of health care. In July 1989, health minister Elinor Caplan confirmed that the province was rethinking its earlier promises on paying for new beds in Ontario hospitals.

But Soldiers' Memorial Hospital pressed on, and the fundraising campaign went into high gear. Hospital officials learned in a December 1989 meeting that the province was dead set against two facilities in Orillia. Yet they did not tell the media or the public about that meeting, and the fundraising for a new hospital continued. Five months after the December meeting, the public learned through the hospital's annual report that the struggle for a new facility had been lost. To make matters worse, the province also withdrew the $30 million for the renovation to the existing hospital.

In the 1960s, as this photograph shows, expansion had begun to overwhelm the original Soldiers' Memorial Hospital. By 1987, nothing remained of the old hospital building, and there were plans to build a new facility. Hospital officials insisted they would get money from the province to build a new facility. Their plans were disappointed and they lost the chance to expand the existing hospital.

The Packet & Times

THE SPIRIT RETURNS

The handwritten label on the file of newspaper photographs showing John Palmer stepping into the mayor's office "Palmer takes charge," and underneath, in brackets "God help us all."

The world's tallest free-standing mayor, as a campaigner once called him, struck fear into friends and foe alike. Everything about Palmer was big - his voice, his stomping walk, his clothes, his furniture, his whimsy, his mistakes. His friends worried about the trouble he would get into and the pressure he would bring on himself as mayor. His foes worried about his mercurial temper and occasional blindness to persuasion.

Everyone wondered how he got elected. The bitterness over the community centre and development in the 1980s had driven apart city leaders. It seemed likely the split between those who favoured large-scale, city-backed growth and those who favoured things staying pretty much the same would carry over into the 1988 election. Mayor Ted Emond stepped down late in the term to give deputy mayor Jerry Wink a better chance of winning. A city businessman, Wink was in favor of spending money to make money. Council watchers picked him as the early favourite to win. When his opponent for mayor lumbered on to stage at the first all-candidates debate in the election, life in Orillia turned into a Leacock story. A former teacher and a newspaper columnist with a loyal following, Palmer had run for council in 1985 but pulled out because of heart problems. Two years later, he led a doomed battle against opening up the city landfill site to waste from townships. But as a mayoralty candidate in 1988, he remained an unknown element. Palmer changed that in his first public speech, accusing a shocked Wink of lying, of running the city with an elitist clique, and of drawing grandiose schemes out of a hatful of expensive consultants' studies. Palmer agreed the city needed more industry, but argued it first needed to protect the 1,500 jobs at the Huronia Regional Centre, which was under pressure to close. It was Ben Johnston and Wib Cramp all over again. His bombastic attacks on the past administration captured the favour of voters sick of the fights over a new arena fights and bitter over failed development plans. No one really expected Palmer to win, because it was hard to figure out whom he was trying to represent. In some ways he represented what has been called the old guard of the city, those who favor the status quo. Talk surfaced that he and other candidates had gained support of some Legion members in return for ensuring nothing be built on the land between the Legion and the shoreline of Lake Couchiching. But Palmer played on his style more than his substance. His own promises of a new style of open government took on less importance than his own personal style. He was big but vulnerable, temperamental but generous. Growing up as the biggest kid in the class made him the centre of attention, not all of it good, Palmer once recalled. Everyone wanted to take a shot at the big kid, so he was unwillingly thrust into many schoolyard fights. As big as he was, he knew vulnerability too, Palmer said. And he also knew how to defend himself.

That combination of strength and vulnerability helped get Palmer elected in 1988 and quickly into trouble. The fun began in the winter of 1989, appropriately enough, at the Stephen Leacock Home. The home was surrounded by bush and fields, part of Leacock's original property. Only part of the author's property had been obtained by the group that saved the home in the 1950s. In 1977, Lou Ruby had sold the rest, about twenty-eight acres, to the city. Ten years later the city asked developers for proposals to build a seniors' village on about eighteen acres of that property. The remaining ten acres would go to the Leacock Home. Not a peep of opposition was raised as council announced in the spring of 1988 that Versa-Care Ltd. of Cambridge had won the contract to develop the Leacock property. The development would provide $500,000 in taxes a year, $1 million in construction wages, $350,000 in improvements and services to the Leacock Home, and best of all, an immediate $1.5 million in city coffers. Versa-Care, an experienced developer and operator of seniors' complexes, planned to build a full-service seniors' community, with condos, apartment units, a lodge, and a nursing home. Palmer inherited this plum that seemed to please everyone. Days after he was elected, the first uneasy questions about the development arose. How close would the condos be to the Leacock Home? Would the complex destroy the peaceful nature of the grounds? Still confused by the answers, the Leacock Home board waited until January 1989 to express worries about the development's borders. It appeared the development would cut through the back of the Leacock Home property and destroy the line of cedars Leacock had planted to separate the formal back yard from the farm fields, and keep the servants out of sight of his guests. Suddenly six city residents started a campaign to stop the development. Palmer was furious. "The deal is made. When I say it's a deal, it's a deal," he told reporters. He called the opponents, the Committee to Protect the Leacock Home, a dishonest "self-appointed collection of grandstanders" whose objections were "totally stupid."

The fledgling committee refused to back down. "The land is beyond price," said leader Gwen Richardson, a transplanted Torontonian and teacher. Before long the city was split into two camps over the development and Leacock himself. All the bitterness about Leacock surfaced. He was nothing but a drunk and a nuisance, said some oldtimers. He was a genius, argued others. Palmer's style reached a fever peak, as he accused the home's board and its curator of working with the committee and threatened to cut off their funding. The committee came under fire for refusing to make the names of all its members public. One member, weekly newspaper columnist Rick Webster, charged city council with nothing less than a coverup over the shady deal. "Two city councils seem to have left their brains in bed," he wrote.

As winter turned to spring, and an appeal of the development headed to an Ontario Municipal Board hearing, the plot's twists and turns filled the front pages of the newspaper and the letters to the editor. One Leacock board member quit to join the committee to save the home, charging the board was nothing more than a social club that did not have the courage to bite the hand that fed it. Alderman Fayne Bullen's wife,

Vera, was chairman of the home board, complicating matters even more. Simcoe North MP Doug Lewis entered the fray and made a point of publicly refusing to help save the property. The board had done nothing to promote itself in twenty years and would not get his help now, said Lewis. Curator Jay Cody arranged a meeting with Lewis to talk about the federal government taking over the home, sparking another tempest at council. National media figures joined the fight. Humourist Gary Lautens, writer Lloyd Dennis, and McClelland and Stewart editor David Staines backed the Committee to Save the Home. Even an exasperated Palmer and an amused Richardson had to admit the battle was one of the craziest things they'd ever seen. "I wish Leacock was here to write about it," Richardson told reporters.

The Ontario Municipal Board hearing maintained the high emotions of the battle. Versa-Care planners called the Leacock property scrubby and garbage-filled. An emigre from Europe testified that as children, she and her sisters had huddled under the bedcovers reading Leacock's Sunshine Sketches of a Little Town and dreamed of someday living in Canada. Consultants and planners played down the significance of Leacock and the home. Writers and editors testified Leacock was the most popular Canadian writer in history. One resident presented his dog, named after a Leacock character, as evidence. The Ontario Municipal Board chairman took the rare step of visiting the home, where an angry planner assailed a photographer for taking pictures of the group.

Each day's hearing in the council chambers of the Opera House drew a packed house, which booed their villains and applauded their heroes. Crusty city lawyer Wharton "Rusty" Russell and Terry Hunter, lawyer for the Committee to Save the Home, attacked opposing witnesses with glee, rolling their eyes in scepticism at some remarks, playing the crowd, putting everything into a performance that had much fewer constraints than a courtroom proceeding. At stake were Leacock's archives, 100-year-old trees, and one of the few waterfront parks left in the city, argued committee witnesses, including editor Staines. At stake were hundreds of thousands of dollars and the city's credibility, argued city and Versa-Care witnesses. In spite of the emotional appeals, the issue came down to planning, and the Ontario Municipal Board ruled the city had followed its tangle of land-use plans correctly in allowing the development. Versa-Care was allowed to build.

As fierce as it was, the battle over the Versa-Care development was quickly overwhelmed by other controversies during Palmer's term as mayor. Over the next two years, council and Orillia grew even more divided. The budget-conscious, especially deputy mayor Clayt French, favoured slow growth and the maintenance of Orillia's small-town appeal, although not necessarily promoting that appeal to tourists. French opposed putting city money into an airport, and letting a developer build on the waterfront. More aggressive businessmen on council, led by Alderman Geoff Hewett, tried in vain to persuade council to put more city money into projects. Palmer generally favoured slow growth, but one could never tell where he stood. Reporters learned to put down their pens when they made their first call to the mayor in the morning. Often they woke him up and in his gravelly voice, Palmer made little sense. Only when an alarmed Palmer called back to find out what he had said did reporters take notes. Throughout council's

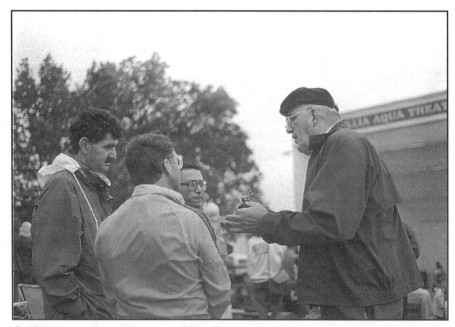

Orillia's seven-foot-tall mayor, John Palmer, insisted throughout the incinerator debate that the energy-from-waste plant would be safe, and waded into groups of opponents to argue his case.

The Packet & Times

term, French gathered more power. His biggest weapon against spending was the city's huge debt. French made a visit to the Packet's publisher each spring at budget time with the latest dire figures, just to make sure the newspaper understood the necessity of making cuts in spending. Tracing the city's debt is a difficult task. Several times in its history, the province had warned Orillia that its debt was too high. The costs of servicing the land annexed in 1967, and upgrading the water treatment and waste water plants had fueled the latest borrowing spree. As the industrial tax base shrunk over the years, it became harder for the city to keep up its infrastructure of sewage and water lines and roads without borrowing.

Given the economic squeeze, city council was pleased to announce in April, 1990 that it had agreed in principle to let a New Jersey waste company, Ogden Martin Systems Ltd., build a $500-million incinerator in the Sunshine City. Few controversies in Orillia's history raised as much anger, craziness, and bitterness as the proposed incinerator. It may have claimed the life of the mayor; it certainly wounded whatever trust the public had in its politicians.

Nothing prepared Orillia for the impact of the fight that first day. City council members had met Ogden Martin officials only three times before secretly approving the proposal. When they unanimously passed the public resolution welcoming the waste giant, aldermen from all camps praised the plan. The energy-from-waste plant would provide $1.5 million a year in business and property taxes and create 150 jobs. The plant's production of 75,000 kilowatts of electricity could slake the entire city's thirst for electricity. Businessmen and other community leaders applauded the plan. A few environmentalists condemned incineration, saying it produced toxic byproducts and discouraged recycling, but their voices were smothered by a chorus of approval. In those days in Orillia, finding a local environmentalist to comment taxed the resources of The Packet & Times newsroom. There just weren't many around. Besides, company pamphlets assured everyone that incineration was so safe, a person had a greater risk of getting sick from eating peanut butter sandwiches each day than living near an incinerator. The emissions would be cleaner than the air around the plant, they said. And for a couple of weeks, at least, Orillia residents took Ogden Martin at its word. At a public meeting and in letters to the editor, most people, even members of a group fighting a dump in a nearby quarry, backed the incinerator. It was easy to understand why. Orillia's landfill site sits on Lake Simcoe, and there were fears that contaminants might leak into the lake. An incinerator seemed to solve the worries over burying garbage.

Then quietly, almost unnoticed by the media, a few city residents began questioning incineration. A Packet reporter attended a meeting on incinerators in Toronto and reported the fears of environmentalists there. A few more letters to the editor appeared, and the group opposed to the quarry landfill, Citizens Against Metro Garbage, announced it was against incineration as well. If Palmer figured incineration would be an easy sell, he got a bit of a shock at a May luncheon of the Kiwanis Club, hardly the place where revolutions usually begin. Several Kiwanis Club members, businessmen mainly, pressed Palmer for assurances the incinerator would be clean and safe. In a typical Palmer reply, the mayor waved away opposition with his big hands and bigger statements.

"In a year, you'll forget it is there. From the outside, it will look like the local high schools. It is the way of the future."

From that day in May, 1990, the smouldering fears and opposition to the incinerator began to catch fire. A day later, both the Economic Development Commission and Citizens Against Metro Garbage hosted separate public information meetings on the incinerator. About 130 people listened with scepticism to Ogden Martin officials pitch their proposal, while 200 people listened attentively to Toronto environmentalists sound warnings about incineration. A new group, Stop Incineration Now, sprang up and drew 400 people to its inaugural meeting. One mother vowed, to thunderous applause, she would not let incineration ruin the health of city children. Palmer showed up briefly to tell the crowd he was hurt by talk that he wanted to harm children. The mayor was heading into this battle the same way he did in the Versa-Care issue, with his heart on his rolled-up sleeves and reputation on the line.

As opposition grew over the spring and summer, council dug in its heels. For the first time in a long time, council stuck together. At first, council members argued residents should wait for more information before making up their minds. But the more information and questions that arose, the more insistent council members became that they knew what was best. The city faced a garbage crisis, and a minority of rabble-rousers, with no better ideas, were making trouble, insisted council members.

In an unusual move for a tight-fisted Thomson newspaper, The Packet & Times sent two reporters to Indianapolis, Indiana, for a week to examine an Ogden Martin incinerator. In all the numbers, comments, descriptions and photographs they brought back, a simple photograph and a typographical error sent a chilling message to Orillians. After five days of negotiating, the two reporters had managed to get a tour of the ash site, where waste from the incineration was stored. Ogden Martin officials had claimed that incineration burns so cleanly that nothing is left but ash. Evidence of an incomplete burn could mean dioxins and other pollutants were released during incineration. At the ash site, reporter Mark Bisset and this author noticed a lot more than ash left over - grass, pieces of carpet, even bits of newspaper. With an official busy elsewhere, Bisset snapped a photograph of his colleague holding a clump of grass found in the ash. When the photograph appeared on the front page, it carried a sentence that was supposed to end in a question mark. Instead, in no uncertain terms, the photograph's caption officially proclaimed the grass was "a link between incineration and dioxins." Environmentalists seized the photograph as proof of their fears.

Still, dozens of protests and meetings with so-called experts on either side could not persuade a wary public that incineration was either totally bad or totally good. Tempers flared throughout June and July. About eighty high school students left their classes and persuaded Mayor Palmer to meet them in front of City Hall by pretending they wanted a civics lesson. Instead they greeted the mayor with chants and protest signs. An angry Palmer suggested he would shoot every one of them if they had skipped his class for such a protest, prompting a protest over his protest of their protest. Orillia had not seen this many demonstrations since the Homes or High Rise protests in the 1970s. Council members said they were called names, harassed, and phoned in the middle of the night with threats. Yet aldermen insisted only a minority opposed the incinerator and planned a public forum in August to present all the facts. Their train was derailed in mid-June, when rookie Alderman Josephine Martensson suddenly announced she was opposed to the incinerator because of the health risks. Her fellow council members charged Martensson with grandstanding and said she hadn't thought it through. At a council meeting a few weeks later, deputy mayor Clayt French told an alderman that Martensson should be kept out of all future meetings on the incinerator. Television microphones picked up the comment, sparking another uproar.

Then came the worst news of all for council. The Orillia Medical Society released a twenty-page report calling incineration harmful and dangerous. Council members sputtered that the doctors were using scare tactics, and their arguments began to border on the hysterical — the incinerator would promote health because of the parks the tax money would buy; the Japanese have lots of incinerators and they are more intelligent than we are. Perhaps council members could see that the doctors' report was the turning point. About 600 people gave Dr. Donald Philpott a standing ovation when he presented the report to the public June 27 at a high school gym. For the next week, doctors and nurses told their patients incineration was unhealthy.

At a Monday, July 9, council meeting, a volunteer group of pollsters presented council with the results of a random phone survey. About 75 per cent of 4,300 residents called were opposed to the incinerator. Ten per cent supported it and 15 per cent were undecided. The same night, Stop Incineration Now handed over a petition signed by 8,870 people against the incinerator. For the first time, council admitted there was no silent majority supporting the incinerator. Four days later, council voted to reject a deal with Ogden Martin. Council did not reject incineration as a way of dealing with city garbage, just the handling of Toronto's waste. Behind the scenes, Alderman Hewett had told council he was ready to publicly oppose incineration because of the overwhelming opposition to it. Faced with crumbling support within their own ranks, council members decided to save some face and kill the proposal.

It was hardly a unanimous decision.

"I'm so damn fed up with what they did," Palmer said. "They get someone yelling at them and they bend over and surrender." Some say Palmer never got over the incinerator debate. "I could find far more attractive ways to fall on my face," he told a reporter. A month later, Orillia's giant complained about pains in his leg and had to undergo surgery for two aneurysms, a weakening and ballooning of the arteries that can be fatal. His lungs collapsed once and congestion sent him back to hospital, but Palmer managed to make it home to Orillia in September, and showed some progress. His body never recovered from the strain of the operations. The city woke up Friday, September 28 to learn Palmer, 65, had died at 4 o'clock that morning. His heart had given out. Palmer's death shocked his friends and adversaries alike. The rumbling and rambling giant mayor seemed as if he would go on forever, and no one doubted his sincerity.

Many still blame the stress of his two years as mayor as the main reason for his illness and death. Palmer took every argument, off-hand remark, and news report to heart, and it was his heart that finally gave up.

The incinerator debate influenced Orillia in several other ways. The environmental movement born of the fight refused to fade away. Some Stop Incineration Now members formed Citizens Acting Now, a group that had helped force the city to adopt a waste management advisory council and a waste management plan that has made Orillia a leading recycler in Ontario. The life of the landfill site on Lake Simcoe was extended, thanks to the diversion of waste.

Palmer's death also cleared the arena for a full-scale battle over the shape of Orillia. Palmer was closer to deputy mayor French in philosophy, but his changing moods made it difficult for French, already in charge of the budget, to win every battle. When Palmer died, it was as if a distraction had been removed for the two most popular aldermen in the city - French and

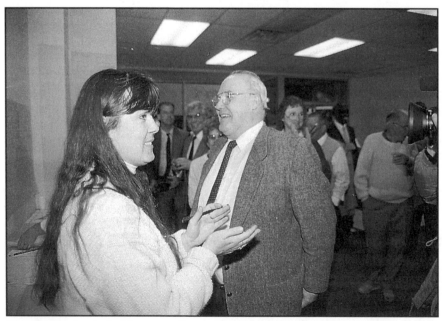

Tough talk about slashing spending and making the waterfront a park got Clayt French elected mayor in 1991. He won handily again in 1994, and with little opposition on both councils, directed the city's affairs with a firm hand.

The Packet & Times

Hewett. They immediately clashed over the waterfront. With Palmer as mayor, council had agreed to expropriate about two acres of the land owned by businessman Ralph Cipolla and his partners for a park. Cipolla was bitterly opposed to the expropriation, and it appeared the city was headed for a nasty fight. (The city's plan did go to an expropriation hearing, which it won. At the writing of this book, the dispute over the value of the land had not been settled.) Hewett disagreed with expropriation and fought for a mixed development, with a privately run hotel on half of the waterfront and a park on the other, with a public boardwalk in front of both. French and Hewett tangled over the waterfront all term, even as the slow process of expropriation continued. Hewett made halting expropriation the key platform of his run for mayor in 1991. French wore the mantle of the saviour of the waterfront for the public, although he had previously supported the Versa-Care development on the Leacock waterfront and expropriation ran counter to his chief platform, cutting city expenses. It was a nasty campaign, with each candidate throwing mud at the other, then complaining about it to the press. Each accused each other of representing, what else, but those old "special interests", and in a sense they were right. A member of the old guard and conservative, French had the support of many seniors opposed to waterfront development and spending of any kind. A member of a group of businessmen that met frequently to discuss city issues, Hewett had the support of younger leaders impatient to get on with expansion. Hewett lost mainly because his timing was bad, and people in Orillia trusted a business leader less than the grandfatherly French.

By 1991, the city's brief economic boom had died, and taxpayers no longer liked the idea of high spending. As it had been for many years, the average household income in Orillia was low, far behind Barrie's, Simcoe County's and Orillia Township (now the Township of Severn). The lower than average income was due in part to a large population of seniors on fixed incomes, but sixty per cent of the workforce had jobs in the two lowest paying sectors; tourism and retail, and trades. In a 1991 survey, residents put affordable housing and poverty at the top of a list of serious problems in the city. In the twelve months leading to the 1991 fall election, about 800 Orillians had lost their jobs. With that kind of outlook, and a recession deepening, residents gave French and his promise to cut taxes an overwhelming election win in 1991. Staying the course and ruffling few feathers earned French and many of his incumbent aldermen another win in 1994.

What is now the Sir Samuel Steele building at 30 Peter Street South has experienced many changes since it was first built in 1894 as the Orillia post office. The federal government paid $14,000 to build the post office, which was constructed by J.R. Eaton. The post office was remodelled in 1914, with a clock tower added. The building was changed again in 1956 when it was turned into a police station. The police moved out in 1977 and the building served a variety of purposes. The 1914 version, in this photograph, is roughly the building the Sir Sam Steele Art Gallery has made its home. A group of art lovers quietly put together the support to open the gallery in 1994. The gallery quickly became popular with city residents.

Several aldermen on those councils had been through the incinerator wars together, and the longer they served together, the more cohesive they became. With a powerful mayor at the head of council, a loyal core of aldermen, and a public nervous of spending, city council turned into a homogeneous group that did most of its business in private session. The debates in Orillia in the mid-1990s did not come from within council, but from the public and media. Those debates lacked the ferocity of the incinerator battle, and, without a business leader on council, the intensity of the waterfront fights.

For example, council decided in 1995 to disband the local police force and negotiate a contract with the Ontario Provincial Police to take over city policing. It wasn't the first time council had considered disbanding the force. In 1949, the town had briefly entertained the idea of having the Ontario Provincial Police take over policing to save money. This time, French's oft-repeated promise the move would save the city $800,000 persuaded the police board and council to disband the city force. A brief flare-up of public opposition fizzled under council's determination to save money. A small burst of public resentment over a new waterfront park fizzled just as quickly. Council had promised to hold a meeting on the proposed design of the park after expropriation was approved. The city began building the park without holding that meeting. When a meeting was finally held in the fall of 1995, months after an amphitheatre and trail had been built, it was too late for critics to have much of an impact.

The opening of the OPP general headquarters in 1995 spelled relief in Orillia. The headquarters provides relatively secure and high-paying jobs, plus $1 million a year to the city treasury.

The Packet & Times

Neither the city's leaders or its ordinary citizens had much to do with the start of the two largest developments of the 1990s - the building of the OPP headquarters and the native casino in Rama. The province decided in May 1990 to move the OPP headquarters and the administration department for the ministry of the solicitor general from several buildings throughout Metro Toronto to Orillia. The city's location at the junction of Highways 11 and 12 and the large property already owned by the province at the Huronia Regional Centre helped Orillia get the OPP headquarters. Orillia's leaders had little to do with the decision, besides welcoming the 900 employees and the more than $35-million a year payroll.

City council had even less to do with province's decision to allow the Chippewas of Rama First Nation to build and operate a casino and resort. The casino and resort are expected to bring thousands of jobs and millions of dollars to Orillia. But it was the Chippewas, not council, that made the deal happen. In fact, many council members first opposed the casino, finally approving it in a private session just before the province chose which band would get permission. This is not to say the councils of the 1990s have done nothing. With the help of the Economic Development Commission, council persuaded Hunter Enterprises, one of the city's larger industries, to build a new factory in the city instead of moving out of town. The deal showed signs of the support industries received in the early 1900s. The city bought the Hunter plant - the old Tudhope car factory - for $1 million and may turn it into a government/commercial centre. In a related deal, the city approved a developer's plan to build a huge mall across Highway 11, close to the site of the Trizec mall proposed in the 1970s. The developer agreed to pay for servicing of the land, annexed from Orillia Township in 1989. It appeared that development of Orillia West, as it was named, was finally going to happen. The original deal fell through late in 1995. While council and developers continued to negotiate a new deal, many in Orillia were left wondering if the city was jinxed when it came to commercial development.

None of these issues - the mall, the park on the waterfront -captured the public's interest or imagination. It left some to wonder what had happened to the Orillia Spirit that inspired great accomplishments and wild debates for the past 150 years. Was it dying? The answer came from two sources, with irony attached to each - that old eccentric Stephen Leacock and the Chippewas forced to leave Orillia more than 150 years earlier.

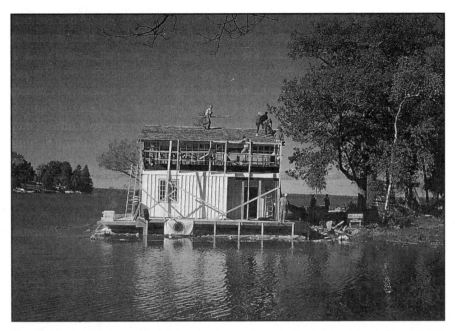

The Orillia Spirit returned in full force on a weekend in September 1995. About 5,000 people raised a replica of Stephen Leacock's boathouse.

The Packet & Times

went to city council. He stressed that no politicians would have to be involved and no public money spent. Council approved the plan. For the next nine months, Dykes and contractor Jim Storey signed up volunteers and construction companies, pressed the flesh at dozens of city functions, and cajoled the media into making the campaign a priority. The idea snowballed. Perhaps because few had seen it, the boathouse had always taken on a certain mystery for Orillians. Leacock often sought the quiet of his two-storey boathouse to write early in the morning. The image of the writer at his large table on the second floor, writing sentences that would delight the world, gave the small building more cachet than any ordinary boathouse.

And the reconstruction would be nothing ordinary, either. Organizers insisted the reconstruction be an old-fashioned barnraising, with entertainment, food, and the entire city invited out to lend a hand. More groups and donations came on board throughout the summer. Typically, a little doubt and scepticism arose. How could they build a boathouse in one

Leacock inspired one of Orillia's most unified moments in its history, in a typically simple way. C.H. Hale., J.B. Tudhope, Pete McGarvey, Ruth Jones, Sue Mulcahy, Mac Carter - they all launched their quests with a simple question: "Why don't we...?" So did Jim Dykes in 1994. Trying to sell his canteen service to the Leacock Museum, a naive Dykes asked to see the boathouse he had admired in Karsh photographs of Leacock at his Orillia summer home. He was told the boathouse had fallen into disrepair after Leacock's death and efforts to convince the politicians to help fix it had failed.

"Why don't we do it ourselves?" Dykes asked Leacock Museum curator Daphne Mainprize. He soon forgot he had asked, until several months later, when Mainprize told him the museum board was ready to hear his proposal. Dykes quickly put together a presentation for a January 1995 board meeting. His idea quickly received the board's approval. Dykes then

Orillia celebrated the 50th anniversary of VE-Day in May of 1995 with a ticker-tape parade down Mississaga Street and a sold-out, big band dance organized by The Packet & Times that rekindled memories and reflected the rebirth of the community's spirit.

weekend? Where was all the money going? Dykes dismissed the rumours and scepticism as last-minute nervousness on the part of Orillians. The weeks before September 9 and 10, construction crews readied the site. When the sun rose Saturday, September 9, a flat, concrete pad welcomed the first set of sleepy workers. When the sun set on Sunday, the boathouse was up. The sunny two-day "barnraising" drew about 5,000 adults and children to help out, watch, and celebrate. What made the accomplishment even greater was that it took place on Leacock's property. It was the first time since the home was bought that Orillians of all stripes shared the same opinion about the old drunk/genius - he was worth something. For many Orillians, it was the first time they had stepped on the Leacock property. The barnraising may have given Orillians a sense they own and are responsible for the home of their most famous citizen. It certainly gave them, for a weekend at least, a sense they own and a have responsibility for the Orillia Spirit.

That spirit was shown again the next year. Months after the Chippewas of Rama First Nation and Carnival Casinos began building a temporary casino, the Conservative provincial government ordered construction to stop. The government said it was nervous about proceeding without certain agreements signed, but the real reason behind the shutdown was the government's desire to change the financial arrangement. The previous NDP government had decided not to take a percentage of the revenues, in order to give Ontario's native bands more money. In that way, the province hoped to help the natives help themselves and avoid any sticky showdowns if native bands decided to set up their own casinos. The Conservatives decided to change the deal and demanded a twenty per cent share of gross revenues.

The provincial Conservatives had received nothing but the blessings of Orillians for the past sixty years. But shocked business leaders, would-be casino workers, merchants, and municipal politicians all cried foul. About 700 showed up to a news conference at the casino site to show their support, and dozens wrote letters to Conservative cabinet ministers in protest. About a month after the shutdown, the province and casino officials signed the outstanding agreements, and the province agreed to let construction resume while negotiating the stickier issue of revenue sharing. It was likely the first time since white settlers forced the Chippewas out of Orillia in 1836 that the two communities had united. While much of the incentive to do so was

money, the effect may run more deeply than the bottom line. Many reacted with disgust over the government's shutdown because it appeared that once again whites were trampling over natives. It appeared some Orillians were prepared to do battle against the government partly because of past wrongs, including their own city's. A casino is hardly the place to find spiritual satisfaction. To the same extent, Stephen Leacock is hardly the man to unite Orillians. Ironically, the casino may have been just be the place and Leacock just the man to rekindle the birth of the Orillia Spirit.

About 150 years after white settlers had the Chippewas moved to Rama, a proposed casino more or less united the two communities. The temporary Casino Rama features native artwork along its exterior walls.

The Packet & Times.

SOURCES

GENERAL

Bisset, Mark, 125 Years in Orillia, a special edition of The Packet & Times, June 27, 1992.

Brillinger, Isabel, The Orillia Hall of Fame, 25th Anniversary Booklet, The Orillia Hall of Fame Committee, 1989, Orillia, Ont.

The William Sword Frost Scrapbook, Volumes I, II, III, Appendices and Explanatory Notes by Leslie M. Frost, Orillia Public Library

Hale, C. H., Notes on general history of Orillia, 1957, in Orillia Public Library Orilliana collection

Ireton, Norah; Thomson, Ruth; Crooks, Grace, ed., Orillia Portraits Vol. 1, The Orillia Historical Society, 1966

Ironside, Allan, Anecdotes of Olde Orillia, ed. by J.C. Grossmith, The Orillia Historical Society, 1984

Ironside, Allan, Around Lake Couchiching Tour (unpublished) 1979, revised, 1981

Leitch, Adelaide, The Visible Past: The Pictorial History of Simcoe County The County of Simcoe, Ont. 1967

Newspapers - The Orillia Expositor, The Packet, The Times, The Packet & Times, The Newsletter

Rushton, Ted, Outline of an Orillia History, 1966 Copy 7, The Packet & Times, It Happened in Orillia, 125th anniversary edition, November, 1995

General source interviews
French, Clayt - March 1995
Hunter, Don - April, September, 1995
Jenkins, Don - March 1995
McGarvey, Pete - July 1995
Mulcahy, Sue - March, 1995

A GRAND VISION

Champlain, Samuel de, Journals of Samuel de Champlain, Vol. III, 1615–1618, ed. H.P. Biggar, University of Toronto Press, Toronto, 1971

Drury, E. C., All for a Beaver Hat, A History of Early Simcoe County, The Ryerson Press, Toronto, Ont. 1959

Hayes, John, Wilderness Mission, The Story of Sainte-Marie-Among the-Hurons, The Ryerson Press, Toronto, 1969

The Jesuit Relations and Allied Documents, Vols. XXXIV and XXXV ed. Rueben Thwaited, Pageant Book Company, N.Y., 1959

University of Toronto Archeological Field School, Cahiague 1961 Public Lecture Series, June 15 to August 15, 1961

AN INEVITABLE CLASH

Douglas, Mark, Interview on history of Chippewas in Rama, May, 1995

Douglas, Mark, Mnjikaning, The Fish Fence at The Narrows, personal account (written)

Drinkwater, Jack, The Drinkwater Family, interviewed by Jay Cody and Dr. Luke Irwin, Feb. 19, 1964

Extracts from the report on Indian Affairs by the Commissioners Rawson, W. Rawson, John Davidson and William Hepburn dated 22nd January, 1844, National Archives

Gaudaur, Jake, My Orillia Heritage, meeting of the Orillia Historical Society, April 21, 1977.

Hale, C. H., The Moffatt Family, paper read to the May meeting of the Orillia Historical Society, date unknown.

Jameson, Anna Brown, Winter Studies and Summer Rambles in Canada Selections, McClelland and Stewart Limited, Toronto, 1965 pp170-172

Letter from Thomas G. Anderson to Colonel J. Givons, 28th December, 1830, respecting Mr. Alley and his school at the Narrow, National Archives

Rogers, Sean, Ancient Fishing Weirs, essay, March, 1994

Steele, Millicent Pollock and Ellen Frances, "Diary of a Voyage from London to Upper Canada in 1833", Ontario Historical Society's Papers and Records Volume XXIII, 1926.

Thomson, Captain John, Extracts from His Diary, Simcoe County Archives

Ware, Titus Herbert, The Titus Ware Diary of a Journal from Liverpool England to Orillia, 1844, Simcoe County Archives

Tiller, John and Winchester, Ian, Modelling a City With a Village, Orillia and Hamilton, 1850-1870 Department of History and Philosophy, Ontario Institute for Studies in Education, May 1977

Village of Orillia, Statement of Receipts and Expenditures for the Year 1868

THE LUMBER BOOM

Annis, Charles; Bingham, Elinor; Ironside, Allan; Leigh, Monty Lumbering in Simcoe County, panel discussion for Orillia Historical Society meeting, March 19, 1970.

Groen, Allan C., Image and Economic Development Within Orillia,

Heels, Charles H., A Brief Summary of the Background of the Railways That Served Orillia, presented at the meeting of the Orillia Historical Society, January 8, 1970.

Illustrated Atlas of the County of Simcoe, published 1881. H Belden and Co. Toronto.

Long, Clare, Longview, The Story of an Orillia Pioneer Enterprise, 1995

Noble, E. J., Entrepreneurship and Nineteenth Century Urban Growth: A Case Study of Orillia, Ontario, 1867-1898, Vol 9. No. 1, June , 1980

Noble, E. J., Barrie and Orillia: The Market Town and the Manufacturing Centre, 1860-1911, in The Country Town in Rural Ontario's Past, ed. A.A. Brookes, University of Guelph, Guelph, 1981.

Washington, Whitney, The Start of the Portage, letter to Orillia Public Library, 1952

Wilson, Mrs. M. E., The Steele Family, Paper Read before the Ontario Historical Society at the annual meeting in Orillia in 1840, published by the Orillia Historical Society, date unknown

THE DRY DAYS BEGIN

Minutes of the Orillia and Oro Division No. 122 Branch of the Order of the Sons of Temperance, 1854 to 1857, Orilliana Collection, Orillia Public Library

CANADA'S FIRST MEDICAL PLAN

The Daily Times, February 25, 1899, October, 11, 1889 Nov. 8, 1889

STEAMING INTO LEGEND

Tatley, Richard, Steamboating on the Trent-Severn Mika Publishing Company, Belleville, Ont. 1978

Tatley, Richard, Steamboating and Lumbering on the Trent-Severn Waterway, speech at the Orillia Historical Society Meeting, Oct. 15, 1981

ORILLIA CHURCHES

Barker, Kenneth, History of Orillia Churches, published in The Packet & Times, 1987.

Orillia Presbyterian Church, Jubilee Sketch, 1851-1901

Orillia Presbyterian Church, Order of Divine Service, July 17, 1932, at the Celebration of the Centenary of the Settlement of the Pioneers in this region, 1832-1932

Pealow, Joan, History of the Guardian Angels Parish, Orillia, 17th to 20 Century, published by Guardian Angels Church, date unknown

St. James Anglican Church, The First Hundred Years, The Story of St. James Parish, 1941

St. Paul's United Church, Then and Now, A History of St. Paul's United Church, 1832-1972

Wilson, May E., Church of St. James, Orillia, 1841 to 1956, published by St. James Anglican Church, 1956

THE ORILLIA SPIRIT

Angus, James T., Severn River, An Illustrated History, Severn Publication Limited, Orillia, 1995

Orillia Board of Trade Minutes, 1910 to 1928, Orillia Public Library

Lamb, David B., The 1912 Tudhope, the all Canadian car, in Driving, July 1974, pp 29-31

Lamble, Bert and Stephens, W. T., discussion of The Smelter on Atherley Road, Nov. 8, 1966 interview by Allan Ironside

Leigh, Jabez Montgomery (Monty), Monty Leigh Remembers, eds. Grace Leigh and Sally Gower, Simcoe County Historical Association, 1983.

McNeice, L. G., The Story of Orillia's Three Power Plants, The Packet & Times, October 31, 1935.

The Orillia Water, Light and Power Commission, A Centennial Look at Orillia's Power and Water Development, 1967

Smith, Gordon E., "Automobile Manufacturing in Orillia", speech at the Orillia Historical Society meeting February 18, 1982

Spencer, John Timothy Tudhope, A Short History of Tudhope Specialties Ltd., Orilliana, Orillia Public Library, 1966.

A MOTORING ADVENTURE

Robinson, A.W., "The First Motor Car Purchased by the Bell Telephone Co." article written for the Bell Telephone employee magazine

Courtesy of Bell Canada Historical Collection

A FAIRY-TALE ENDING

Phantoms of the The Orillia Opera House, 1895-1995, compiled by Don Jenkins, Orillia Opera House Management Committee, 1995

KING BEN

French, Wib, History of French's Stand, 1920-1980, for The Packet & Times, 1980

Ironside, Allan, As I remember it, series of articles published in The Packet & Times, August 11, 1990.

McGarvey, Pete Notes on the 1950s

"ALL MUSSED UP"

Mulcahy, Teefy, Reminiscences of Teefy Mulcahy, speech to Orillia Historical Society, 1966, Courtesy of Sue Mulcahy

Tudhope, M.B., Personal Reminiscences sent to Mrs. George Blackstone, in 1938, Orilliana Collection, Orillia Public Library

Watson, G.A., as told to Don Jenkins That's Y (booklet, publication date unknown) Orilliana Collection, Orillia Public Library

THE FINEST POSITION IN THE DOMINION

Lapp, D.A., "Preface to a report for the Orillia Public School Board," January 28, 1967, in Orilliana Collection, Orillia Public Library

Skeaff, Bruce, The Compleat Centennial History of Orillia and District Collegiate Institute after 100 years on "The finest position in the Dominion", paper, 1978

CHASING RUM-RUNNERS AND NAZIS

Clark, Gregory, Herbert Ditchburn and the Famous Boats He Has Built at Orillia and Gravenhurst, The Toronto Star Weekly, January, 1928, reprinted in The Packet & Times, January 26, 1928

Hunter, Don, interviews, June 1995 to March, 1996

The Weekly Times, Nov. 21, 1929, interview with Herbert Ditchburn

ANYTHING WAS POSSIBLE

Barons, Harry, Interview, September, 1995

Carter, Mac, Interview, July, 1995

Cohn, Barry, Interview, July 17, 1995

Department of Industries, Orillia, Ontario, Facts and Figures, 1965

Howes, Kenneth, Interview, June, 1995

Jones, Ruth, Interview, June, 1995

Lightfoot, Gordon, Interview, May 30, 1995

A LEACOCKIAN TALE

McGarvey, James A. "Pete, The Old Brewery Bay, a Leacockian Tale, Dundurn Press, Toronto, Ont. 1994

SOME DREAMS JUST WON'T DIE

Environmental Consulting Services Limited, Centre for Environmental Studies, Orillia, Ontario, Phase Two Development Plan, Final Report, Oct. 30, 1991

Post, Isabel, interviewed by Sally Gower, April 11, 1975.

Town of Orillia City Status Report, Glendinning, Gould & Co., Chartered Accountants, January 26, 1968

BIG CITY DREAMS, SMALL TOWN REALITY

Balmer, Crapo and Associates, Inc. Orillia Master Plan for Parks, Open Space and Recreation Facilities, July, 1978

Coates, D.E., A Demographic Model of Simcoe County, Ontario for the Purposes of Projecting Demand for Post-Secondary Education, revised July 1979, York University, Toronto, Ontario

City of Orillia Economic Development Commission, Orillia, Community Profile, November, 1982

Inducon Consultants of Canada Limited, City of Orillia Downtown Improvement Program, Nov. 20, 1978

Marshall Macklin Monaghan Limited, Institute of Environmental Research, John W. Prince & Company Inc., Orillia Tourism, Recreation and Culture Master Plan, Summary Report, August, 1988

Mayor and Members of the Orillia City Council, The City of Orillia in the Toronto-Centred Plan, (a brief to the Treasurer of Ontario and Minister of Economics, Charles S. MacNaughton) 1970

Moore/George Associates Inc., City of Orillia Waterfront Concept Plan Final Report, June 13, 1985

Richmond, Randy Under the Waterfront, Dec. 21, 1991 The Packet & Times, p 3

Simcoe-Georgian Consultants, Simcoe-Georgian Area Task Force, Final Report of Development Strategy, July, 1975

Willard, Joseph W., Inquiry into the Management and Operation of the Huronia Regional Centre, Orillia, A Report to the Honourable James Taylor, Q.C., Minister of Community and Social Services

THE SPIRIT RETURNS

City of Orillia Economic Development Commission, List of Industries and Major Employers, January, 1994

Dykes, Jim, Interview, September 1995

Mainprize, Daphne, Interview, September, 1995

INDEX